CW01674565

Adventure in Art

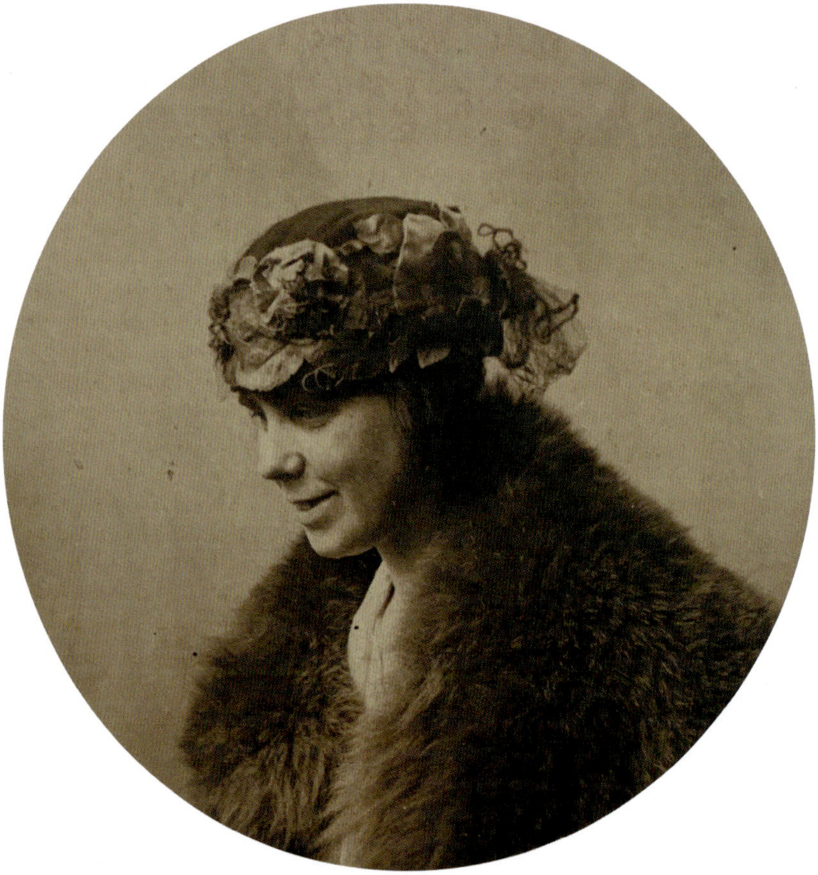

In memory of my friends
Christopher Wood, Kenneth Hall
and Helmut Kolle

ADVENTURE IN ART

BY

LUCY CARRINGTON WERTHEIM

WITH ADDITIONAL ESSAYS BY

FRANCES SPALDING, ARIANE BANKES AND KAREN TAYLOR

TOWNER Eastbourne

UNICORN

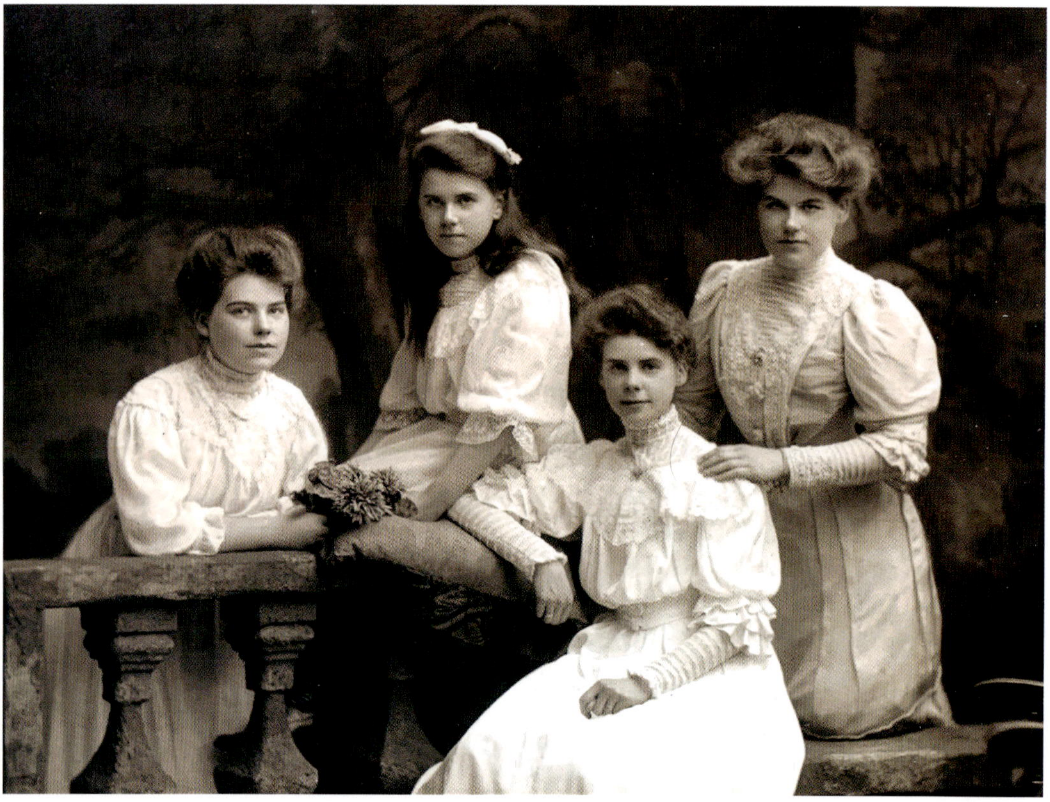

Lucy Pearson (later Wertheim), seated front right, and her sisters Hilda, Theodora, and Phyllis, portrait photograph by N.S. Kay of Bolton and Manchester, *c.*1905
The Lucy Wertheim Archive

Previous spread: Lucy Wertheim, portrait photograph by J. Braakman, *c.*1930
The Lucy Wertheim Archive

Foreword

Lucy Wertheim was my maternal grandmother. She was a forceful, albeit somewhat remote and enigmatic presence through the first fifteen years of my life. Since then, I have learned much about her and feel great pride in the exceptional adventure of her life. Though she and her husband Paul, the Dutch Consul in Manchester, had three children, life for Lucy did not revolve around family. Her artists became central to her very being.

An early group portrait photograph of Lucy and her three Pearson sisters shows them as archetypal elegant Edwardian young ladies – four peas in a pod. Lucy alone was to break that mould as she came to embody a certain high-bohemian attitude – unconventional, wilful, with a singularity of character and purpose that set her on her remarkable path as a champion of young artists. Her 1947 memoir *Adventure in Art* – to the new edition of which I feel honoured to write these words of introduction – gives us the vivid flavour of her energy and spirit, of the depth of her passion for fresh, vibrant, and expressive art, and of the commitment and generosity with which she embraced her young protégés.

This republication of *Adventure in Art* coincides with a major exhibition at Towner Eastbourne, devoted to Lucy Wertheim as collector, gallerist, and patron. I thank the exhibition's curator Karen Taylor and historians Ariane Bankes and Frances Spalding for their insightful essays that give context to Lucy's career and consider her legacy. I am grateful for their precious contributions to the growing recognition of my grandmother's extraordinary life and achievements.

Lucilla Garner, 2022

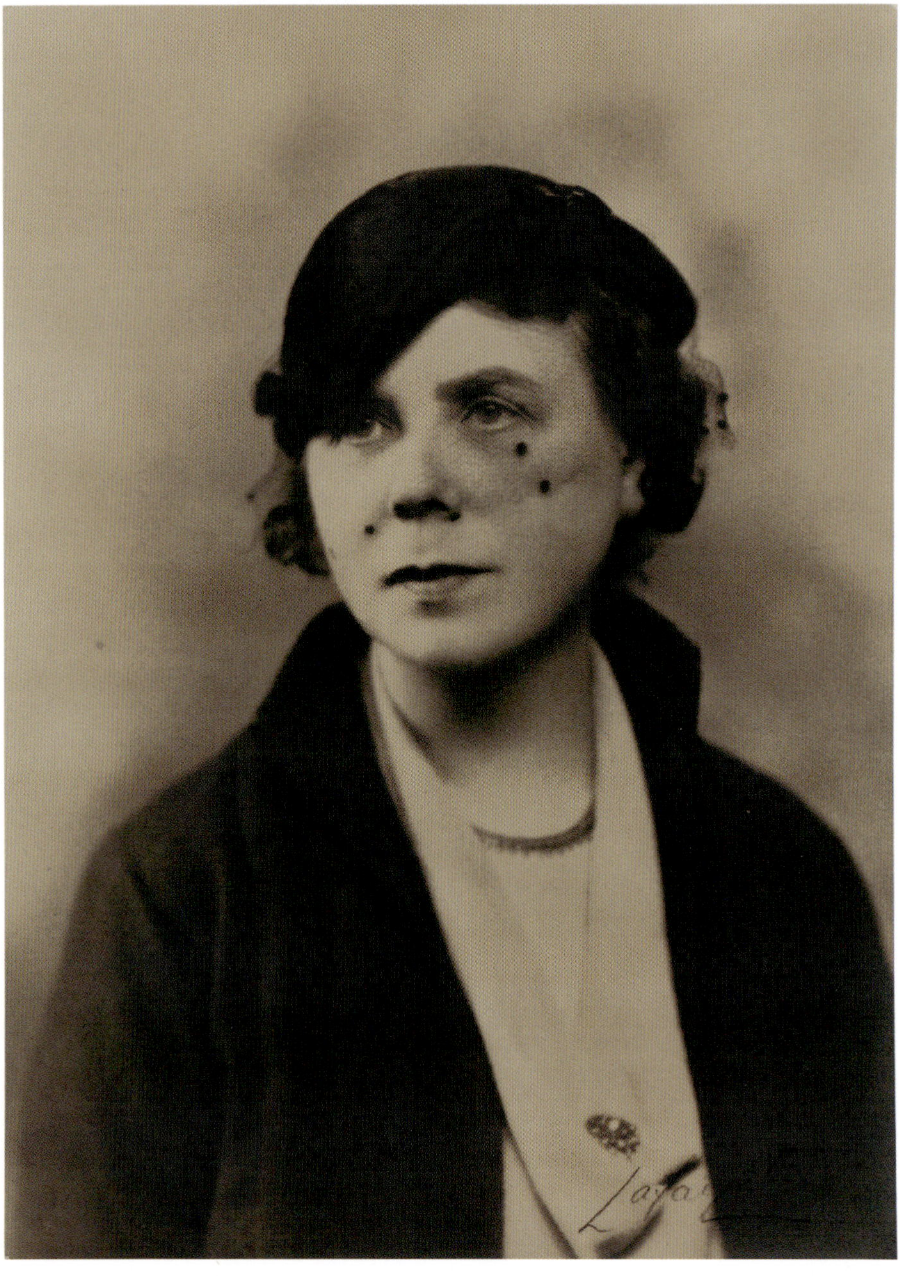

Lucy Wertheim, portrait photograph by Lafayette, 1938
The Lucy Wertheim Archive

Author's Note

Adventure in Art was begun in 1938, completed in 1939, laid aside during the war years and revised, with slight additions, this spring.

To the younger generation, many opinions expressed in this record may seem strange but it must be remembered that in the days when I opened my gallery there was no British Council, no Council for the Encouragement of Music and the Arts, no British Institute of Adult Education and no BBC talks on modern art. In 1930 it was a pioneering job to sponsor the unknown British artist.

The attitude of the public has undergone a complete change in the intervening seventeen years. A new generation of curators is taking over. Committees grow ever less conservative in their outlook. Loans of modern pictures to schools are no longer looked on askance by our educational authorities.

It gives me keen satisfaction to peruse my 'Twenties Group' list and see how many of these young people have achieved recognition. I grieve that Kenneth Hall is not among the number. By his untimely death last year, England was robbed of a very great artist.

The paintings, watercolours and drawings herein reproduced belong to my own collection, with the exception of *The Yellow Man*, which I sold to Mr Brinsley Ford, and *Mending the Nets*, which I sold to Miss Cecily Debenham. Many are familiar to the public, due to their inclusion in provincial and travelling exhibitions. I acknowledge my indebtedness to all the artists whose pictures I have made use of to illustrate my text, and take this opportunity of expressing the pleasure their work has given me.

Lucy Wertheim, 1947

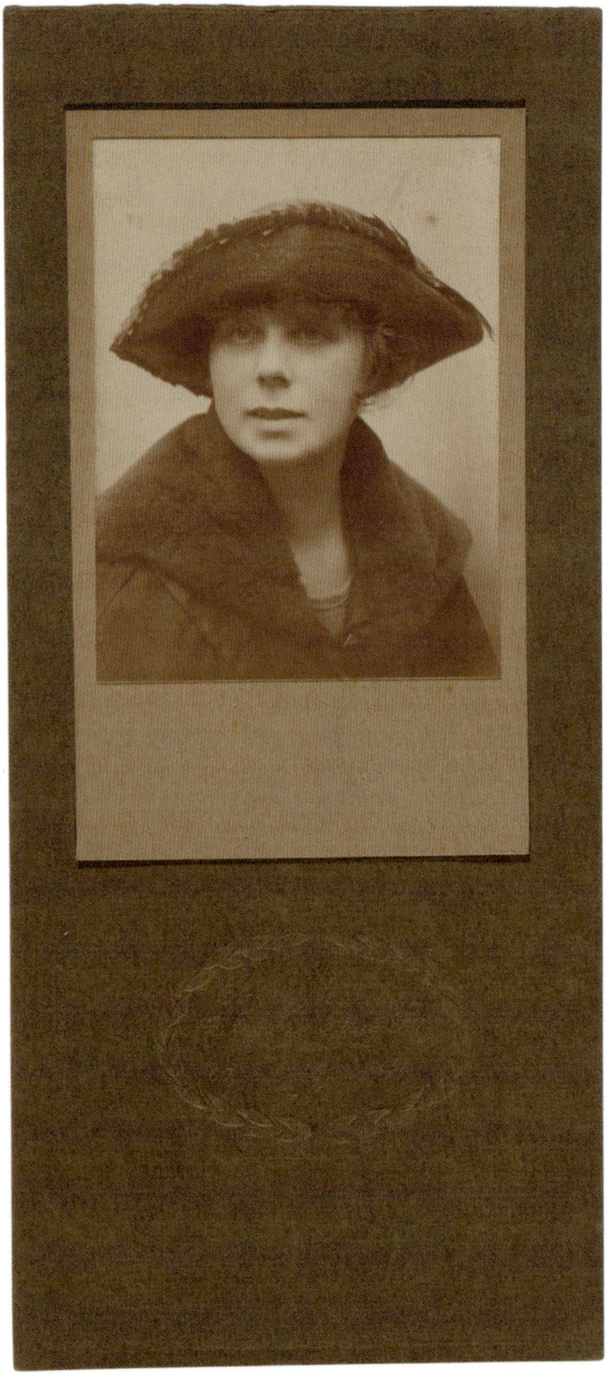

Lucy Wertheim, portrait photograph
by Elwin Neame, *c.*1920
The Lucy Wertheim Archive

Contents

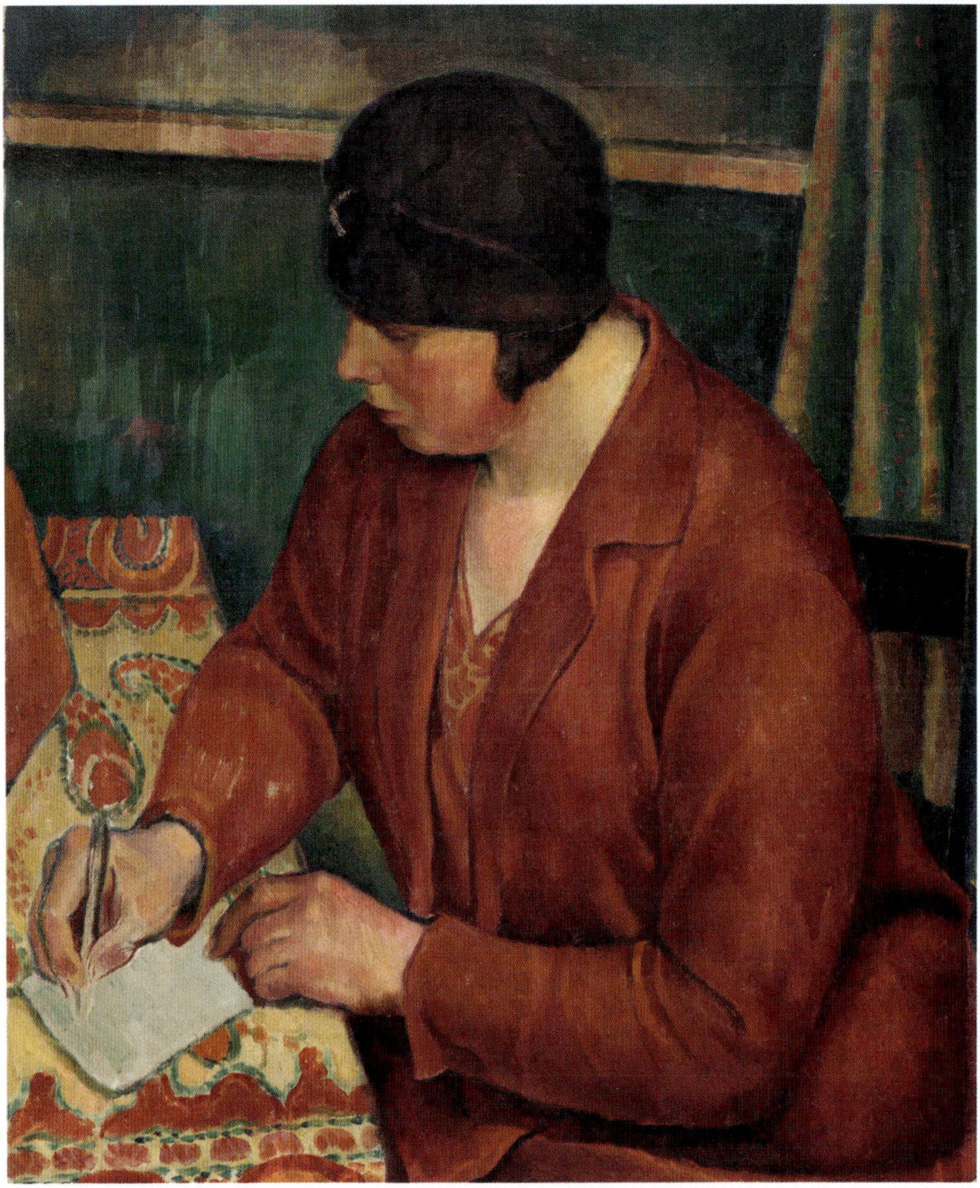

Roland Pitchforth, *Portrait of Lucy Carrington Wertheim*, 1927
Auckland Art Gallery Toi o Tāmaki, gift of Lucy Wertheim, 1948

Thus It Began...

I sometimes say I was goaded into opening my gallery in London. Having maintained with fervour to my Dutch in-laws and to many cosmopolitan friends that Young Art in England was in a healthy state and could hold its own with that of other countries, I was often asked *Where could this work be seen?*

In the spring of 1930 I made the round of the London galleries in the company of a Frenchman, and no dealer could be cajoled into showing us a representative selection of modern painting by young English artists. Sporadic examples of Augustus John, Wilson Steer, Walter Sickert, Matthew Smith, yes, but these were the painters who had 'arrived', whose work was already commanding three figures for a slight example. Where were the painters of promise I had talked about so much, the painters of the future?

The *English Artists under Forty* exhibition arranged by the *Daily Express* in 1927 had proved that a considerable amount of really good modern English painting existed at this time.

It was at this exhibition that I first became acquainted with the work of Christopher Wood, and I remember the impression of tremendous vitality and of an unusual personality that I got from it. Among other contributors who have since achieved fame were Edward Wadsworth, Paul Nash, Charles Cundall, Roland Vivian Pitchforth and Winifred Nicholson.

A young artist named Humphrey Slater was represented by a set of paintings called *The Idealist's Progress*. Some quality in his painting thrilled and excited me, a quality difficult to define but enormously to do with the artist's enchanting colour sense. I bought this set, and on taking it out of store the other day, got the same thrill and pleasure renewing its acquaintance.

Apart from the critic Reginald Wilenski and one or two artists, no one at the time I bought it had a good word to say for this painter's work, and as for my family, so much were these particular paintings disliked by my immediate circle that the word 'Slater' gradually grew to be synonymous with a picture that was anathema in the home.

In the year 1927, the words 'modern art' conjured before the mind of the average English dealer a cubist or abstract canvas for which he had little feeling. Most dealers regarded it as a passing craze which would be over in a couple of years' time. They did not recognise it then as a return to the Great Tradition in painting, to what has been called by Clive Bell 'significant form'.

Frances Hodgkins

Looking back to that period and trying to recall special events that had a bearing on the opening of my gallery, perhaps my friendship with Frances Hodgkins was as big a factor as any.

I recall vividly the very first time I met her, at Withington House, the home of the Dreys in Manchester. I had been taken there to tea by a friend. I remember the immediate *sympathie* between us: her wit, the charm of her warm voice, her felicity of expression. I felt that I had made a friend.

As we left the house my companion remarked, 'What an odd little creature!' But I had not seen her as odd, only as lovable and exceedingly amusing.

I was invited to a one-man show of her paintings the following day in a large, pleasantly decorated basement in Manchester, lent by that generous friend of artists, Edward Hardy. Frankly, most of the paintings bewildered me and at that time only a few of them gave me any real pleasure.

It was an unhappy afternoon. Frances had had a disagreement with her friend over some trifling matter. There was a feeling of tension in the air, and I was thankful to escape after half an hour.

Although much of her work I did not understand, her painting made a deep impression on me and a few weeks later I bought a lovely watercolour by her from Jackson's gallery in Manchester. It enchanted me when I chose it and it enchants me still. I remember how happily it took its place

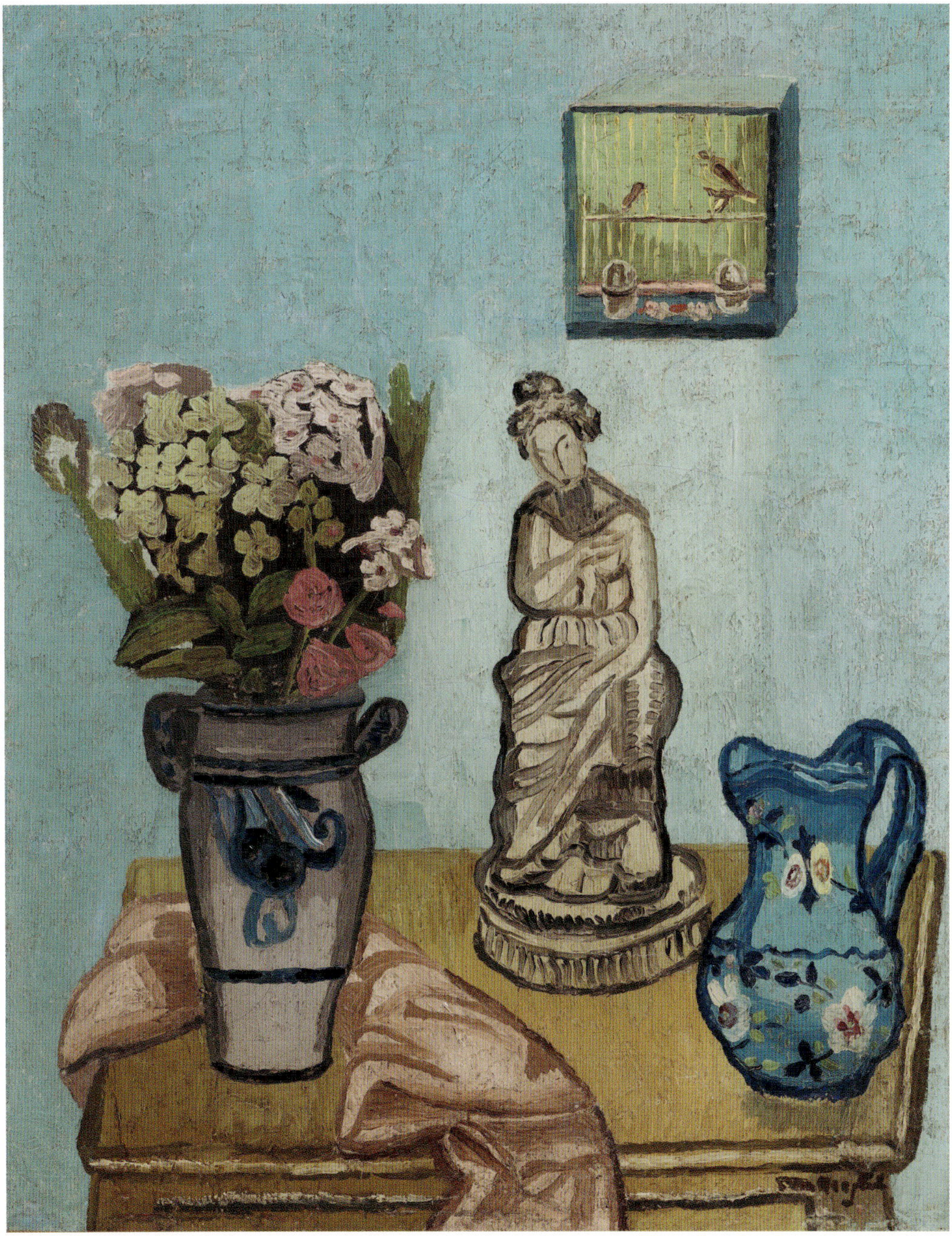

Frances Hodgkins *The Birdcage* (or *Blue Still Life*), *c.*1929
Fletcher Trust Collection, New Zealand

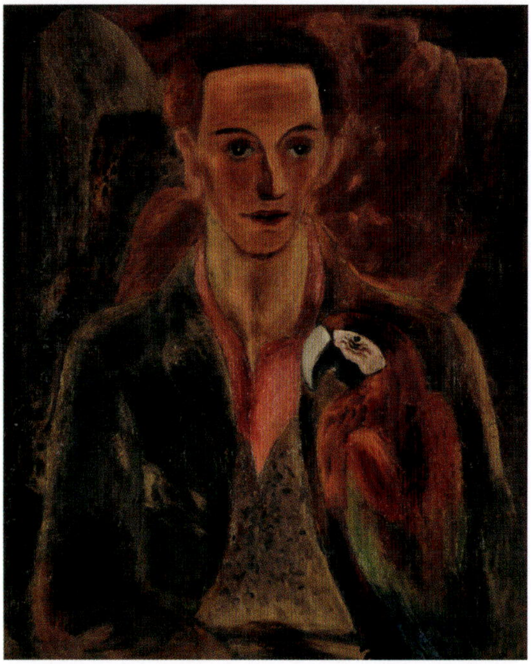

Frances Hodgkins, *Portrait of Cedric Morris*, 1930
Towner Eastbourne, The Lucy Wertheim Bequest, 1971

in a room in which hung some prints and an early Sickert of Dieppe.

I was expatiating on its charms and trying to explain why it enthralled me so one Sunday afternoon when half a dozen friends and Frances Hodgkins herself were having tea in that same room (in Manchester). Suddenly Frances exclaimed to my husband, 'Your wife should open a gallery for us poor artists: her enthusiasm would make it a success!' And I remember my husband's laughing rejoinder: 'One thing I am sure of – she would be her own best customer!'

Those words, however spoken more than half in jest, sowed a seed in my mind that was to bear fruit later.

Humphrey Slater

Through my purchase of his paintings I became acquainted with this artist and my admiration for his work proved a bond between us which ripened

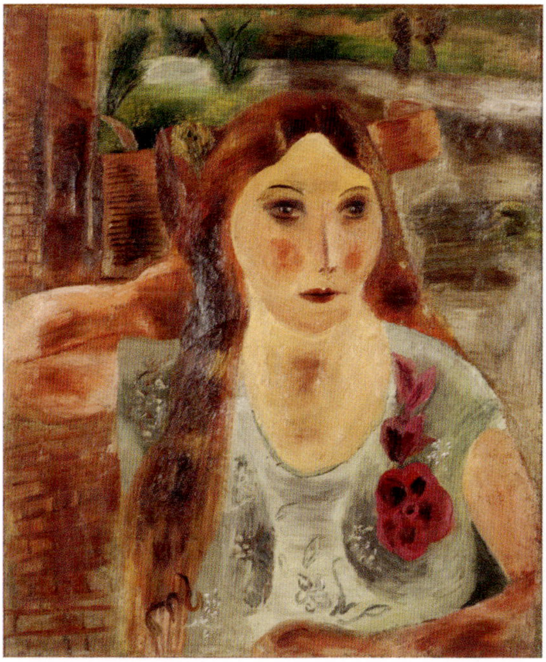

FRANCES HODGKINS, *THE FARMER'S DAUGHTER*, *c.*1931
CANTERBURY MUSEUM, NEW ZEALAND

into a delightful friendship, culminating in a long weekend with my family in Manchester. Slater was then in his early twenties.

Of all my friends none understood the art of conversation better than he, but because he made such outrageous statements as, 'The National Gallery would be a more valuable institution if it were weeded of half its boring Old Masters and modern art hung in their place,' he was thought didactic and conceited.

Actually his idea was carried out to some extent by the young Director, Kenneth Clark, and an improvement thereby effected. Out of the mouths of babes!

Humphrey Slater was the first painter to rouse my interest in surrealist painting. I well remember his delight when later I chose a purely abstract painting from his studio in Paultons Square for my first exhibition.

It was a breath-taking, daring innovation to show abstract work in London in 1930!

Edward Wadsworth

I am not a great admirer of the work of Edward Wadsworth. He is too intellectual a painter for my taste, but nearly twenty years ago he and his wife did much to jolt me out of what I can only look back on as a decidedly self-complacent outlook on art in general.

In our house in Manchester hung paintings by Géricault, Zoffany, John Sell Cotman, Sickert, Henry Lamb, Philip Padwick, Bertram Nicholls and Henry Rushbury. I remember Fanny Wadsworth looking round my walls and exclaiming with a faint disdain in her voice, 'Lucy, have you never heard of Picasso?'

Edward was cousin to my brother-in-law, Walter Wadsworth, who had married my younger sister, and we were seeing a good deal of them at this time. They stayed at our house in Manchester and Fanny invited me to pay them a visit later at their home in Kensington.

I had been brought up by a mother who had strict ideas on the subject of hospitality. Judge of my chagrin, therefore, when I turned up on the day arranged and by the train agreed upon to find no hostess to greet me, and a surprised host partaking of tea in the garden in a rather detached manner. I felt extremely ill at ease, especially as no one offered to take me to my room. When Fanny arrived an hour or so later I got still more the impression that they thought I had dropped in to pay a call. Perhaps it dawned on them gradually that a suitcase implied at any rate a stay overnight, for after a while I was shown to a bedroom and told where to find the bathroom and lavatory.

Fanny was full of her domestic trials and described very feelingly a dinner party she had given the previous night. Two pounds of smoked salmon at what seemed to me a fabulous sum bought to serve as hors d'oeuvre had been *boiled* by her cook, and served *hot*. That had been the chief catastrophe! They had guests to dinner and I heard more – shall we call them sophisticated – stories during the evening than I had heard in all my life before. As I didn't see the point of half of them, I know they thought me gauche and country-cousinish, but twenty years have not changed me much in this direction and I still think a story of that kind must be *very* funny to justify its vulgarity.

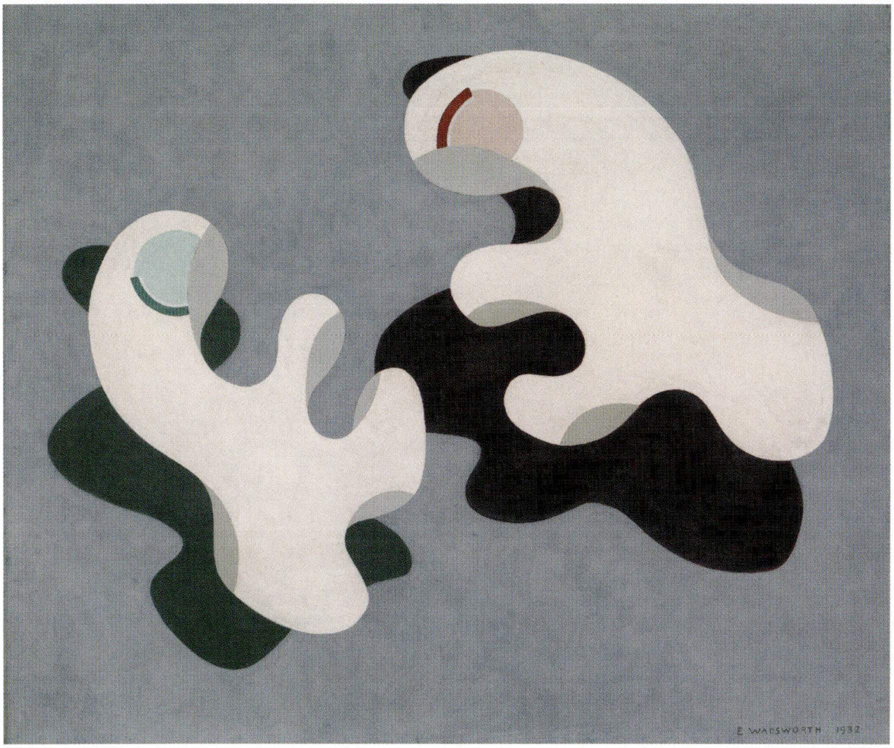

EDWARD WADSWORTH, *DUX ET COMES I*, 1932. TATE
A painting from Wadsworth's Dux et Comes series was included in the Wertheim Gallery's 1936 exhibition *Yorkshire Artists*.

In my bedroom hung an early drawing by Edward and when I came down to breakfast the following morning I remarked how much I liked it. 'Well, you can buy it if you like,' said Edward. 'I'll sell it to you for three guineas, frame and all.' So the drawing became my own and it still gives me great pleasure.

The walls of Edward's 'den' were decorated with a collection of paintings by his friend Wyndham Lewis. Living with these and other (to me) ultra-modern pictures at close quarters for a number of days had a definite influence on my taste at that time. No more really restful pictures for me in the future! I craved exhilaration and stimulation. Picasso had triumphed! Thank you, Fanny. Thank you, Edward.

Sickert

I have always been rather hazy about dates but it was about this time that I made the acquaintance of Richard Sickert (he called himself Walter in those days).

My husband and I were having a little house built near Worthing, to be used for the family's holidays. I had been going through the plans on the site with the architect and was returning to Manchester.

It must have been winter, for I remember I was wearing a short black sealskin coat and an artist cousin who saw me off at St Pancras exclaimed how much she liked my little soft round hat and the plum-coloured scarf to match, adding that she would like to paint me in that 'get up'.

Having settled myself comfortably in the corner of the diner, I began to read (the volume was A.P. Herbert's *Man about Town*). I had just got to that story of the man at Tattersall's who finds he has bought a horse through blinking his eye, when I raised my own eyes and I suppose with a smile in them – for I was greatly amused by the book – looked into a pair of eyes that smiled back at me. These belonged to an arresting face on the opposite side of the diner a few tables lower down the car. I was embarrassed – the man had surely thought the smile directed at himself! I settled myself down to my book again. When a little while later our meal was served the eyes that had been smiling before were fixed upon me with an intent but strangely impersonal gaze – a gaze at which it was impossible to take offence. He began to talk to his *vis-à-vis*, and presently this man, of whom I could only see the shoulder and back of his head, rose, and fiddling with his valise on the rack also took a good look at me. When he sat down again I got the decided impression that they had been discussing me.

The following evening I very much wanted to attend a lecture entitled 'Straws from Cumberland' by Sickert, at the Manchester City Art Gallery. My husband was convalescing after an operation. Was it very selfish to leave him when I had barely returned? I said I wouldn't be away for more than a couple of hours and saluting him with that added warmth of affection that a guilty conscience can impart, I bade him *au revoir*!

I arrived at the art gallery just as the lecture was about to begin. The room was crowded. My friend William Batho, assistant curator, welcomed me, giving me his own seat near the door. Judge of my surprise when I looked towards the platform – the lecturer was my interesting-looking fellow-traveller of the evening before!

It was a delightful discourse and at the end of it Batho asked me if I would like to be introduced to Mr Sickert. I said indeed I would and he led me towards the lecturer. As he opened his mouth to effect the introduction, Sickert exclaimed 'The Renoir lady of the train! I said to my friend Wheatley, "Look round, Wheatley, and see for yourself if there isn't a woman behind you who might have sat as model to Renoir!"'

The following morning I was in Manchester shopping and happened to call in at Jackson's Gallery. Sickert was there and we had a further talk. I think he was rather pleased to know that I possessed two of his paintings and several of his drawings. I invited him to stay with us any time he was visiting Manchester, and in the meantime hoped that he would come and dine with us one evening with his friend Jackson.

They both accepted. An evening was fixed. It was a busy time of the year, nearing Christmas. Jackson rang up to say he was detained and that they would be a little late.

I had an excellent cook and a very special little dinner had been prepared. Time went on. Eight o'clock, nine o'clock came, no Jackson, no Sickert. The meal was cleared away. The maids had asked earlier in the day if they might go out that evening. There was only Nannie upstairs with the children. I was alone, my husband in Holland.

An hour later, after I had given them up, a ring came at the door – there they were! Jackson profuse in his apologies. He explained that one thing after another had kept him, and though Sickert had wanted to come on alone he had persuaded him to wait and let him drive him in his car. Sickert looked the picture of misery. What remained of the carefully prepared dinner by this time was stowed away in the larder in the basement. In the circumstances, I could only offer them drinks.

Sickert cheered up for a moment when he saw his own painting of Dieppe and remarked that he didn't remember he had ever painted anything so good. Later that picture had to go to the sale room to enable me to pay my rates at the gallery. I was heartbroken to lose it.

Our next encounter was at Central Station, Manchester. I had been seeing a friend off to Liverpool. Sickert had just arrived from London and had a couple of hours to spare before his evening class. My car was waiting outside and I invited him to drive home with me for tea. He accepted readily and half an hour later we were sitting chatting over a comfy fire.

My little daughter just in from a walk with Nannan and still wearing her outdoor clothes entered the room. Her hat (from Paris), striking in its severity, was of stitched brown velvet, with a long pheasant's feather. Sickert rose and gravely shook hands with her, remarking as he did so, 'I see you are wearing Louis XI's hat.' I recounted the story to Frances Hodgkins, who exclaimed, 'Very clever – how like Sickert to note the resemblance.'

Sickert asked me if I would sit for him at his studio at Islington, but I said I preferred to retain his friendship. Other artists who had tried to paint me had become so exasperated in the process that the sittings had always ended badly. They complained that all expression left my face when it was in repose, I told him. To which Sickert rejoined, 'But I won't paint you in repose. I'll paint you walking about, talking to me as you are walking about and talking to me now.' But I resisted his blandishments.

Sometime later I was travelling from Manchester to London and, meeting on the train, Sickert invited me to join him at his table for lunch. I don't remember what we laughed at but it was one of the merriest meals I've ever enjoyed – my companion was full of good stories. The incident that sticks in my memory was his telling the waiter to take away that synthetic stuff and bring him real salt.

As the train wound its way through the lovely Derbyshire Dales, Sickert observed that it was a part of the country he had often planned to paint,

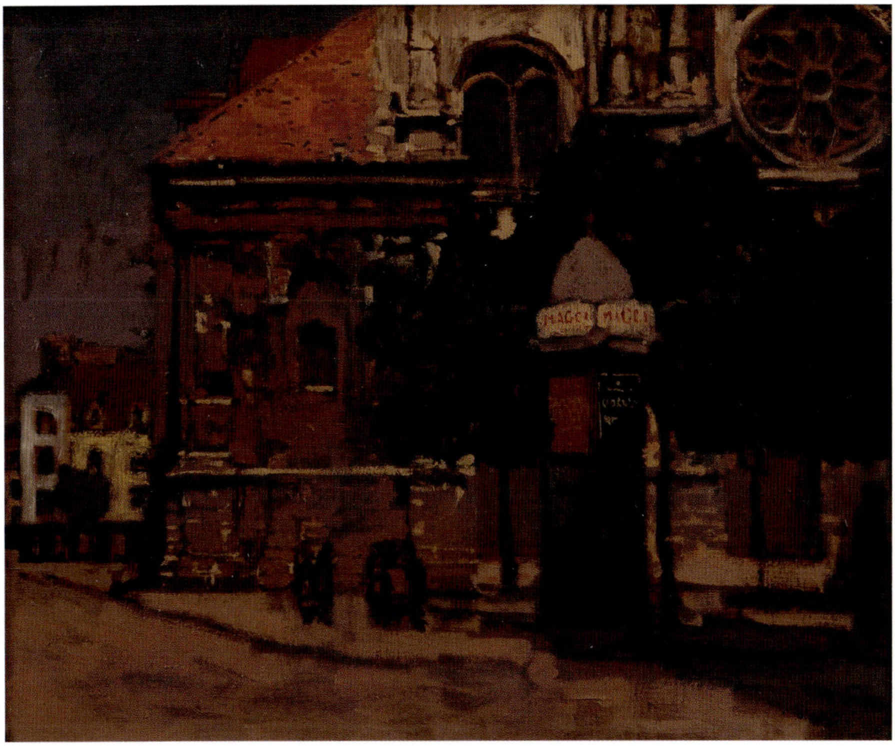

WALTER SICKERT, *SAINT RÉMY, DIEPPE*, *c.*1910. JERWOOD COLLECTION
Wertheim exhibited and owned a painting titled *Dieppe* by Sickert, though it remains unidentified.

adding that he might carry out his idea that year. I said if he cared to make our house his headquarters, I would put our car at his disposal and he could make daily trips to Ashbourne and Darley Dale. We arranged that I would contact him on my return to the north. Later, in reply to my invitation, he telegraphed as follows: 'Grateful and delighted *vive Renoir*, Sickert.' But the visit never took place. On 6 April 1926, I received the following telegram: 'Very sorry am not able to come to Manchester ordered a rest, Sickert.'

In a letter from Frances Hodgkins to me about this time occurs the following: 'Sickert comes no more to Manchester. He slipped silently away from his last class without farewells.'

I never met him again.

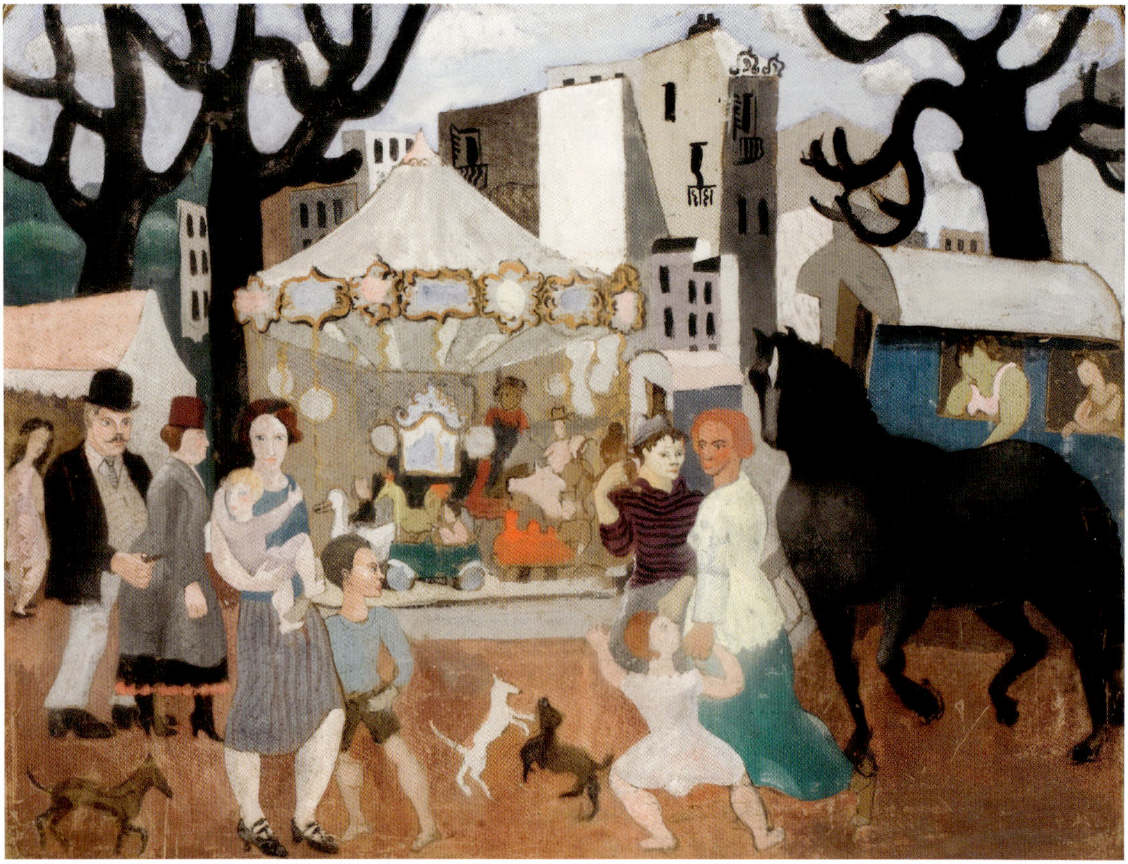

Christopher Wood, *Fair at Neuilly*, 1922
Towner Eastbourne, The Lucy Wertheim Bequest, 1971

Christopher Wood

A chance encounter in the Spring of 1929 had the effect of altering the whole course of my later life. I had bought a few days earlier at Tooth's in Bond Street a small painting by Christopher Wood, at a one-man show of his work being held there. The subject: a purple crocus in a pot, the canvas about 14 inches square, the price 12 guineas – surely not such an important thing as to be the cause of an obsession. Yet looking back on that morning it seems to me that I did become obsessed by the paintings of the artist from the time I bought this little picture. I was filled with an utterly unreasonable fear that something would happen to prevent it becoming my very own. I thought about it all day long and developed a sort of nostalgia for it.

I had bought it early in the morning of the private view. Later I paid another visit to the exhibition to reassure myself of its existence. I remember that it seemed incredible to me that so much joy could be mine by the mere transference of 12 guineas to the coffers of Messrs Tooth. I was absorbed in the picture, rapturously feasting my eyes on it when the assistant approached me in the company of a young man.

'Madam, the artist wishes to be introduced to you!' Before me stood a tall, rather fair, young man of obvious breeding and great charm of manner. Looking back over these years and recollecting that first impression – 'easy on the eye', as the Americans would say – best described him. The grace with which he moved, in spite of a slight affliction to the knee, the beautifully poised head, the inimitable way he wore his well-cut clothes and last, but not least, the extraordinary intelligence of his face, gave him an Apollo-like quality. I felt that I was in the presence of a very unusual personality, sensitive yet dynamic, and we seemed to become friends from the moment of the introduction. I remember as other people came into the show and our conversation was interrupted, he exclaimed impatiently, 'When can we go on talking?' I asked him to return to lunch at our flat in Regent's Park. He at once accepted but added that he would have to rush away immediately afterwards. (How often have I made use of this cliché in order to extricate myself gracefully should I be bored.)

My husband was in London at the time and I knew that my woman, according to custom, had left the table laid and a lunch just ready for the finishing touches should either or both of us turn up for a mid-day meal. My husband did not return that particular morning, somewhat to my relief, as the subject of modern art frankly bored him, and Christopher and I were still talking twenty to the dozen on this fascinating subject when he put in an appearance towards tea-time. (Was it a cliché?)

At this time art was a subordinate interest to my three children (the youngest aged ten) but as I had an excellent Nannie who had been with me since the first baby was a few months old and who was devoted to all three of them, their responsibility did not irk me unduly and I was free to spend days, or during term time even weeks, in London or on the Continent. My husband was considering retiring from business, and frequently we took pleasant holidays away from our Lancashire home. The Regent's Park flat at this time was no more than a *pied-à-terre*, but as I made the acquaintance of more and more artists and felt as time went on, more and more drawn to this circle, gradually I began to feel happier there than I had felt in all my life before.

Christopher Wood said that my long, low living room with its flat Georgian windows and simple furnishings had a more restful effect on him than any room he knew.

The next painting I bought from him was *Dieppe*. This I chose when the paint on it was hardly dry from the studio of his tiny house in Chelsea. He asked me if I thought £45 too high a price, as he believed it was the best painting he had done up to date. I said not if my husband would give it to me – which he did.

I recall very clearly that visit to his little house in Minton Place, Bury Street. I had made the journey by taxi and remembering how much he loved

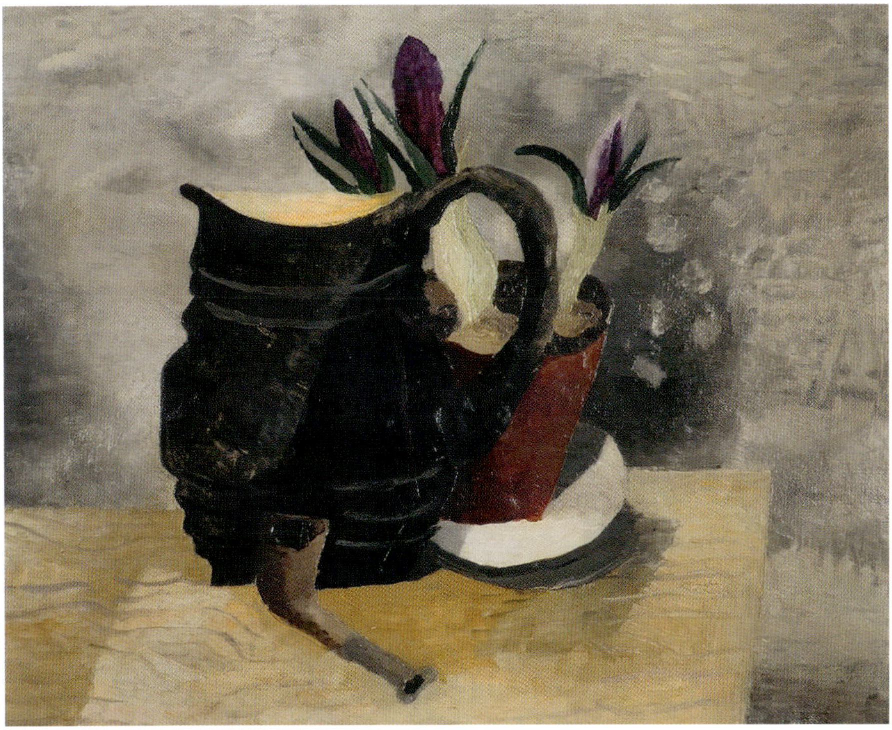

CHRISTOPHER WOOD, *BLACK JUG AND PIPE*, 1929. PRIVATE COLLECTION
This is one of several works by Wood owned by Wertheim featuring a purple crocus.

flowers, I had pulled up at a florist's nearby in the Fulham Road so that I could get him some. My arms were quite full, and he was so overcome with delight that he gave me a quick spontaneous kiss when he knew they were for him.

'I shall paint them,' he said. 'I'm going to paint you too, but that will have to wait: I am leaving London as quickly as I can – I am too troubled here by people. I want to be by the sea in a quiet place, and alone – perhaps Cornwall!' He went on to tell me that his mother's people were Cornish and that he got his love for the sea and for boats from his Cornish ancestry.

With some people one arrives so quickly, so unfalteringly at such a basis of understanding that subsequent absence or series of absences can do nothing to impair the complete sense of intimacy that has been established. So it was in my friendship with Christopher Wood. During the next months my only reminder of his existence, apart from my *Purple Crocus* and *Dieppe*, was an occasional postcard from him.

In the spring of 1930 he was back in London and I find these entries in my year-to-year book:

28 March 1930	Cochran's Revue.
29 March	Morning with Christopher Wood at Minton Place. Buy a painting from him (*The Yellow Man*).
31 March	Christopher to dinner at flat.
1 April	Matinée, Cochran's Revue.
3 April	Christopher expected to dinner at flat to meet M.E. Friend telephones he is ill.

Kit in London

Christopher was coming to dinner with me at my flat. I had prepared a meal with extra care. It was chilly enough to have a fire and I thought my living room had never looked more inviting as I came in through the wide double doors and watched the flames playing on the pale old orange Dutch tiles of the hearth. The walls were parchment colour, the carpet a matt brown, and curtains and covers the shade the French call 'bile'.

A huge bowl of amethyst-coloured glass by Powell on a low round table held the only flowers in the room. A painting of Djerba, *The Mosque* by Cedric Morris, given to me by the artist himself, hung over the fireplace. It was of soft whites and browns and greens and fell harmoniously into the decorative scheme of the room. Between the windows hung *The Birdcage*, a blue still life by Frances Hodgkins. Pavel Tchelitchew, visiting me a few weeks later, said it was the finest modern painting he had seen in England.

Over the narrow walnut chest alongside the door was Christopher Wood's *Dieppe*. What a thing of joy! To the left of the fireplace hung my *Purple Crocus*, and on the other side another flower painting, a gift from the artist Frank Freeman. Its title? We had had an argument over the plural of ranunculus, of which I had recently taken him a bunch when he was ill.

Frank: What lovely ranunculuses!
Lucy: Can you say ranunculuses?
Frank (quickly): No. It should be ranuncul*uci*.

So the picture was known as the *Ranunculuci* from that day on. A lovely head in bronze by Henry Moore, christened by my husband for some obscure reason 'Emma'; a warm-coloured stone carving by John Skeaping, *Femme Enceinte*; a stone tablet, a gift from Eric Gill, 'cut with my own hands', with the inscription 'Dilige Deum et fac quod vis' (free translation by a young member of my family when asked what it meant: 'Advice to do what she likes and land herself in quod'); and a T'ang horse. These, after my children, were my most precious possessions.

Do you see this room in your mind's eye? It figures often in letters received from Christopher Wood and other visitors who came to see me about this time. Among these were Frances Hodgkins, who stayed for months at a time at my flat, Henry Moore and his lovely Russian wife, John Skeaping, Barbara Hepworth, Cedric Morris, Lett Haines, John Alford, William Plomer, Leon Underwood, John Gould Fletcher, Pavel Tchelitchew, Theodore Komisarjevsky, David Fincham and his wife Sybil, Jim Ede, Frank Freeman, George Bissill, Anita Berry, and James Bolivar Manson.

To this room then should have come Christopher this particular evening. The meal had been fixed for eight o'clock. At nine o'clock he had not arrived. About ten o'clock the telephone bell rang. Peter Spencer, if I wasn't very much mistaken (I thought I recognised his voice though he gave no name) said, 'Christopher is not well, and hopes you will excuse him.' Nothing more.

The next day, 4 April, was my birthday. At a restaurant in Piccadilly, my elder son Michael, my daughter Hilary and a friend were sitting down to a festive lunch. Christopher had been invited but after the telephone message of the night before I was uncertain whether to expect him.

After waiting for him half an hour we decided to begin. A few minutes later he rushed up to the table and thrust a picture into my arms. 'For your birthday, Lucy dear. Can your son lend me half-a-crown for my taxi ticking away at the door. I have no money at all.' This little matter settled, the various introductions effected, for he had not met my family before, lunch proceeded.

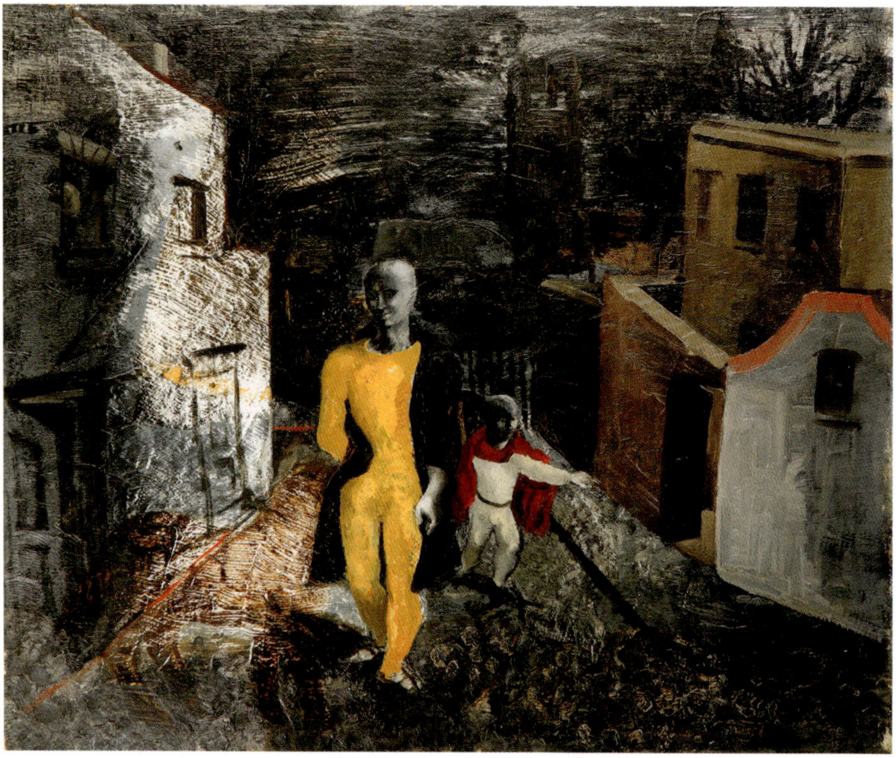

CHRISTOPHER WOOD, *THE YELLOW MAN*, 1930. PRIVATE COLLECTION

It was a strange little meal. My own feelings were a mixture of elation and embarrassment. I was enchanted with my birthday gift, a lovely flower painting in a maple frame which bore the inscription: 'To Lucy for her Birthday with love from Kit', but Kit was obviously not his normal self. He had one very black eye and several bruises on his face, which was puffy and swollen. He said he had had a fight the night before and for his own self-respect had been obliged to lay a man out.

He insisted on drawing his chair close to my own and at one moment laid his head on my shoulder. My children looked on half-amused, half-concerned. Kit seemed oblivious of being in a public place. He barely tasted food and at times spoke as if he were in a kind of trance. He made a statement during this meal which made a great impression on my mind. 'I am sometimes clairvoyant,' he said, 'and today more than I have ever been. I know that my

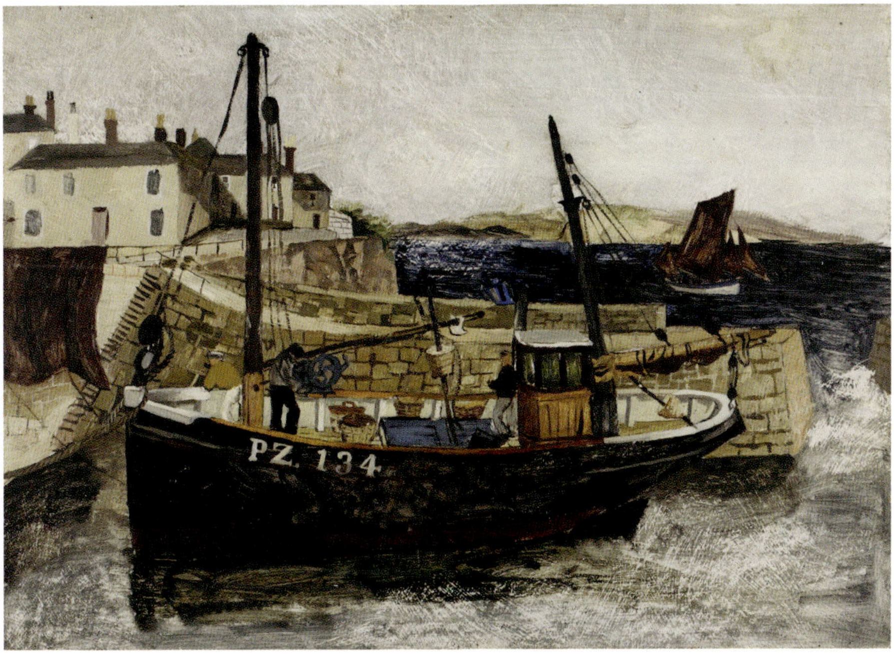

Christopher Wood, *PZ134*, 1930
Towner Eastbourne, The Lucy Wertheim Bequest, 1971

future as a painter from now on will be bound up with your own, and *I shall become great through you!*'

The next painting I bought from Christopher Wood was *The Yellow Man*, for which I paid him £35. It did not take me five minutes to decide that it was quite the best thing he had painted up to date.

When I bought this picture, the plan of starting a gallery in London to help recognise the young English painter was only just beginning to take shape in my mind. I had mentioned casually to Christopher one day that Frances Hodgkins had suggested it to my husband. Immediately he saw its possibilities and became tremendously enthusiastic. Indeed, from the moment the idea was mooted he assumed that it was a settled thing and would never refer to it as a mere possibility. It was always 'when we have our gallery', for from the beginning he intended to take an active part in its affairs.

Kit in Paris

On Sunday 11 May, I crossed to Paris, the chief object of my visit being to see Christopher's exhibition at the Georges Bernheim Gallery. Christopher knew that I was travelling that day but I did not mention the time. Judge of my surprise then when arriving at the Gare du Nord I found him awaiting me on the platform. 'How did you know I was coming by this train?' 'I didn't *know*, just hoped you would,' said Christopher. Was it another instance of his clairvoyance? I thought he looked tired to the point of being ill, and the fact that he had not shaved that day heightened the impression. He made it obvious that he was extraordinarily pleased to see me, but I remember that in the taxi on the way to my hotel he hardly spoke except to exclaim a couple of times, 'You dear Lucy!'

I dined alone and later Christopher called for me at my hotel, and we spent the evening on a quiet boulevard sitting and strolling by turns: Kit in an excited and happy mood, full of his exhibition and his plans for the future – modest yet confident of himself.

It would be pleasant to record here that the art-loving crowd of Paris had the wit to recognise in Christopher Wood the makings of a great painter but if one chronicles with truth the effect of his work on the public in that spring of 1930, one must reluctantly admit that apart from the plaudits of his personal friends and a handful of critics the exhibition was not a conspicuous success. In the early summer of that year already there were presages of the coming slump and many friends and acquaintances whom Kit had been counting on for practical support failed to do more than visit his show and make the usual polite and complimentary remarks.

It is true that one friend went so far on the morning of the private view as to offer to buy at a reduced figure *The Yellow Horse*, '*if the artist would consent to repaint the background*'. But to this suggestion Kit retorted excitedly that he would be damned if he would and only calmed down when I interposed, saying that I liked the painting better than any other in the exhibition and would like to buy it for myself.

I have often wondered since if that would-be purchaser repented his ill-timed remark.

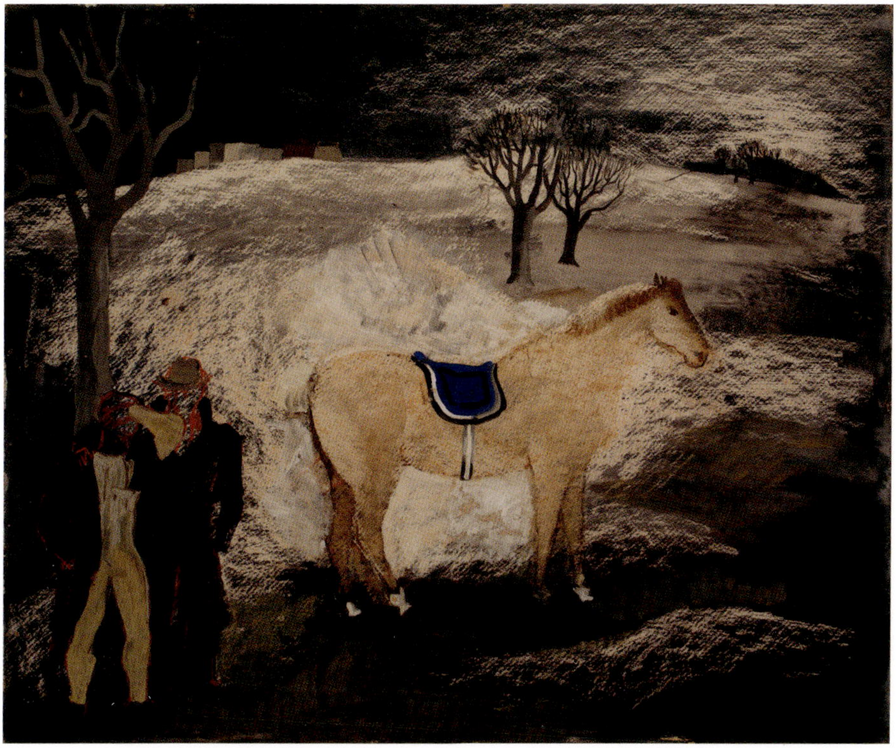

Christopher Wood, *The Yellow Horse*, 1930. Private Collection

All work possessing that dynamic personal quality that is the very essence of Christopher Wood's painting is bound to have an effect that is almost exacerbating on those who look upon it for the first time. There are very few, even among the most ardent art lovers, who can stand the impact of a terrific personality and respond to it sensitively and sympathetically the first time they are brought into contact with it.

At Kit's 'vernissage', I heard one man say to another, *'Pour mot c'est trop anglais,'* and the other warmly agreed with him. I wanted to tell them that it was the very quality that he described as '*trop anglais*' that, if they only knew, gave the paintings their distinction: a lyrical quality that their own countrymen could not hope to emulate, but I held my tongue, dreading lest my French should not prove equal to the occasion.

I bought four other paintings on the opening day of Kit's show, and it was agreed that neither of us should mention who the purchaser was, trusting that the sale of these five would have a psychologically beneficial effect and induce others to follow suit. However, there were few further sales. The days lengthened into weeks, and no one bought. I believe on the closing day of the show Kit sold two small canvases, which he was wont to describe as 'babies', for next to nothing. His own disappointment was feelingly described in one of his letters to me.

At the close of the exhibition I bought five more paintings, the price being fixed by Georges Bernheim.

All these paintings I bought for my private collection.

I have always had a certain admiration for those folk who have the patience to keep a diary chronicling their daily thoughts and doings, for personally I could never take myself seriously enough for it to seem worthwhile the effort expended. But looking back over these years and realising with how many people I have had personal contact who are very much in the public eye and whose doings and sayings would certainly have made interesting 'copy', I now regret my diffidence or laziness.

Over these years, however, of 1929 and 1930, I did make a serious effort to put into use a little year-to-year book given to me by a friend for a birthday present. It seemed a shame not to use it, seeing she had been so sweet as to give it to me, and finding it tucked away in a drawer not so very long ago I had reason to be grateful to her, for it brought back many little happenings over those two years that would have otherwise escaped my memory, and that have a decided bearing on my friendship with Christopher Wood.

During these weeks that I spent in Paris, I got to know Christopher and to understand him better than ever before. I found that he shared my own dislike of social functions, and whilst reluctant to hurt the feelings of his friends he would often escape, when possible without giving offence, from any sort of party even when given in his honour.

'I've got to be present at the dinner,' he said on one occasion, begging me to keep my own evening free, 'because half a dozen people will be there who have been invited to meet me, but I can get away soon afterwards,' and he would turn up later and take me to his favourite boulevard, the name of which I no longer remember, and we would sit and walk by turns. A restless energy seemed to impel him to keep moving whilst the knee that troubled

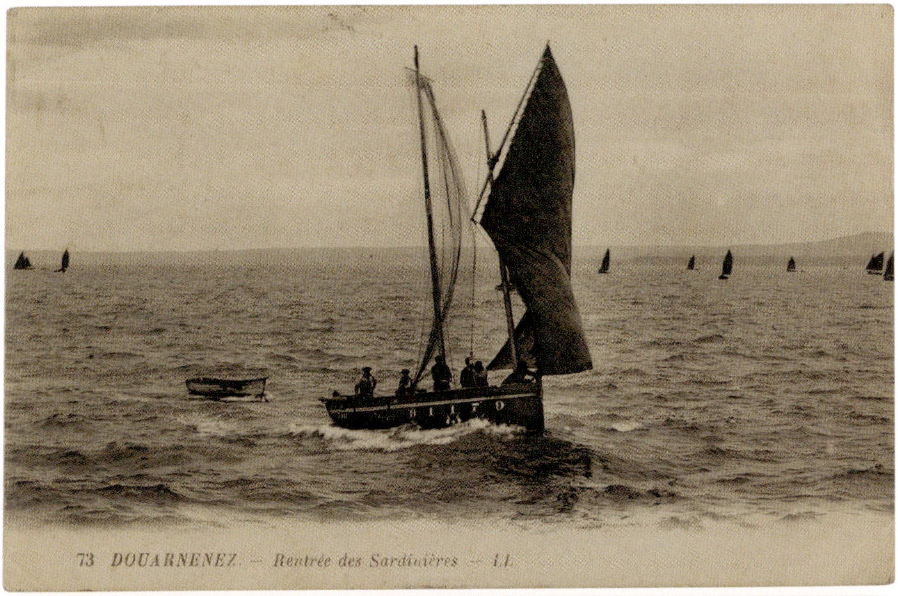

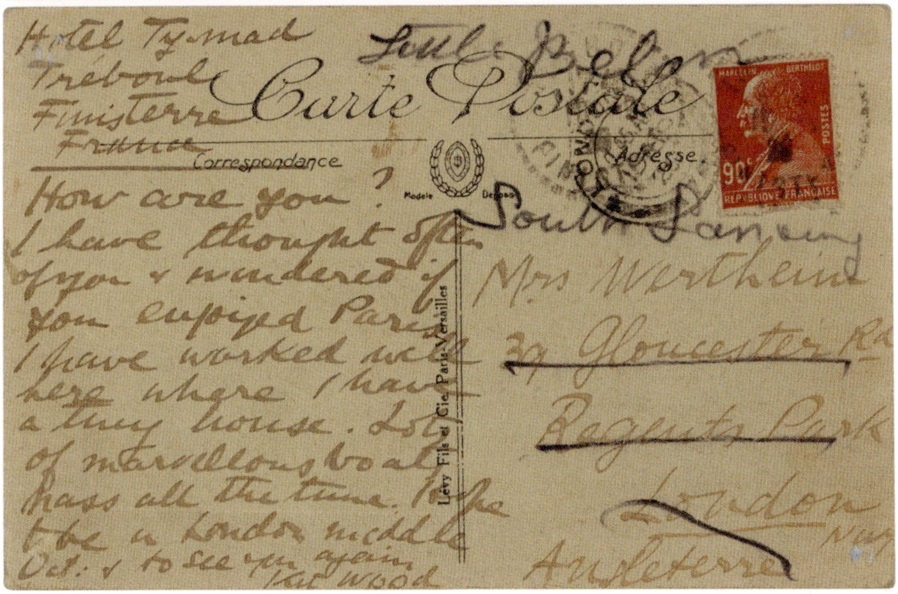
Hotel Ty-mad
Tréboul
Finisterre
France

Carte Postale
Correspondance
Adresse
Modèle Déposé
Lévy Fils et Cie, Paris Versailles

How are you? I have thought often of you & wondered if you enjoyed Paris. I have worked well here where I have a tiny house. Lots of marvellous boats pass all the time. Hope to be in London middle Oct: & to see you again Kit Wood

Mrs Wertheim
39 Gloucester Rd
Regents Park
London
Angleterre

MARCELIN BERTHELOT
POSTES
90c
REPUBLIQUE FRANÇAISE

Postcard sent from Tréboul, France,
from Christopher Wood to Lucy Wertheim, August 1929
The Lucy Wertheim Archive

'How are you? I have thought often of you and wondered if you enjoyed Paris. I have worked well here where I have a tiny house. Lots of marvellous boats pass all the time. Hope to be in London middle Oct: & to see you again Kit Wood'

him obliged him to take frequent rests. On such occasions Kit did most of the talking and I was very content to listen.

His language was simple and dynamic like himself. He had a vivid power of description and an extremely personal way of telling you things about himself that made them live for you in your mind's eye. The evenings of my stay in Paris thus spent are unforgettable.

It was Kit's earnest wish to make a trip to Berlin and there introduce himself to Alfred Flechtheim, the well-known gallery director, whom he wished to interest in his painting. He asked me to accompany him and I said I would if he arranged the journey so that I could be back by the time my family's holidays began. This he promised to do.

'I want you to go with me because you are the only person who never bores me,' said Kit. I quote this because it was a very Kit-like statement. I am sure he meant it when he said it, but I do not flatter myself that it was true.

On one of these evenings he confessed to me his terror of being left alone when a certain mood that he had come to dread descended on him. Kit extracted from me a promise that if he sent for me when he went away to the country to paint, I would go to him if it were humanly possible. He attached so much importance to my answer that I felt I could not do otherwise than give him this assurance. Actually, a request came by telegram to join him a few weeks later in Britanny at Tréboul, but when I found what a long journey it was I wired asking if he would not meet me half-way at St Malo. By the time Kit got my answer the mood had passed and he had become so engrossed in his work that I should have been regarded as a thorough nuisance had I taken him at his word.

I have kept about a score of Kit's letters, but I might add here that much of our correspondence was conducted by telegram.

Luna Park

I saw Cochran's 1930 Revue four times and on each occasion the little ballet, *Luna Park*, for which Christopher Wood did the *décor* seemed the chief item around which the show revolved. It made a deeper impression on me as a spectacle than anything I had ever seen on any stage. It remains as clearly in my mind now as if I had seen it last night, yet I remember very little else that went to make up the revue, unless perhaps the haunting little melody, 'With a song in my heart'.

Luna Park had the same effect on Kit's mother. Kit had intended taking her to see his ballet, and when through his precipitated journey to Paris he could not do so I proposed that I should invite her to go with me, and stay overnight with me in London. Kit jumped at the suggestion, and it was in this way that his mother and I became acquainted.

On the morning of 22 May, Mrs Wood travelled up from Salisbury, had lunch with me and we went to a matinée of the Revue, returning to my flat where we talked until the small hours. That night I learnt much about Kit's childhood; his intelligence, his prowess at games, his musical gifts (he became an adept on the flute during his long illness), the trouble with his knee caused through septicaemia, and how at one time the doctors had wanted to amputate his leg and it was only through her own determination and Sir Robert Jones's skill that this was avoided. That Kit's leg was spared was obviously due to months of untiring nursing and devotion on his mother's part. No wonder he adored her! I thought when I took her breakfast to bed the following morning how pretty and seductive she looked as she lay propped up against the pillows. It was difficult to imagine that she had a son in his thirtieth year.

So impressed was I with the quality of Christopher's painting after seeing his exhibition in Paris that immediately on my return to London I began to look round for suitable premises in which to open my gallery. For a little while I considered a house in Berkeley Square, and alternatively a house belonging to Lady Diana Fitzherbert, close to the Langham Hotel. But my friend R.A. Walker, assistant-editor of the *Print Collector's Quarterly*, whom I was seeing frequently at that time, strongly advised me to 'dig myself in' within 100 yards of Bond Street. 'The critics won't be bothered to go farther afield,' he said, 'and you will be very dependent on them – especially in the early days of your venture.' So finally I decided on a large room on the entresol at 3-5 Burlington Gardens. It was probably the most spacious room in London, apart from public galleries, for showing pictures and before long the lease was signed and I had committed myself to an overhead expenditure of approximately £1,000 a year.

I should like to make it clear here that I had no intention whatever of becoming a *dealer* in pictures. (I infer that a dealer is one who buys and sells again at a profit.) My idea in taking this room and establishing a secretary there was to give the English artist the opportunity of exhibiting his paintings and a chance of making his reputation whilst still young, a chance that had been hitherto denied him. I let it become known that I was forming a group of young English artists and soon I was inundated with requests to look at work.

My husband had guaranteed my rent for the first three years. Later he acknowledged that at the time he was convinced that I should be heartily sick of the scheme at the end of a year and be thankful to return to a life of domesticity. A condition attached to his financial help was that I should keep myself free for my family during their school holidays, roughly a month at Christmas, a month at Easter and two months in the summer. I had given my promise as to this condition and felt myself bound by it. Almost straight away my sense of honour was put to the test. Lady Diana Fitzherbert invited me to meet Serge Lifar at her house and suggested that I should open my gallery '*the first week in September*', with a show of Lifar's private collection of paintings. She pointed out that the exhibition would immediately make the gallery well-known and that excellent publicity would result. After the agreement with my husband I could but refuse, and I am afraid I caused offence both to Lady Diana and to Lifar. But I could not help myself.

I decided to open the gallery on 7 October with a one-man show of the latest paintings by Christopher Wood. The exhibition was mainly to consist of the paintings that he had done at Tréboul with this show in view. It was to be held on a commission basis, all overhead expenses in connection with it being undertaken by the gallery.

At this time I had no business experience of any kind. My husband was never tired of teasing me about my arithmetic. I hardly ever arrived twice at the same answer in adding up figures or working out a rate of interest and to this day a balance sheet or column of figures which have to be personally examined by me induce in me a feeling of nausea.

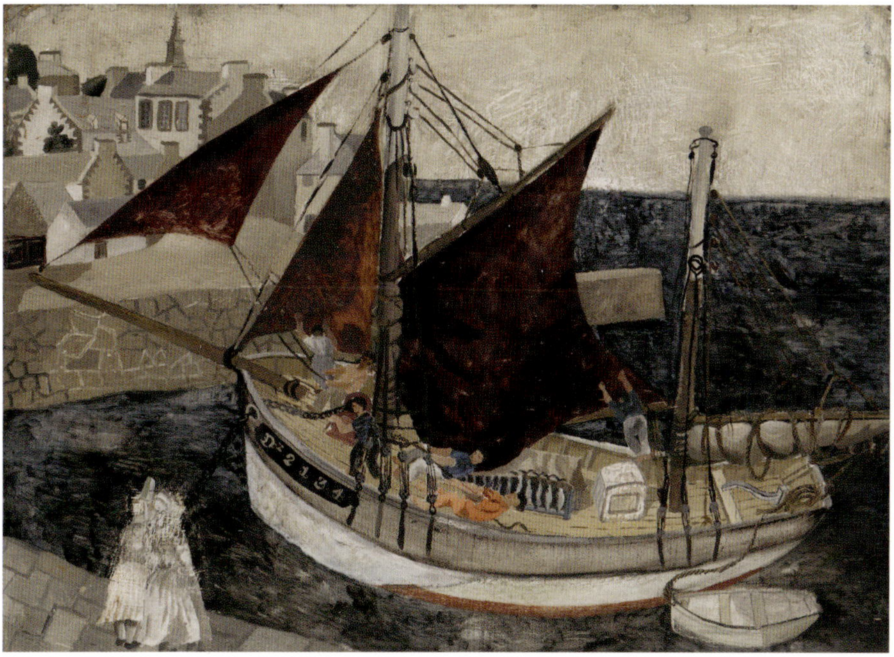

Christopher Wood, *Boat in Harbour, Brittany*, 1929
Tate, gift of Lucy Wertheim, 1962

43 Boulevard Lannes

On Sunday 27 July, I crossed to Paris with the express purpose of choosing the paintings of Kit that I wanted for my opening exhibition.

I had written to him the time I intended to arrive and invited him to dine with me the same evening at my hotel, suggesting he should keep open the following day, Monday, and that we should devote it to making a selection of his work. Kit was there on the platform when my train drew in, and I remember how taken aback I was by his tired, overwrought appearance. It did not mend matters when on finding he was expecting to spend the evening alone with me I had to break the news to him that others were dining with us – Bertie Jacoby, whom he knew already, and a man named Lemasle, a friend of Jacoby.

Kit was very much put out that I had made this arrangement. At first his mood seemed to me unreasonable, but afterwards, realising that he had literally been counting the hours to showing me his pictures, I blamed myself very much for my stupid lack of imagination in not keeping free that first evening. He was too sweet-natured to sulk, but his obvious disappointment acted like a wet blanket on my spirits, and I felt like one might who has unintentionally done some hurt to a child.

The following morning Kit called for me at my hotel and took me to 43 Boulevard Lannes, there quietly to go through his paintings. He was in a tense, highly nervous state and my own nerves were quivering in sympathy and under stress of emotion as he placed one painting after another on the easel for me to pronounce judgment on.

Since that day I have had to do with many hundreds of artists who have submitted their work to me for approval or criticism, and I have learnt what an ordeal it is for most – but it is hardly a greater ordeal for the artist than for myself.

My first feeling as Kit placed a large new canvas on the easel in front of me was one of dismay. I had got so used to the sombre depth and colouring of the paintings I now owned by him – *The Yellow Man*, *The Yellow Horse*, *Purple Crocus*, *Dieppe*, *Boat in Harbour*, etc. – that this new mood in which he was painting came to me as something of a shock.

There was a bright, glittering quality about the new canvas that in the first surprise of seeing it actually jarred. The subject was a large boat, keel upwards, in the process of being built. When I saw this picture again in the recent complete Christopher Wood exhibition, it had almost the same effect on me (*Building the Boat*).

Another painting equally high-toned and metallic followed. I could not bring myself to speak. It was no good simulating an enthusiasm I did not feel. Kit would at once see through it. My heart was heavy with disappointment and I avoided looking at him.

The next painting he placed on the easel had a softer, more translucent quality, but I got no thrill from it comparable to the thrill my own *Dieppe* had given me. The chilled feeling persisted in my consciousness. I don't know who was the unhappier, Kit or I. Then in a rather deprecating tone he wondered how the next one would appeal to me. He had done it more or less to amuse himself, he said. It was a small canvas and painted with all the spontaneity and magic I had come to associate with his work –

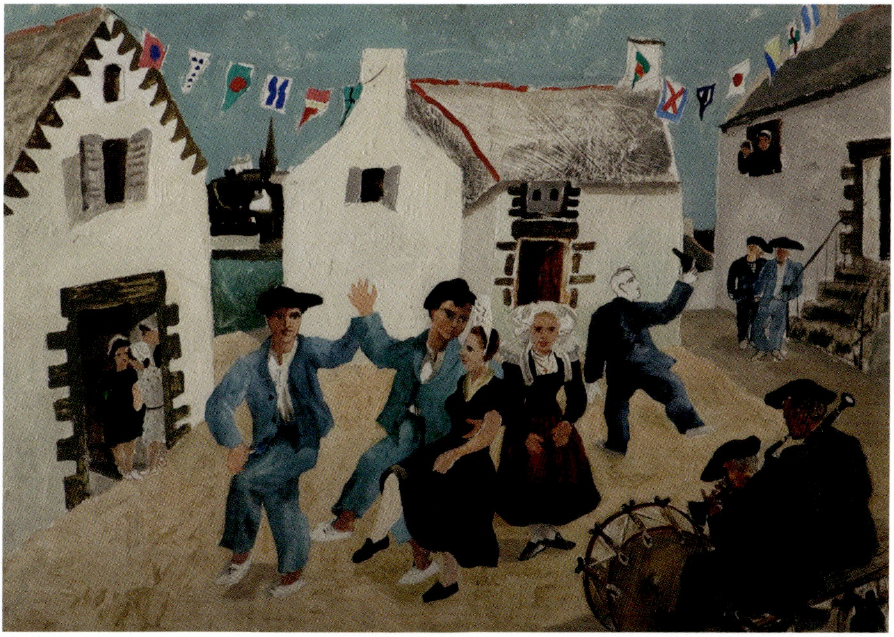

Christopher Wood, *Dancing Sailors, Brittany*, 1930
New Walk Gallery, Leicester

The Dancing Sailors. It was Kit's inimitable self. I heaved a sigh of relief.

My spirits soared as he showed me canvas after canvas, each as lovely as the last. 'The exhibition should stagger London, Kit,' I said, meaning it from the bottom of my heart.

Restaurant Marius

This was Monday 28 July. I did not see Kit the following day, but on the Wednesday he came to have lunch with me at the restaurant Marius, close to the hotel at which I was staying. He arrived in a tense, overstrained mood, and there was a rather wild look in his eye. I can remember my perturbation. We seated ourselves at a long table just inside the restaurant, Kit on my right. There were strangers opposite and I remember wondering if others remarked anything unusual in his appearance. He hardly touched his lunch. We talked in a rather desultory way about his paintings and the coming exhibition at my gallery. Sickert, John and Matthew Smith were mentioned and I said we would ask the same price for Kit's paintings as these artists were obtaining, my idea being to force the public to take his work seriously.

Gradually the room became deserted. After a long pause Kit said, 'Luce, I hate talking to you about money, and I know you hate it too, but I want you to promise to guarantee me £1,200 a year from the time of my exhibition, £100 a month being the least I can live on. If I can't have this sum I've made up my mind to shoot myself.'

In my time I have had to do with many unpractical artists, but this demand of Kit's quite took my breath away. I told him sharply that his threat was most unfair, that it was cruel to hold me responsible for the sale of enough work to bring him in such an income when up to that time I had never sold a picture m my life. I reminded him that I had been the only serious purchaser at his show at the Georges Bernheim Gallery earlier in the summer, also that he had told me that £8 (or the equivalent in French money) was the highest price ever offered him by a Paris gallery for any of his canvases.

Kit calmed down, and presently begged me to forgive him for upsetting me by his threat. He asked me to return with him to 43 Boulevard Lannes and we took a taxi there. We went through the paintings a second time that we had selected on the Monday for his exhibition with me in London, and I was more impressed with his work than ever. By this time he was in a gentle, contrite mood. I think he realised that I had been very much upset by the conversation at lunch. He asked me to accept from him as a gift the last little picture he had painted.

The following day, haunted by his threat, I posted him a cheque for £50 before leaving France.

Requiescat

It was August and the children's holidays. My husband and I were with them at the little house in Sussex. There had been some question of Kit joining us there and I was expecting a letter or telegram from him daily.

My son Michael had gone in the car to Worthing to do some little

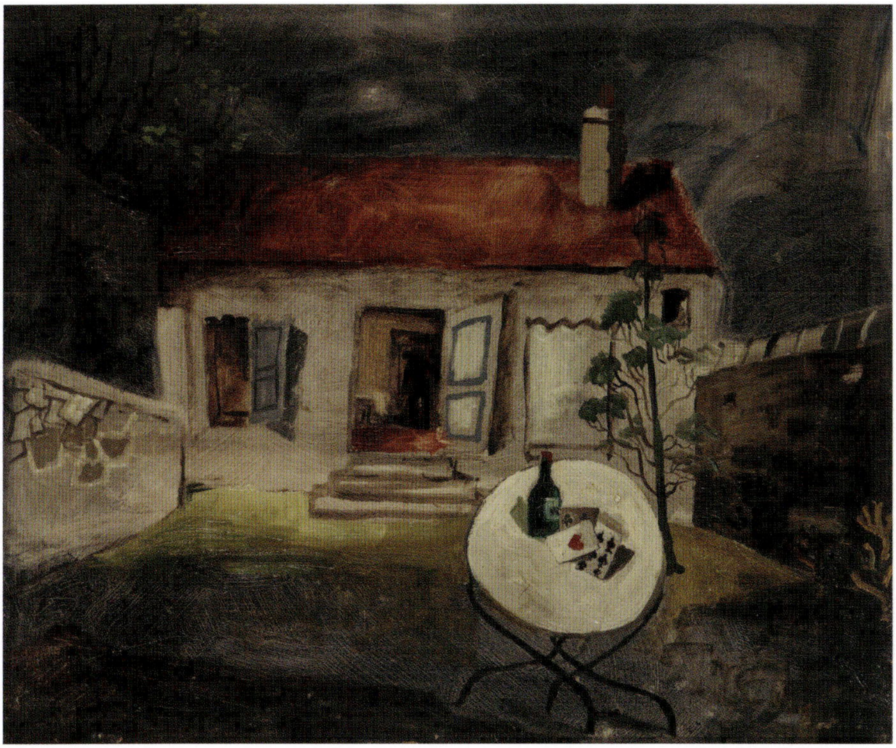

Christopher Wood, *Little House by Night*, 1930. The Lucy Wertheim Estate

errand for me, and his father had called after him to remember to buy an evening paper.

I was in my bedroom trying on a last year's hat, wondering if I could do anything with it to bring it up to date when Michael returned, paper in hand. His face was so grave that I sensed immediately that something was wrong. He came up to me saying: 'There's some bad news, Mum, news that will hurt you. I'm sorry.'

He pressed the paper into my hand and I read in the Stop Press column the news of Christopher Wood's death earlier in the day. He had fallen under a train at Salisbury Station.

I remember a feeling of numbness overcoming me. What mattered my gallery now? Only then did I realise how much I had come to count on Christopher's co-operation and the éclat of his work to make good in the eyes of the world my claims for the English Painter of Today.

I remember that my first reaction to the news was to cancel my lease and call the whole thing off. This was Thursday 21 August. Kit was buried on the Saturday two days later. On the Sunday I motored to Broadchalke to spend some hours with his mother. An atmosphere of peace pervaded the house. Mrs Wood's calmness made me ashamed of my own misery. We walked and talked in the garden. She showed me with pride some of Kit's very early paintings and kept reiterating how beautiful he had looked in death: 'So young, so peaceful,' she said. She pressed me to go on with my gallery and especially my plan for opening it with a one-man show of his recent paintings. 'Just as if Kit were still here – it is what he would have wished,' she said. But I dreaded the publicity that his untimely death would cause, and begged to be allowed to defer his exhibition till the following year.

His influence

I opened my gallery that autumn with a mixed show featuring Frances Hodgkins, Matthew Smith, Sickert, Cedric Morris, Tchelitchew, Kolle and Vivin, and in the following February arranged an exhibition of the paintings I owned personally of Christopher Wood.

Later, another gallery had the honour of holding his Memorial Exhibition and showing the paintings Christopher Wood had painted for the opening exhibition of my own gallery, and in 1938, Mr Nan Kivell, Director of the Redfern Gallery, arranged in the Burlington Galleries a comprehensive exhibition of the artist's complete works.

Perhaps because my gallery became known for my collection of his paintings at a time when no other gallery possessed examples of his work, it was frequently affirmed that I 'discovered' Christopher Wood. I took care to refute this statement, saying that 'discovered' was hardly the appropriate word to apply to an artist who at the time I made his acquaintance was already holding his second London exhibition. Nevertheless, I believe there was no one apart from myself who during his lifetime claimed that Christopher Wood would one day rank among the immortals in English painting and eventually take his place with Hogarth, Gainsborough and Constable in our National Gallery.

His importance as a painter was quickly shown in the early days of running my gallery by the extraordinary effect he had upon the younger generation. During my exhibition of his work in February 1931, young artists and art students began literally to haunt my gallery, and his influence soon began to be apparent in their work. They would come day after day, never tiring of enthusing over the 'wonderful qualities' of this artist's painting, and I, equally enthusiastic, never tired of showing them my treasures.

The older generation was less susceptible to the charms of Christopher Wood. They would often compare his work with that of popular Royal Academicians, always to C.W.'s detriment.

I remember a famous admiral coming to the exhibition on the morning of the private view. I handed him a catalogue and took him round the gallery personally. I could see him grow more and more irritated as he stood in front of my enchanting *Dieppe*, fascinated in spite of himself, yet distrusting the picture as it did not follow any of the canons of what he would have described as 'good painting'. At last he exclaimed impatiently, 'Mrs Wertheim, you will never convince me that this painter's boats were *seaworthy*.' Obviously he was not prepared for my rejoinder: 'Christopher Wood once boasted to me that he could *build* a boat as well as he could paint one.'

I have often maintained that artists make one another's reputation. I think this was particularly true in the case of Christopher Wood. In the early days of running my gallery few but artists enthused about his work. An exception was the Lady Ottoline Morrell, who perhaps among the laity did more than anyone to make Christopher Wood's name famous. She coveted several of my most treasured paintings and frequently brought her friends to see them. Her favourites were *The Yellow Man*, *The Breton Sailor* and *The Crocus*, all three in my private collection and inscribed on the back 'Not For Sale'. My own passion for his paintings grew and grew, and I would spend whole evenings gloating over them. Folk would ask if I wasn't lonely away from my family all week from Monday till Friday but I was never lonely with my pictures round me. I used sometimes to wonder which I should rush to save if the place caught fire. I could never make up my mind.

When some stranger enquired if he might be shown my paintings by Christopher Wood, I dreaded his almost inevitable question: 'What is the

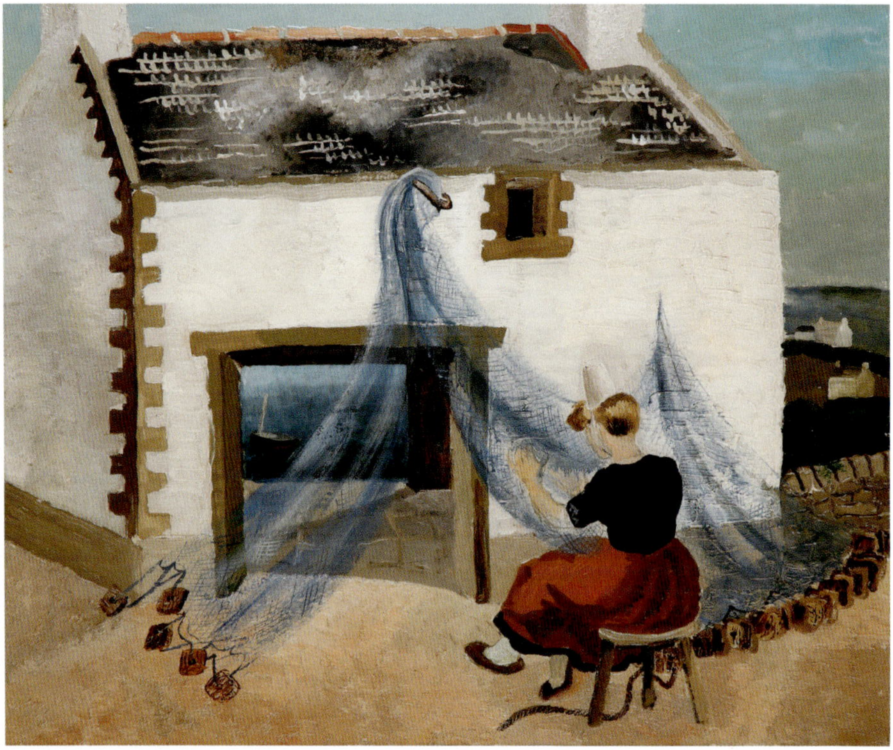

CHRISTOPHER WOOD, *MENDING THE NETS, TRÉBOUL*, 1930. PRIVATE COLLECTION

price of that one?' Panic would seize me at the thought of losing it and I would say desperately, 'Oh, that is one I keep for exhibitions – I don't want to part with it', or make some equally lame excuse.

There were visitors to my gallery who thought the reluctance to sell my pictures was a pose. I was chaffingly told by a friend that it was a well-known dealer's ruse!

The first really important example of Christopher Wood's work that I sold was *Mending the Nets*. The purchaser was Miss Cecily Debenham. What a pang it cost to affix that little red 'sold' spot. Her cheque felt like dross in my hand. Had it not been that my overhead expenses were already far exceeding my income, I doubt if I could ever have brought myself to part with it.

Later the same year Mrs Elmhirst of Dartington Hall purchased three of my finest paintings, *Man in Cart* and *Little House by Night* being the two most outstanding.

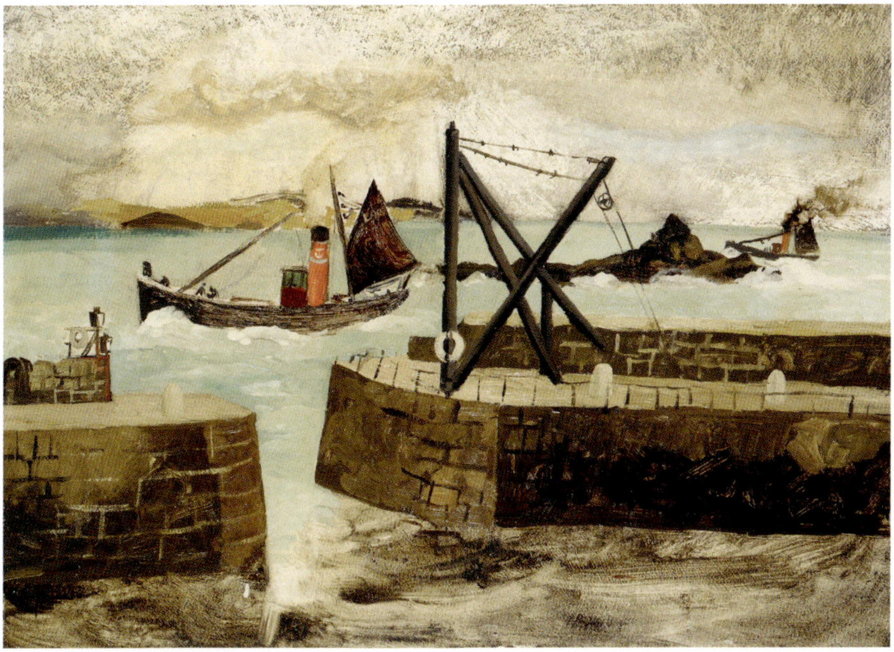

Christopher Wood, *Red Funnel*, 1930. Private Collection

This acquisition must have greatly enhanced the artist's reputation.

Not all Christopher Wood's work is distinguished by the 'classic' quality of the above paintings.

I remember one morning a well-known collector waylaying me as I entered my gallery where half a dozen of my best examples were awaiting consideration by a curator from Canada – *Red Funnel*, *Newlyn*, *Cornish Sailor*, *Clivia*, *The Innkeeper*, *Breton Sailor*. This man said his ideas as to the merits of this artist were completely transformed after seeing these paintings, and for the first time he agreed that the title 'genius' might justifiably be applied to Christopher Wood.

The artist's output was prodigious considering that he died at the age of twenty-nine. Better one superb Christopher Wood in a public gallery than half a dozen mediocre examples of his work.

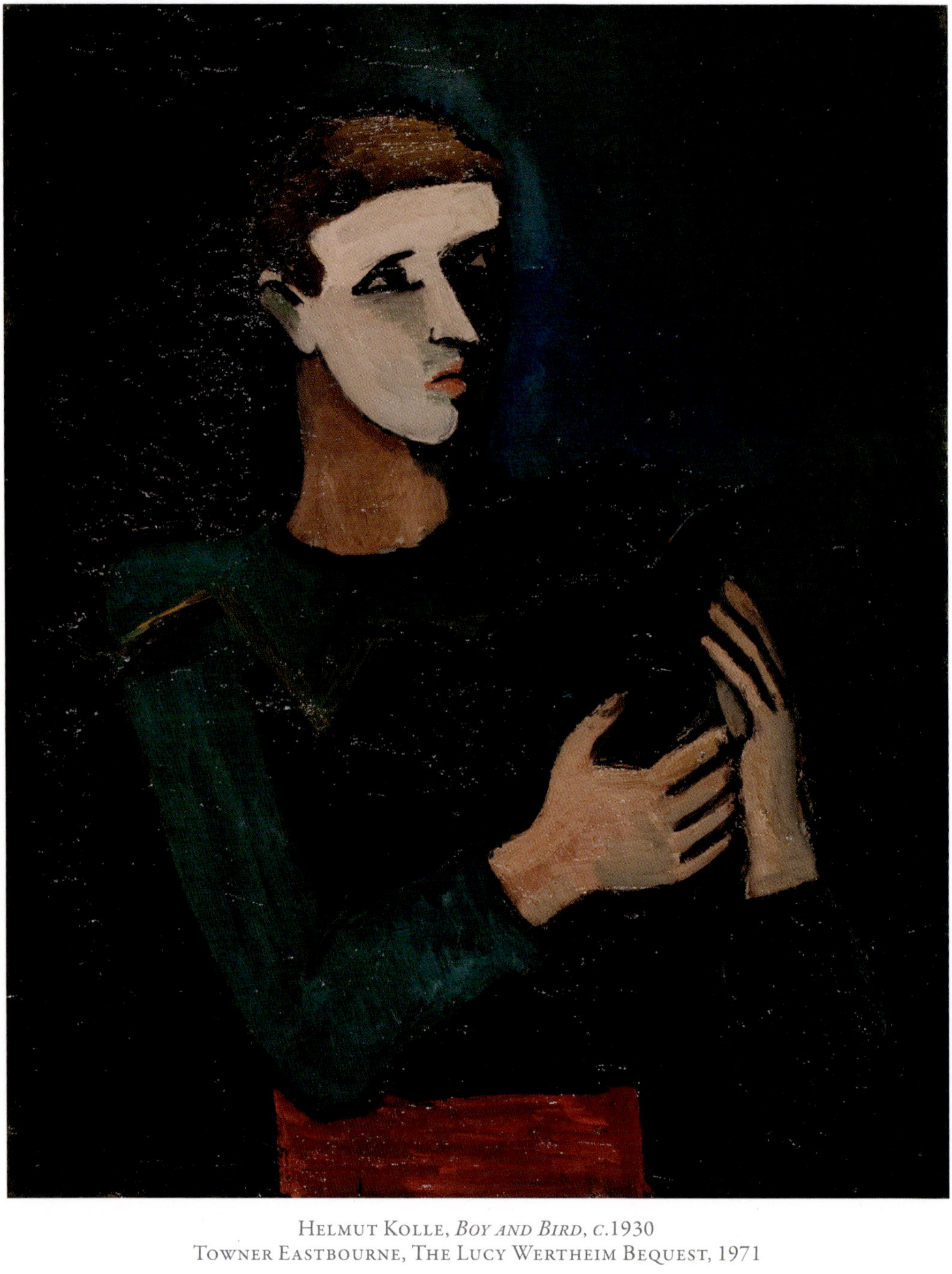

Helmut Kolle, *Boy and Bird*, c.1930
Towner Eastbourne, The Lucy Wertheim Bequest, 1971

Kolle

Strange how a chance word spoken in jest can stupendously affect a number of lives.

In the early summer of 1930 I was taken to see the paintings of Kolle, at the house of M. Uhde, at Chantilly. This introduction was effected indirectly through my friend Charlotte Urquhart, of Manchester, who, teasing me about my odd taste in art, said I ought to make the acquaintance of her nephew, Bertie Jacoby, whose enthusiasms were very similar to my own. Aware that I was just off to Paris on a holiday, she spontaneously inscribed a few eulogistic lines about myself to hand to him on my arrival, adding, 'He can be the most uncordial of people if he doesn't like you, but if he does happen to take a fancy to you there'll be no end to his kindness.'

Most fortunately for me I seemed to fall into the latter category, for we became good friends immediately and though he was many years younger than myself I was able from the beginning to look up to him for counsel and advice as to who were in Paris the most interesting of the unarrived painters. His extraordinary intelligence and versatile mind, and a particularly pleasant capacity of remaining silent if neither of us felt like talking, endeared him to me from the time we met.

The project of starting a gallery in London to help to recognition the young painter was slowly maturing in my mind. As I unfolded my plans to this new friend, he entered whole-heartedly into the scheme and donned his thinking cap to some effect to help me. First I must make the acquaintance of M. Uhde, who it seemed had a young protégé, Helmut Kolle by name, who though not yet thirty was a very remarkable painter and was already regarded seriously by persons of discernment. He would borrow his mother's car and take me to Chantilly the very next day if Uhde could receive us. As it happened, Madame Jacoby's car was in use and we made the journey by train – to me a much more comfortable mode of travelling.

On arriving at Chantilly we made our way to the house of Uhde. It was an old house, very plain yet gracious looking, giving on to a square. I remember that we went straight upstairs and the room that we were shown into had a warm enveloping air of friendliness. There was a round table in the middle of the room with a printed cloth on it. On this was set a bottle of wine and some glasses. The square, flat window was a good size and the room full of light. On the wall opposite to me was a very large painting (I imagine over life-size) of a male figure – in greyish hues. Though very strange and quite different from any other painting I had ever seen, it entered my consciousness comfortably, and I looked round to see if there were other paintings from the same source. Yes, there were others, and through the wide, open doors – or were they just walls knocked down (for three rooms gave spaciously one into another) – there were more paintings equally exciting and they were surely by the same artist. The walls were plastered with canvases, and so beautifully arranged that they did not give an air of over-crowding. Rather, it was the lovely effect of a lovingly worked patchwork quilt. I learnt that the paintings that dominated the rest were by Kolle, the man whose acquaintance I had hoped to make.

Uhde saw very quickly that the work was sympathetic to me, and possibly by some prearranged sign communicated this news to Kolle, who appeared a few minutes later. Knowing his shyness, I feel sure that had Uhde not been convinced of a cordial welcome for his protégé, he would have refrained from making the introduction. As it was, I can only say that rarely in my life – and I have made quite a few spontaneous friendships – has my heart gone out so fervently yet humbly to anyone as it did to Helmut Kolle that afternoon.

I see him now as vividly as if it were but yesterday – a *debonair* grace about the slight, boyish figure that gave it an almost elfish appearance. There was a *faux air* of the English public schoolboy about him; his way of wearing his London tailored suit, his English tie and his English walking stick. In spite of his slightness of build and his air of delicacy, there emanated from him a curious dynamic force. He had a gay, infectious laugh, yet in his eyes there

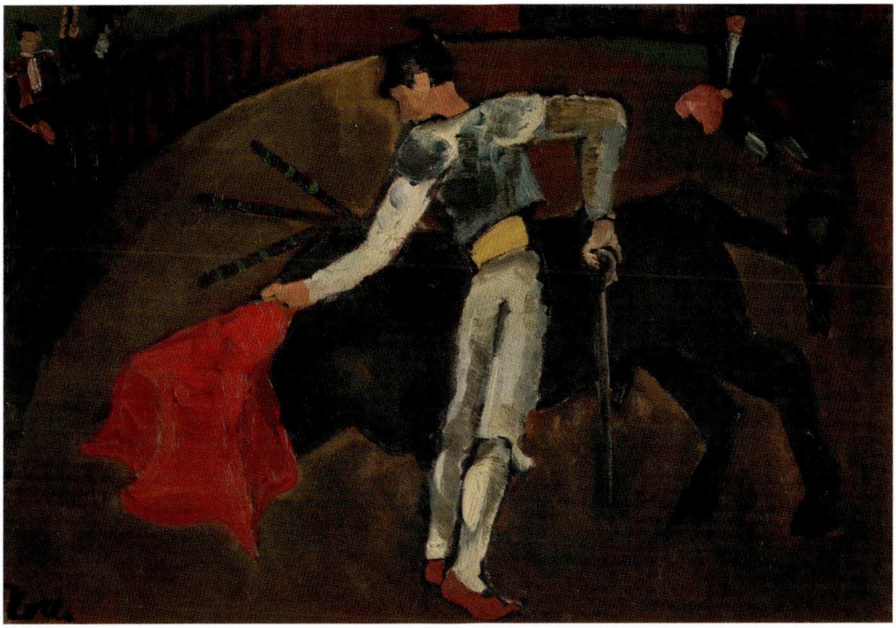

HELMUT KOLLE, *BULL FIGHT*, *c.*1930
TOWNER EASTBOURNE, THE LUCY WERTHEIM BEQUEST, 1971

was an expression as sad as any I have ever seen. One got with him a tragic feeling of solitariness. My heart warmed to him as to a motherless child.

I understood that he had been at school in England. Eton bad been mentioned. English, therefore, would seem the natural language to converse in but his English was of a fragmentary nature. He was very self-conscious and finally we lapsed completely into French.

I cannot remember that we talked pictures that afternoon. But it was arranged that I should return a day or two later and take lunch in the town with Uhde and Kolle. I remember a day when they met us (Jacoby and myself) at the station, and the four of us went to a little restaurant where we partook of a simple yet well cooked meal. That day after lunch we went carefully through a selection of Kolle's paintings and I chose six which I said I would like to buy. Among these was the *Spahi à Cheval*, which Uhde said he wanted to keep for himself, and it was some time before he would agree to part with it. It is one that I also would now feel distressed to lose.

These six paintings I definitely purchased, and I selected another six which

I said I would buy if I could find the money in a few months' time. Uhde was to hold them for me for three months until I could come to a decision.

I returned to England and doubt began immediately to assail me. Had I not done a mad, scatter-brained thing to buy paintings that I had seen for less than an hour and by a comparatively unknown artist? What had possessed me? Pavel Tchelitchew, living in Paris and over in London for a holiday, to whom I mentioned the transaction, thought it was a pity if I was going to show such work in my gallery – the paintings of Kolle had such a coarse, brutal quality.

Three months later I paid another visit to Uhde, at Chantilly, and the moment I re-encountered the paintings of Kolle I fell more deeply than ever under their spell. It was no use reasoning about it. Doubtless it was a crazy thing to do, but I'd just got to have those other six. I told Uhde that if he gave me time somehow I'd manage to pay for them.

If I wrote here that I had loved and been loved by many artists, the statement would be misconstrued by certainly the majority of my readers. Nevertheless, there is a *sympathie* so intense between the creative artist and the sensitive 'appreciator' that I think only the word 'love' describes this emotion. I felt always in the presence of Kolle a deep tenderness mingled with humility and a passionate longing to serve him, or at any rate protect him from the hard, stupid, unseeing world. He seemed such a tragic, defenceless figure.

His paintings became to me animate things. I think before I had never really dreaded dying, and the act of dying had no fears for me, but the passing out from this world and leaving behind my lovely Kolle paintings neglected and misunderstood became for me a nightmare.

In the early spring of 1931 I held in my gallery a one-man show of the work of Kolle. Uhde and Kolle were to come to London for a few days over the opening. I had put my flat at their disposal. We had sent out over a thousand invitation cards for the private view and a small cocktail party had been arranged on the evening of the opening day, to which a number of Uhde's and Kolle's personal friends as well as my own had been invited. The day arrived and word came from Chantilly that Kolle had got 'flu and was too ill to travel. It was a bitter disappointment to me, as my room looked so lovely hung with his work and I was longing for him to see it.

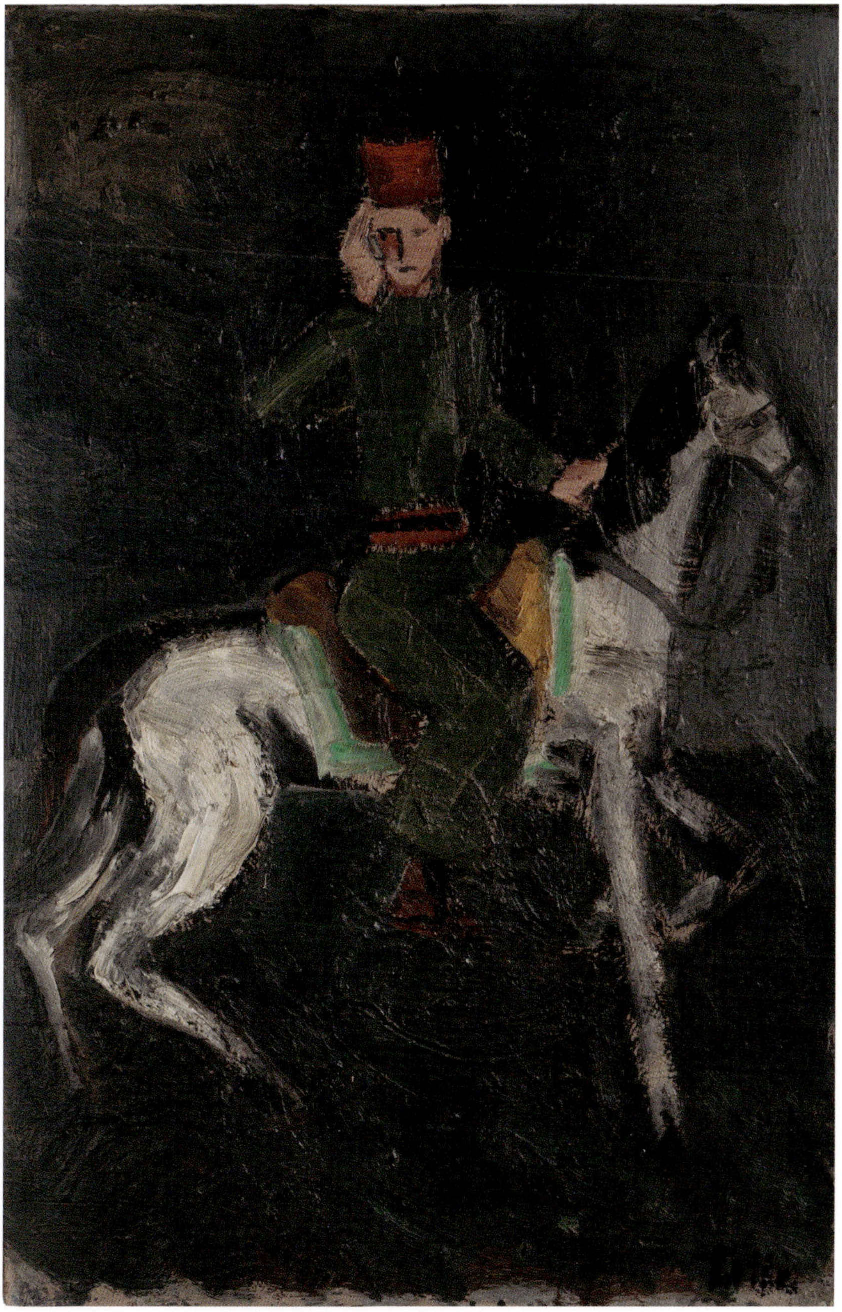

Helmut Kolle, *Spahi A Cheval*, c.1929
The Lucy Wertheim Estate

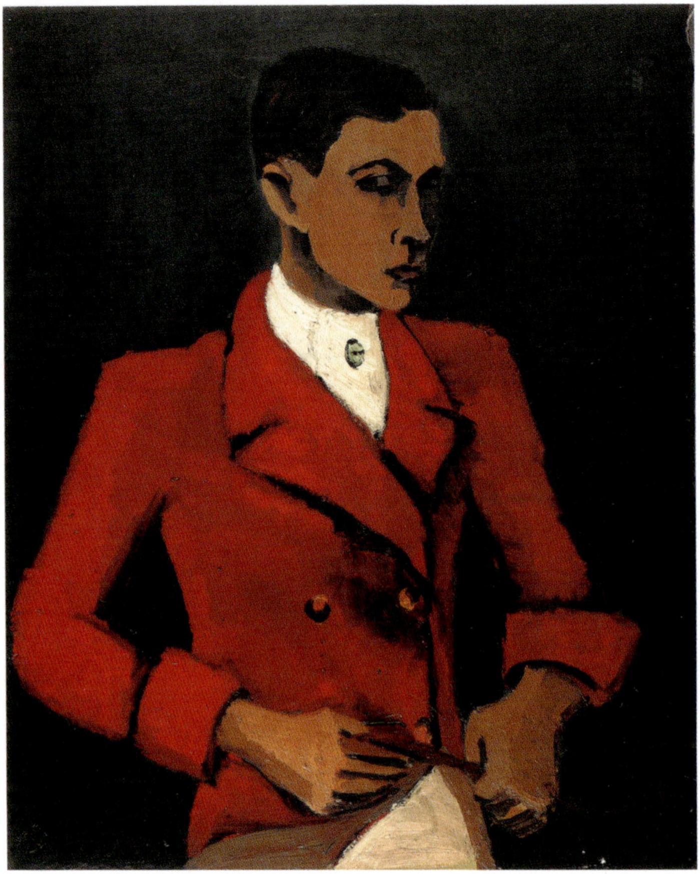

Helmut Kolle, *Self-Portrait in Hunting Kit*, c.1930
Private Collection, Hamburg

The exhibition lasted three weeks and Kolle grew worse instead of better. I remember imploring Mr Marriott, *The Times* critic, however he felt about his work to refrain from saying anything that might hurt the artist, as he was counting so enormously on a success in London and would read the notices so avidly and take them so much to heart. Marriott gave him a sympathetic notice and I have never ceased to be grateful to him for that kindly act.

The exhibition was not liked by the public and many were the harsh things said both by the critics and by the ordinary visitor. My feelings were jarred day after day and I could only be thankful that the artist was not present to hear the stupid, unintelligent remarks made about his painting.

Les Lierres

Later in the spring of 1931, I went to Paris to choose a school for my daughter. I took this opportunity of going over to Chantilly to see Kolle – visiting him for the first time in his little home, *Les Lierres*. It was a small, old-fashioned house approached by a long, narrow garden path. There were a heap of rough-haired, prize-bred fox-terriers rushing in and out, scrambling upstairs and out into the garden again, quite uncontrolled in their habits, evidently adoring their master and equally adored by him.

Kolle was in bed and at my first glance at him my heart contracted. He was obviously so desperately, desperately ill. I went and sat by his bed and begged him to tell me what I could do to help him to get better. He asked me to buy the *Self-portrait in Hunting Kit* that hung in his sitting room downstairs. He offered it to me for a sum in francs equal to a little more than £40 in English money. I said I would, and his gratitude was infinitely touching. He told me he was longing to get away – if possible to the South of France, where he felt much better than at Chantilly.

He was living alone. A woman came in daily to attend to his wants, and the sister of M. Uhde, who lived nearby, did what she could to ease conditions for him.

As he lay there propped up on his pillows, fearfully weak and obviously feverish, he yet had the energy to abuse a cruel fate that cut him off from his painting. He railed bitterly at the treatment ordered by his physician – a series of injections and a diet that he said made life unbearable.

Had I followed the dictates of my heart, all my skill as a nurse (and I had had considerable experience as such) would have been dedicated there and then to trying to get him well. I longed to roll up my sleeves and take charge of that sick room. Surely the passionate desire on my own part to get him well combined with his own will to recover would have succeeded? As it was I had no choice at the time but to return to London, and I did not see him again for several weeks.

An SOS from my daughter imploring me 'not to let her be a boarder any longer' took me to Paris in May, and the day after arriving Kolle met me and we spent a quiet hour together at a little restaurant. He looked extremely frail but was in better spirits, his doctor no longer insisting on the strict *régime* of formerly. M. Uhde told me that by this time the physicians had given up all hope of a cure and were letting him end his days as peaceably as possible.

He died a few weeks later.

Vivin

It was to M. Uhde that I owed my introduction to the paintings of the artist Vivin. I saw them for the first time at his house at Chantilly in the summer of 1930 and in less time than it takes to tell had fallen a victim to their charm. I say 'victim' advisedly, for I could not rest until I had persuaded M. Uhde to transfer some of his most treasured examples to my own collection.

It would be difficult to describe the fascination of these paintings; indeed I cannot attempt to *explain* their charm. And I have known a number of people who detested them at sight or regarded them as unworthy of serious consideration. My husband belonged to this category. I hung a Vivin *Winter Scene* in a living room in our house in Manchester and he exclaimed on seeing it: 'Do take that picture away. I can't bear it.' We compromised. I moved it to another room where it would not meet his gaze at every meal time.

Half a year later I took the picture to London for inclusion in an exhibition at my gallery and on my return home at the weekend he inquired querulously what had become of the French snow scene he was so fond of!

The press cuttings that came in over that first exhibition of Vivin's work in London (February 1931) show that neither the critics nor the public were yet attuned to the naïve vision of this artist. I believe Marriott was the only critic to give him an informed and intelligent write-up. A few enthusiasts (among them Jim Ede from the Tate Gallery) were frequent visitors to the show, and one young man used to dash in every evening just when we were on the point of closing to feast his eyes on a particular canvas that had taken his fancy. (He said he had not the remotest chance of acquiring it.) To many people he would have seemed a trifle mad, but how well I understood his infatuation!

Vivin was then about seventy. He had been a sorting clerk in the French Post Office, and had painted entirely for his own pleasure.

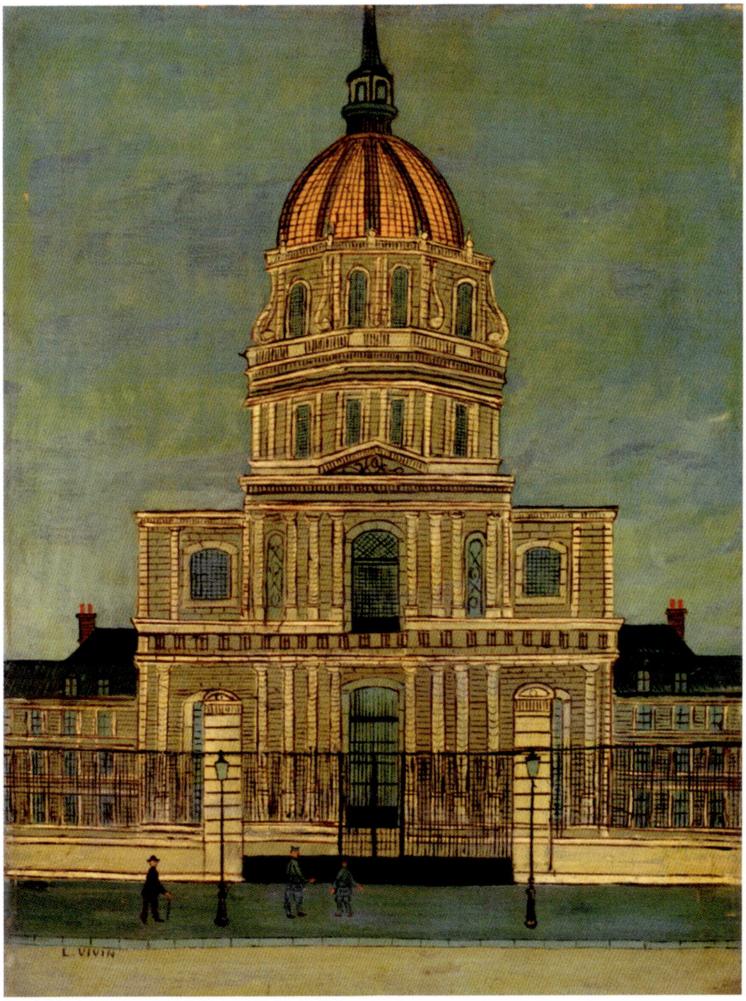

LOUIS VIVIN, *LES INVALIDES*, *C.*1925-30
SOUTHAMPTON ART GALLERY

Mrs C.B. Cochran, dining with us one night in Manchester, admired my favourite painting of Vivin, *The Pleasure Park*, which at the time hung in our drawing room, exclaiming, 'I like it better than any modern painting I've seen!'

Vivin's work is gradually becoming known and finding its way into famous collections. But up to the present I would definitely place him – in England at any rate – in the category of the artist's artist!

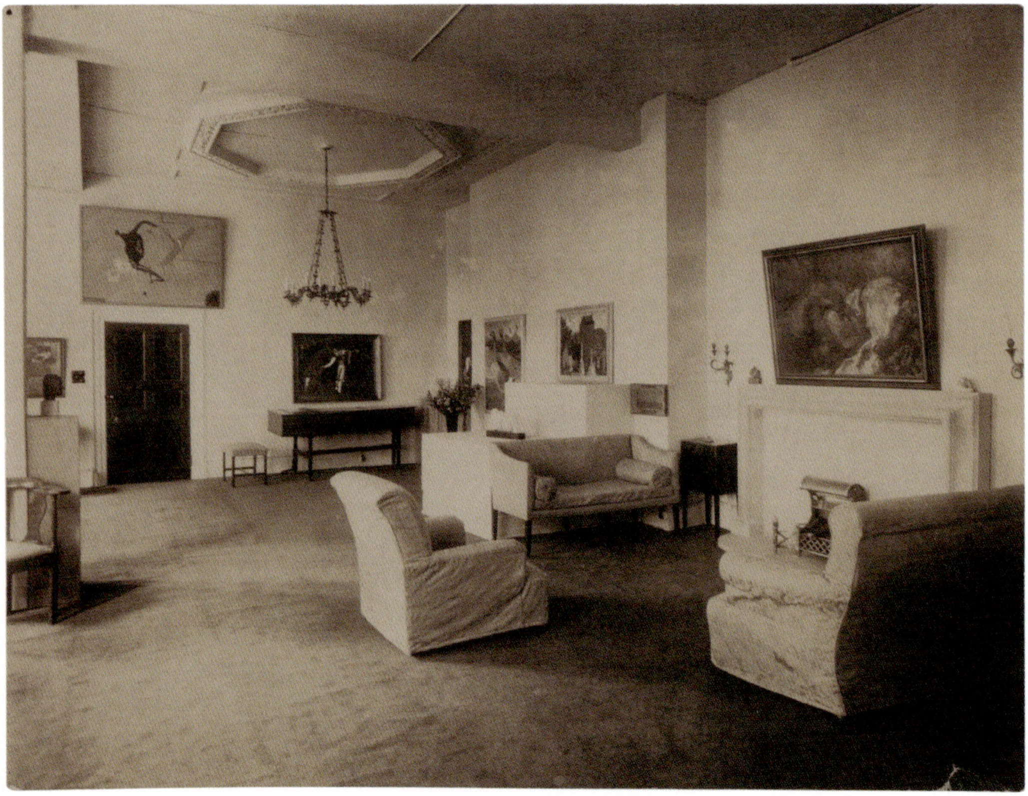

The Wertheim Gallery, exhibiting *Modern Paintings*, October 1930
The Lucy Wertheim Archive

Oiled Wheels

What fun it must be running a gallery! How often was this remark made to me in the early days of my venture and what a compliment it implied of serenity and *joie de vivre*!

That the gallery seemed to run on oiled wheels was due in large measure to the perfect co-ordination of its personnel: myself, my secretary Eve Disher and my assistant Biddy McNay.

I, as director, was responsible for its policy, the choosing of the work and the arranging of the exhibitions. Eve Disher, with her tact and charm and fund of worldly wisdom, constituted a good antidote to my own north-country forthrightness, loathing for expediency and (at that time) somewhat naïve trust in humanity.

I can hear Eve now pensively murmuring as an arrant flatterer took his departure, 'I wonder what he wants.'

The stranger had observed: 'Your gallery is quite the most charming in London; all Paris is talking of it!' The remark left me elated, Eve sceptical! I remember protesting at her cynicism.

'Love of admiration will be your undoing, my child,' my father had been wont to say to me, and perhaps it is because I realise how an artist revels in the sunshine of appreciation (and flattery!) that I get on so well with this genus of the human species. I like people saying pretty things to me, even if they aren't always entirely true!

Biddy, not yet eighteen, became a cogent force in the gallery from the moment of its inauguration. Her pretty ways and soft Irish voice made her extremely popular with visitors, added to which she possessed the charm of complete unselfconsciousness. She was the daughter of a dealer in antiques and the atmosphere in which she had been brought up tended to make her shrewd, cautious and level-headed. Biddy could weigh up a business proposition with the acumen of a woman twice her age. She had a most steadying influence on myself, who did my 'acting first and thinking after'! Would that I had taken her advice more often!

She was at her happiest doing all the things I hated doing – putting tabs on pictures, making out lists and lay-outs, measuring mounts and frames, pasting in press cuttings, dealing with gossip writers, busying herself with the hundred and one routine jobs that make for the smooth running of a gallery. We used to call her 'our Court Circular', on account of her extensive acquaintance with royalty and the peerage, and her amazing knowledge of the ramifications of marriage and divorce in 'High Society'.

Biddy was an omnivorous reader of memoirs and reminiscences, and knew more about the lives of famous people than anyone I've ever met. Yet withal there was no trace of snobbery in her make-up. When receiving visitors in my absence, I could rely on her being at her ease with any type or class. I remember coming in one afternoon, and glancing at my visitors' book saw 'MARY' inscribed on the page – no surname or address accompanying the word. It had fallen to Biddy in my absence to receive Princess Mary and Lord Lascelles. Biddy's report to me later was that they had proved most entertaining and delightful guests!

Rival Claims

Although to outward semblance my gallery was running so tranquilly, certain creakings of the oiled wheels began to manifest themselves about this time.

That perennial topic of the women's journals – 'Career or Family' – took on a personal significance.

In the spring of 1931 my husband assumed the duties of Consul for the Netherlands in Manchester. This involved more entertaining in our home in the north and our joint attendance at consular and civic functions. If I excused myself from accepting invitations on account of 'prior engagements', he was hurt and occasionally resentful.

A son at Cambridge and a younger son and daughter at boarding school also created their individual problems. The report of an injured knee would send me dashing across the country to ascertain for myself the extent of the damage, or a disquieting temperature would keep me on tenterhooks awaiting developments. Prize Days, Confirmation ceremonies and the like made desirable my attendance at school, and often these clashed with private views and appointments at the gallery.

'I could do with half a dozen lives!' I exclaimed impatiently to my husband one day.

'Other cats have nine lives,' was his sly rejoinder as he regarded me with pen in hand ruminating on an article I had entitled 'What I Want From Life'.

After cogitating for half an hour to the strains of the *Washington Post*, and more Sousa ditties from my neighbour's wireless overhead, I decided my only 'want' from life was a sound-proof ceiling and I changed my caption to 'Count Your Blessings', which theme required no deep reflection, wrote on:

Seven blessed gifts the gods have seen fit to endow me with.

1. Good health.

2. A happy disposition with an insatiable joy of living.

3. A congenial job with lots of hard work attached to it.

4. A tolerant husband who having put up with my vagaries for twenty-odd years protests he loves me still.

5. Three children (two sons and a daughter), intelligent and not ill-favoured, who tease me unceasingly, which I am assured on good authority is a sign of deep affection.

6. Tried and trusty friends, some from my childhood days, who laugh with me, and at me not too unkindly, and who depend on me as I on them in times of stress.

7. Sufficient means to assure me shelter, warmth and food and a certain amount of privacy.

My list completed, I made a silent resolution that, please God, my 'career' should not jeopardise these blessings.

My appointments book (in Biddy's hands) from then on was splashed with red ink crosses emphasising the precedence of family claims.

Some days later a consular luncheon involved a mid-week journey to Manchester. Owing to my absence, I missed the arranging of an exhibition of Epstein's *Genesis* drawings. He came into my gallery to discuss dates and not finding me available fixed his exhibition elsewhere.

Psychology

Running a gallery should by rights turn one into something of a psychologist. It certainly affords opportunity for developing one's powers of observation. But I confess my own deductions occasionally fell wide of the mark.

One day I was turning over a series of drawings on the portfolio stand for a well-dressed young woman standing by. She expressed herself particularly interested in a drawing of a horse by L.D. Rust. 'What is the price of that one?' she asked. 'I should like to have it for my little son's room.' 10 guineas,

I replied. She had been studying it apart from the others and at this point returned it to the portfolio, her interest in the drawing seeming to diminish. Thinking it was the price that was prohibitive I offered to reduce it. She bought it.

My client was Barbara Hutton, Countess Reventlow, the richest woman in the world.

Talking of powers of observation, ever since I was a child I have been extremely interested in hands. A distinguished visitor to one of my early shows was the Rt Hon David Lloyd George. He bought a picture from me by Frieda, wife of Sir Percy Harris, who was holding a show in my gallery at the time. Lloyd George came in one morning with his daughter Megan, and having selected a painting that he liked, fumblingly drew out his purse from his pocket and with extraordinary clumsiness counted out notes in payment. I shall never forget the incident. Such maladroitness seemed so incongruous in a man of Lloyd George's mental stature.

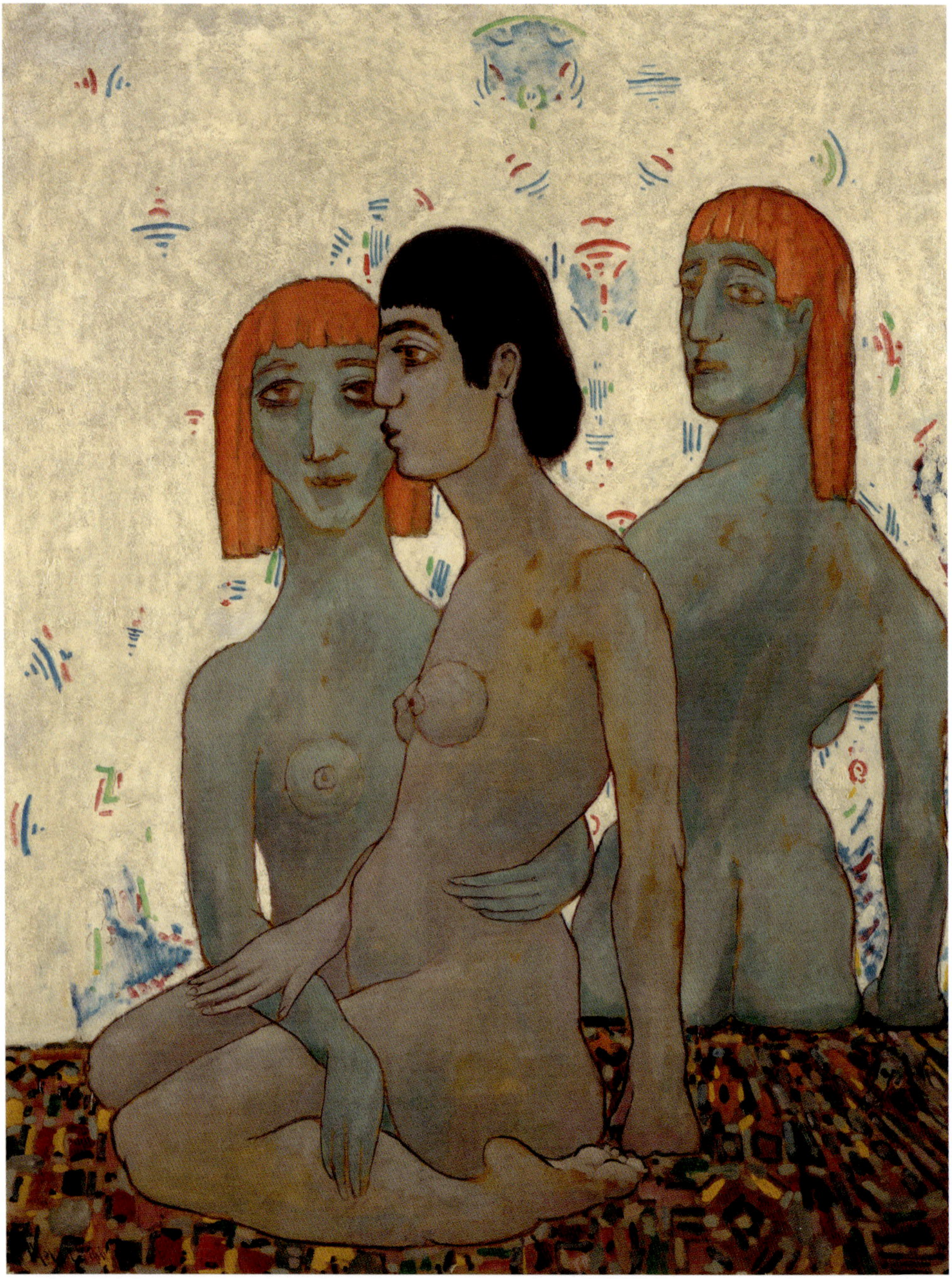

Phelan Gibb, *Three Graces*, 1911
Towner Eastbourne, The Lucy Wertheim Bequest, 1971

Phelan Gibb (born 8 April 1870)

The English artist still living whose work probably is of the most permanent value is Phelan Gibb.

One day Phelan Gibb will doubtless come into his own, and his finest paintings take their place alongside examples of Manet, Cézanne, Picasso, Kolle and Christopher Wood in international exhibitions of modern art.

Not all his work is of this calibre, but what really great artist is consistently good? I have seen paintings by Van Gogh that would shame the least gifted of my 'Twenties Group'.

It was in the early spring of the year 1931 that I first made the acquaintance of Phelan Gibb.

Late one afternoon during the exhibition of Kolle there entered the gallery a rather tall man of slight build wearing a plus-four suit of somewhat emphatic check. He had what is ordinarily known as a fresh complexion, bright blue eyes and exquisitely glossy white hair beginning to recede from the temples. At first glance I took him for a country squire and saw him in my mind's eye thoroughly at home in the hunting field or with a fishing rod. (This impression faded on deeper acquaintance. Phelan Gibb is artist first, country gentleman second.) We entered into conversation, and after a while I learned the aim of his visit. Would I go to his studio in Chelsea and look at his paintings? There was nothing indefinite in the request. It was imperative that I should accompany him there and then.

Now it was not easy to accede to this demand, because an hour later a little party was being given in the gallery by Mrs Byng-Stamper and Miss Byng-Lewis, assisted by their cousin Major Longden, and I was invited to be present. However, my secretary said, 'If you go there and back in a taxi you'll just have time.'

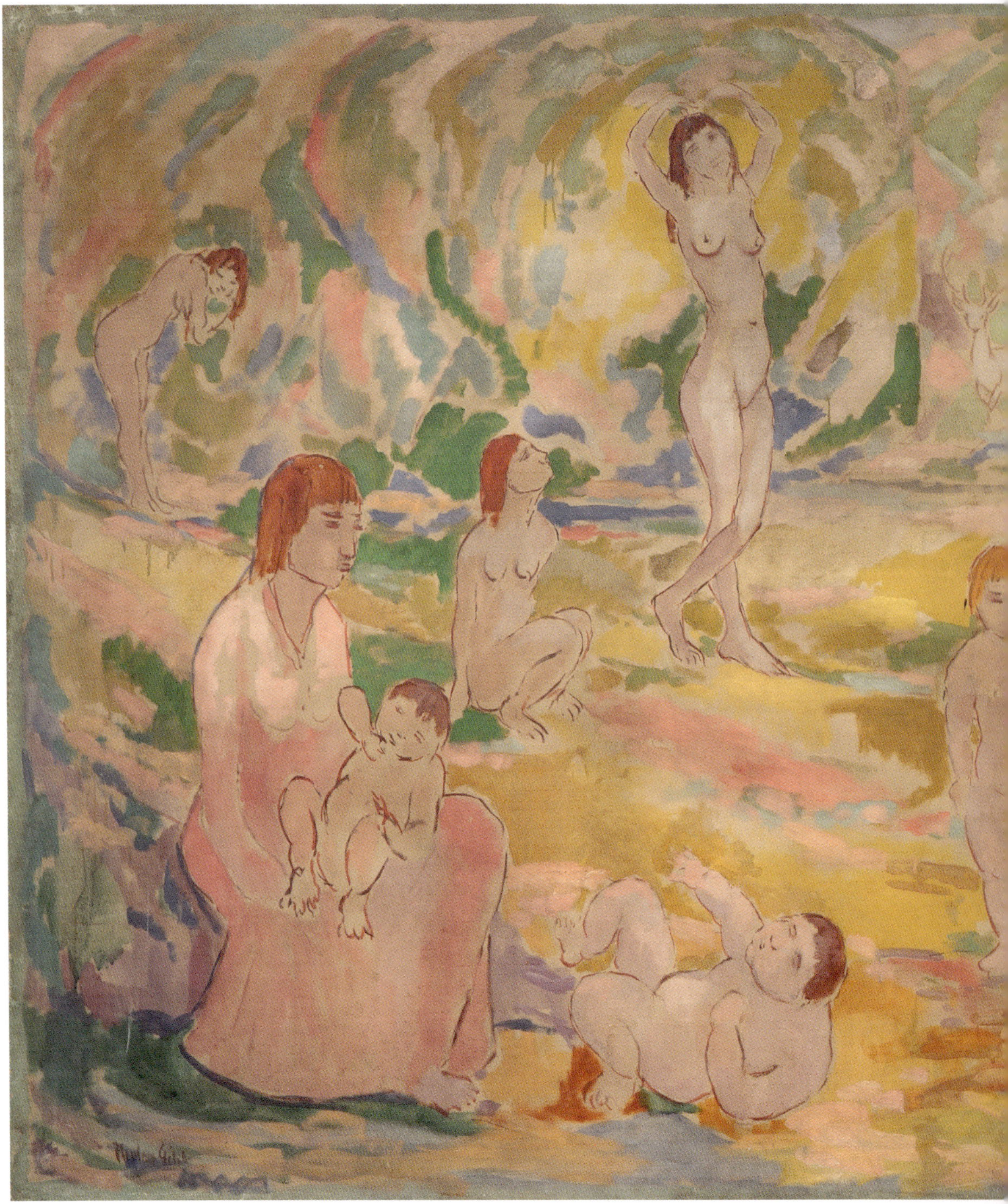

Phelan Gibb, *Rose Nudes in Landscape* (or *Pastorale*), 1916
Towner Eastbourne, The Lucy Wertheim Bequest, 1971

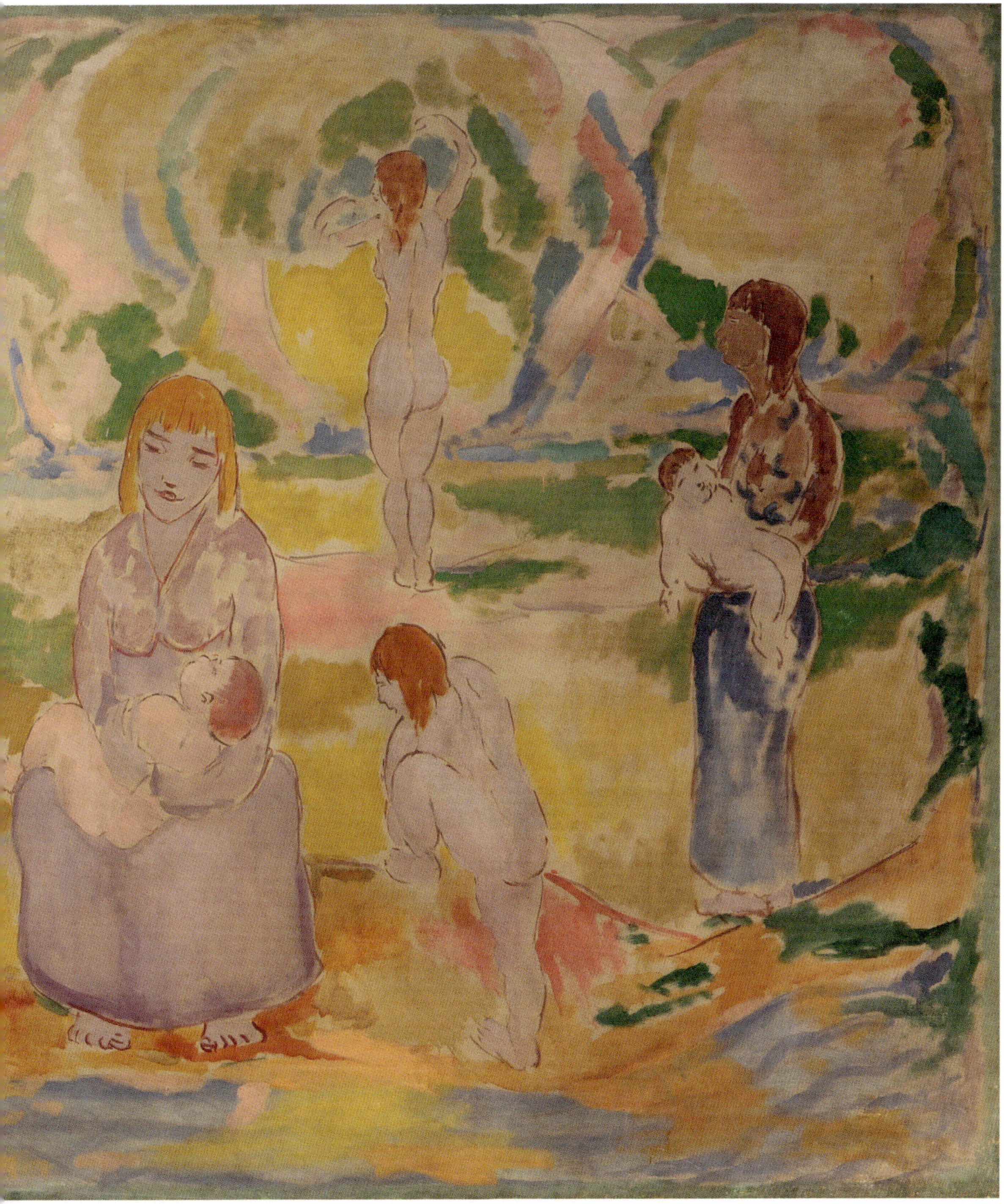

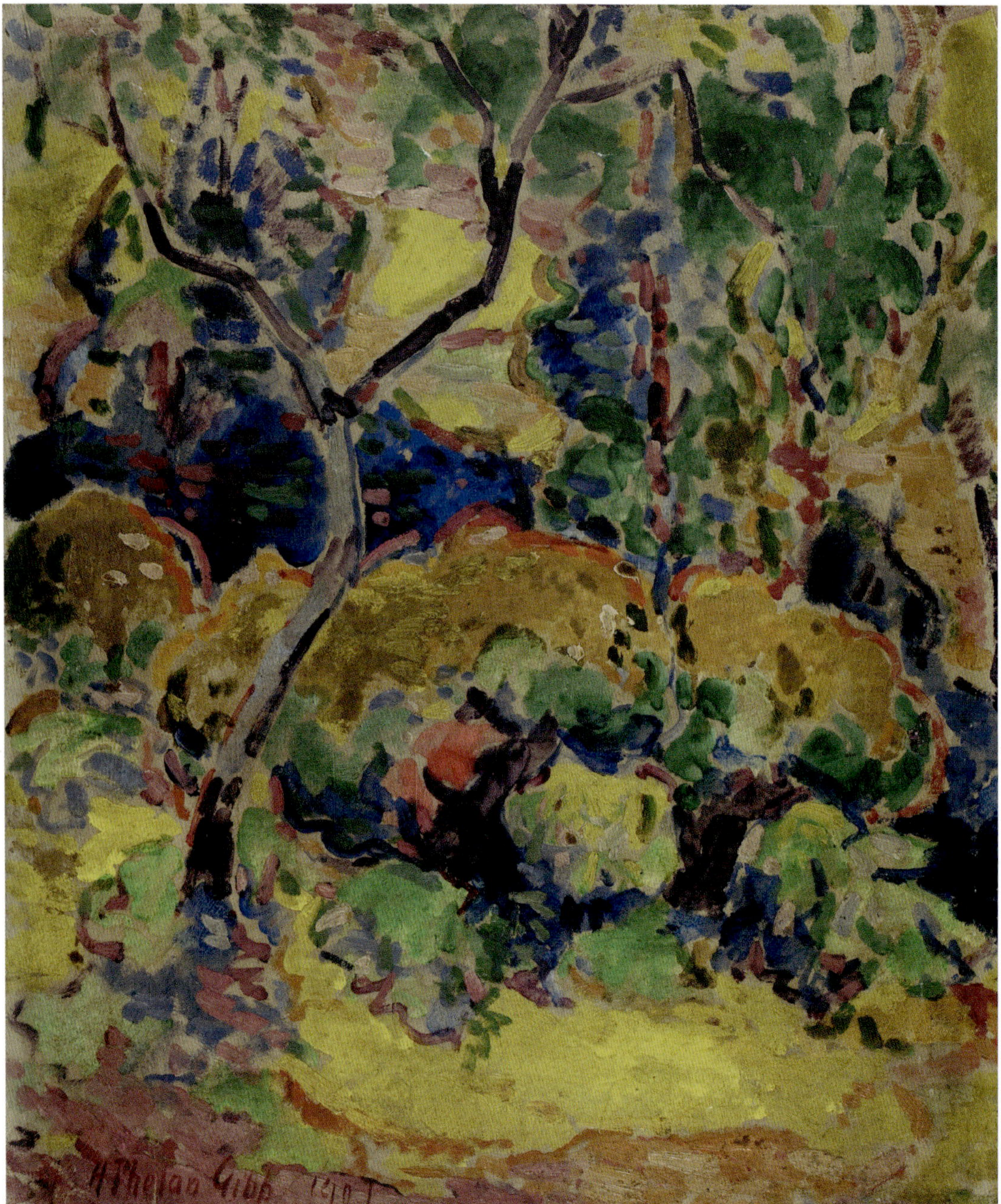

Phelan Gibb, *Paysage*, 1907
Towner Eastbourne, The Lucy Wertheim Bequest, 1971

Think of all the early-April born people you know, then ask yourself if you could have held out against the persuasive powers of any one of them!

Impetuous, self-willed, dynamic Phelan Gibb waved aside all my objections and a few moments later I was being whirled to the Fulham Road to see these paintings, of which until a few moments before I had never heard.

Most of the artists I have known have been hard put to it to find their taxi-fare from Piccadilly to Chelsea and it has come naturally to me, if accompanying them, to pay it, but there was such an air of the *grand seigneur* about Phelan Gibb that I was afraid he would be offended if I offered those few shillings and I refrained.

To the redounding credit of my companion, the taxi-man was paid with an air of considerable resources to draw upon, yet many a laugh have Phelan and I since had over it when he has reminded me of the fear and trepidation with which he watched the taximeter mount in threepences.

When the driver had been paid and a modest tip added, Phelan had exactly twopence-halfpenny in the world.

I was led through a door, along a pathway to a ground-floor studio. The room was large and lofty and a welcoming fire burned on the open hearth. There was an air of well-being about the place. A few good pieces of furniture, some pleasant hangings and soft Persian rugs imparted to the room a look almost of opulence.

How amazingly an artist reveals himself by his paintings. At the end of a very short time I realised that I was in the presence of a painter of no mean stature. There were bad and good canvases on the walls (I know no other great painter as uneven as Phelan Gibb), but there was a quality in the finer ones that was extraordinarily arresting. Here, evidently, was a real personality, a man with something to say and who said it in no uncertain fashion.

I forgot all about the party at the gallery. Later, in an apologetic tone, Marjory Gibb, Phelan's beautiful wife, invited me to stay to a meal with them. I remember how charmingly it was served and the lovely handmade pots – mostly odd ones – that we used and that Phelan made a salad, the dressing of which was evidently a solemn ritual, as was the making of the coffee later. In addition to the salad and the coffee, I think we ate something out of a tin.

I was too excited by Phelan's paintings that evening to concern myself much with the inner man, though at ordinary times food is important to me.

During my visit Phelan broached the subject of my buying a quantity of his work, and I agreed to the proposition on the understanding that I paid him in instalments spreading over a couple of years. (How difficult that became later!)

My appreciation of Phelan Gibb's work was the foundation of a lasting friendship for himself and his wife Marjory. From that time onwards I was always *persona grata* in their little household. Later they moved to the wilds of the country and some of the happiest weekends of my life have been spent in their tiny cottage in Bucks.

How the tongues of the three of us would wag, often into the small hours of the morning. Or Marjory and I would listen fascinated to Phelan's accounts of his boyhood days in Northumberland and his early life in Paris. Phelan, gifted mimic and raconteur, had a seemingly unending fund of stories of his contemporaries in the art world of Paris – Picasso, Juan Gris, Matisse, the Douanier Rousseau, Gertrude Stein, Katherine Mansfield, and the dealers Vollard and Sagot.

Three anecdotes that linger in my mind are: Phelan relating how Matisse shook him warmly by the hand and thanked him for introducing to him a client who paid him 100 francs for a drawing.

Roger Fry buying an abstract drawing of Phelan's for the Contemporary Art Society, which caused such a row that Fry bought it back for himself. (Clive Bell liked the drawing, but Phelan and Roger Fry quarrelled over the incident.)

Gertrude Stein renewing her acquaintance with some of Phelan's paintings after a number of years exclaimed, 'Oh, Harry, I did not remember they were half so good.'

Phelan had been anxious for me to meet Gertrude Stein from the time I began to be interested in his work. They had been very great friends during his long sojourn in Paris, and Gertrude had evidently played a vital part in his artistic life. He had a high opinion of her judgment.

In the spring of 1931, on the strength of my first cheque Phelan and Marjory went off to La Rochelle on a holiday. I was in Paris at the time

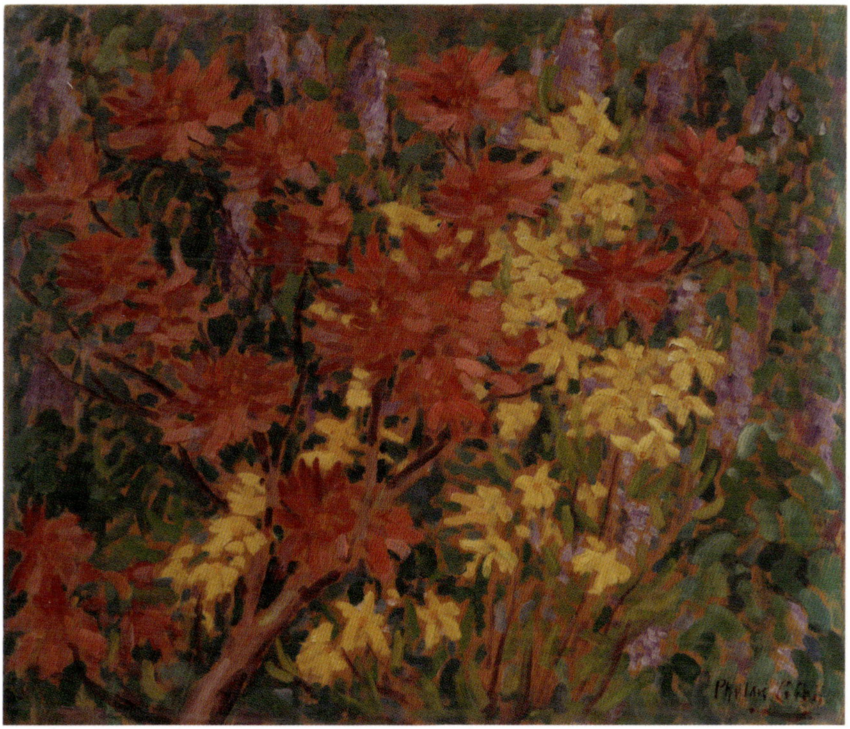

Phelan Gibb, *Flower Study*, c.1910. The Lucy Wertheim Estate

they passed through and Phelan took me to call on Gertrude Stein at her *appartement*. I found her more entertaining than *sympathique*, and apart from being thrilled by her very beautiful early Picassos, which were even lovelier than I had been led to believe, the afternoon was not a great success. I am often at a disadvantage with very brainy people.

Salon d'Automne

But to return to earlier days, the Salon d'Automne made Phelan Gibb a Sociétaire in the year 1909, a greater honour then than it became later.

At this time Sir William van Horne, Engineer of the Canadian Pacific Railway, was one of his patrons. Phelan had a studio off the Boulevard Raspail, and Sir William bought from him two paintings, for which he

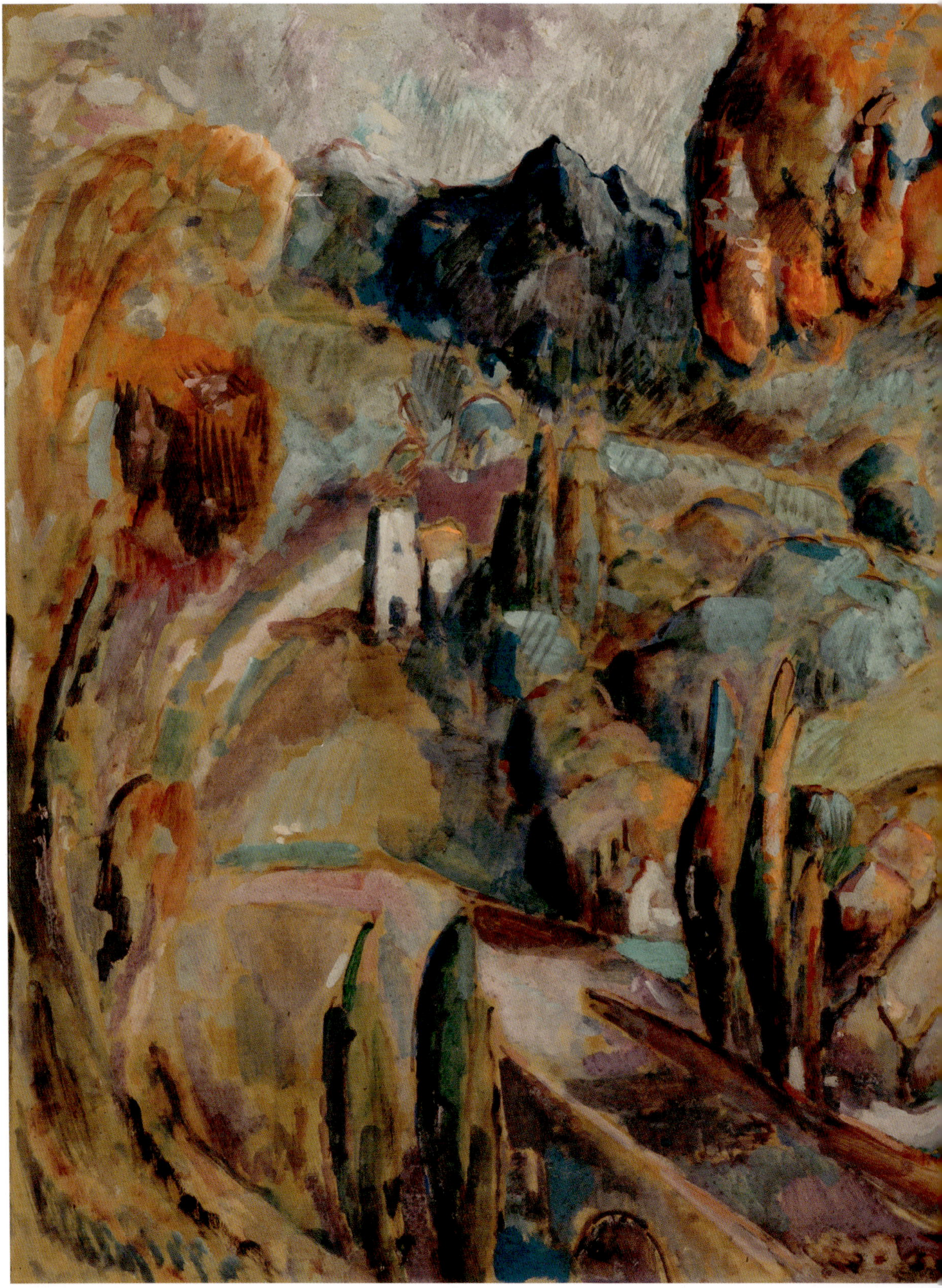

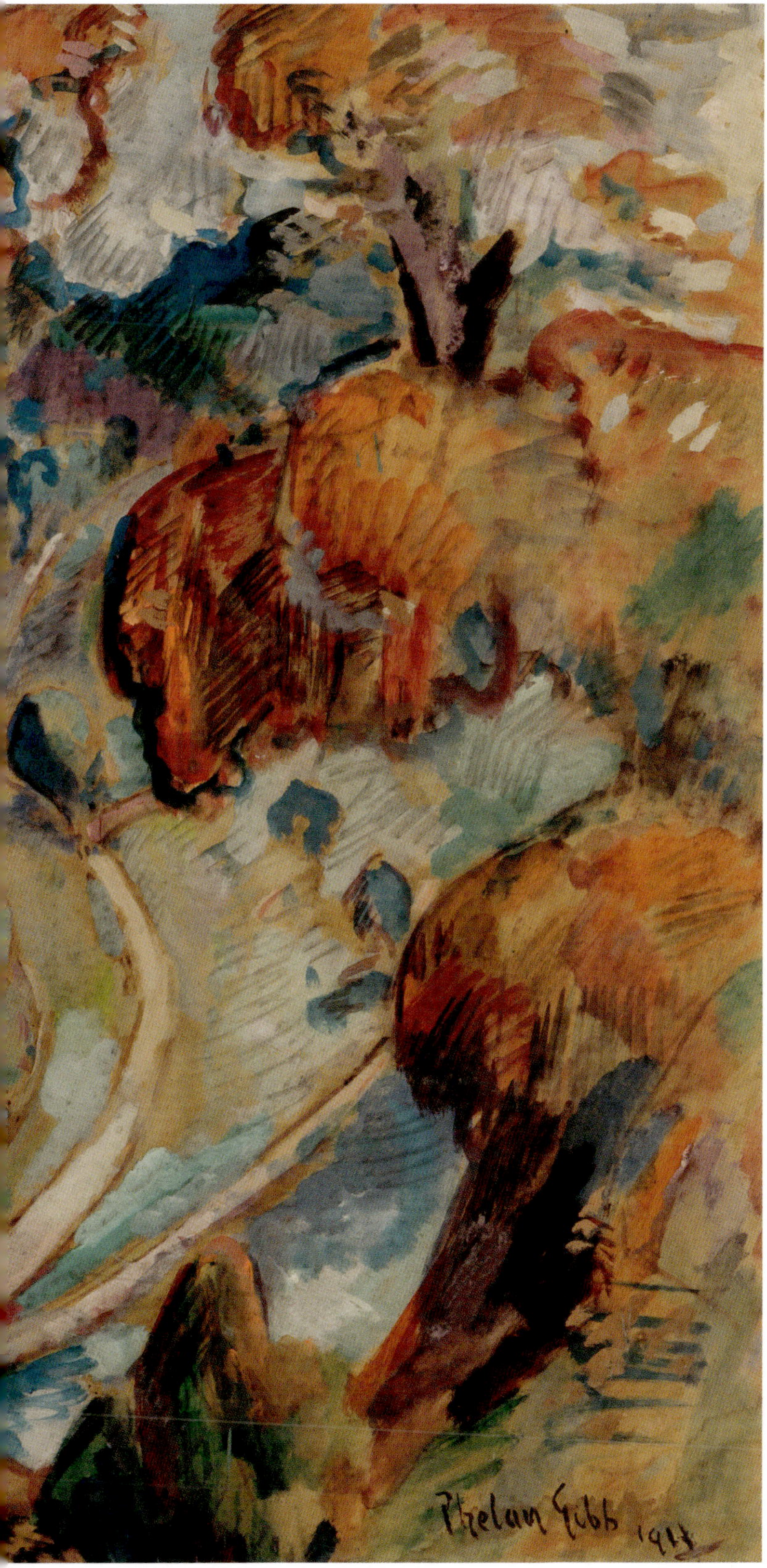

Phelan Gibb, *Landscape*, 1911
The Lucy Wertheim Estate
Exhibited in the Armory Show,
New York, 1913.

paid 100 guineas and 75 guineas, remarking to Phelan that he was a little too far ahead of his public! Van Horne had just added a fine Murillo to his collection and Phelan, aware of this, inquired of him: 'How, Sir, come you to buy one of *mine*?' 'It carries me into another world,' was Sir William's reply.

This was in Paris in the year 1909.

Robert Ross, art critic of the *Morning Post* and stalwart defender of Oscar Wilde, was also one of Phelan's early admirers. It was through him that Phelan came to hold a one-man show at the Carfax Gallery, in Jermyn Street, but so much antipathy was shown to the paintings he exhibited that it closed down at the end of ten days.

In 1913, an exhibition of his paintings held at the Galerie Bernheim-Jeune in Paris was transferred to Dublin at the invitation of Count Markievicz and Dr St John Gogarty. This exhibition was actually closed down before it opened! Phelan recounts that never before had he met with such violent hostility.

His next exhibition was held at the Alpine Club Gallery, in 1917. One day Phelan was feeling very depressed and disgruntled at the lack of appreciation shown by the critics and the public – one visitor had just irately torn up the catalogue and thrown it across the room, exclaiming: 'An insult to the British Public!'

At this moment entered a rather ordinary looking individual with a very live eye who was obviously favourably impressed with the paintings.

Phelan, tentatively: 'You appear to be interested, Sir.' The answer being in the affirmative, Phelan enlarged on the antagonism of the critics and continued: 'After all, I am an Englishman and I would like a little appreciation from my own countrymen. Wouldn't *you*?' 'Yes,' came the diffident answer. A moment after he left the gallery Phelan discovered his visitor's identity. It was H.G. Wells. The following day Wells turned up with his friend Arnold Bennett and a collection of art critics, saying 'Mr Gibb, may I present your enemies!'

Later Phelan and Arnold Bennett had to be almost forcibly separated, so heated became their argument. It must be recalled that Arnold Bennett painted very pretty little watercolours!

Endless are the amusing anecdotes Phelan recalls of past days when modern art was anathema.

On one occasion Mrs Edmund Gosse took him to lunch with Sir Alma-Tadema, who inquired of him: 'Who is the most interesting figure in the Paris Art World at the moment, Mr Gibb?' 'Possibly Cézanne is the most discussed,' replied Phelan. 'What! *That* man!' Tadema barked, 'who can neither draw nor paint – he knows nothing about Art.' *Tempora mutantur*.

Photographed in Phelan's memory of that luncheon party were the panels designed by Tadema in his grand piano, each of the panels painted by an R.A.! One panel had not yet been filled in.

In 1931 I arranged with much pride an exhibition of the paintings of Phelan Gibb. His ultra large canvases, or murals, looked very beautiful in my spacious room and more than one young artist was thrilled with his work.

One enthusiast was Dudley Wallis, that *rara avis*, a curator of discernment, who was much impressed with his drawings, and had he had his way would have acquired one for the Whitworth Gallery, Manchester, of which at the time he was Director. Years later this honour was conferred on Phelan, but not by Dudley Wallis.

Another admirer was James Bolivar Manson of the Tate. An example of Phelan's work can be seen in this gallery. The artist is also represented in the Victoria and Albert Museum and certain galleries in the north of England, among others the Salford Gallery and Cartwright Hall Art Gallery, Bradford.

I had hoped that this exhibition would put Phelan Gibb 'on the map' financially, but his work was not appreciated by the public and he had only a *succès d'estime*. His canvases for the most part were so large that they were only suitable for inclusion in public galleries. I remember I had specially to rent a room at the top of 3-5 Burlington Gardens in order to have them at hand should anyone be interested in acquiring them. They are still awaiting 'homes'.

John Bigge and John Banting

Another outstanding show of those early days was that of John Bigge and John Banting, who held a joint exhibition of their work in my gallery.

Surrealist painting at that time (1932) was so rare in London as to create

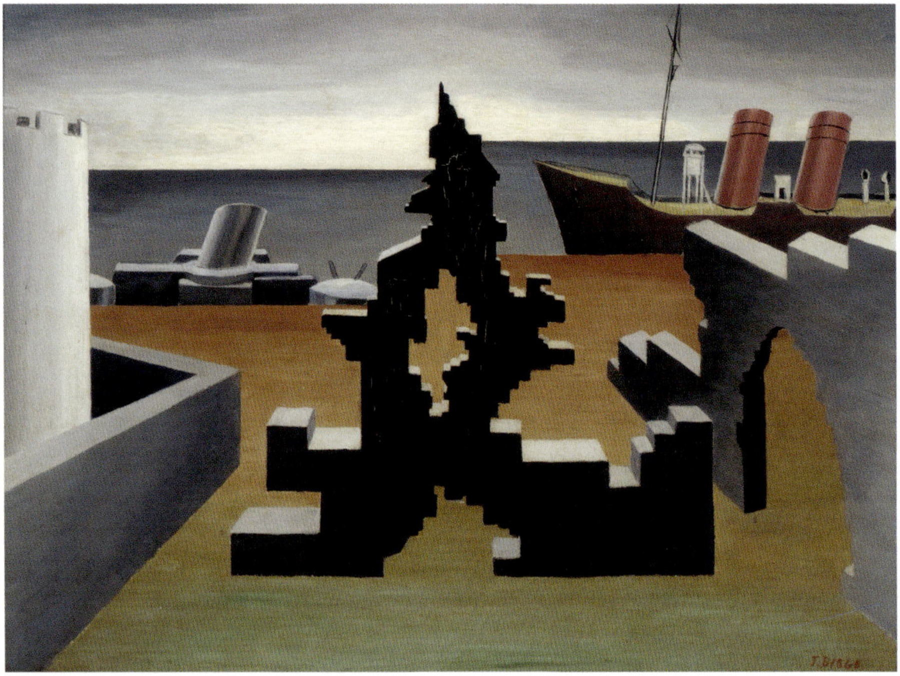

John Bigge, *Dieppe*, 1931. Tate

a sensation. Both Bigge and Banting are creative artists of a high order and it was exasperating in the extreme to have many visitors during the period their work was on view insist on regarding the exhibition as a stunt.

I was able, however, to place a few of the paintings with serious collectors, and bought for my personal collection some of John Banting's drawings. I have shown these in many exhibitions and they continue to give me great pleasure.

Roger Roughton, a boy poet, still at school, who used to frequent my gallery at this time, was mad about the drawings of this artist. He longed to possess one. But he also had a great enthusiasm for a drawing by Helmut Kolle. In order to indulge his passion he sold his collection of stamps and I was so touched by this act that when selling him the one drawing, I presented him with the other. We were great friends ever after.

At the end of a year other duties devolved on Eve Disher, my secretary, and I engaged in her place Ala Story, a Viennese girl, whose enthusiasm for her new job proved an asset to the gallery.

Ala was at her best with chic and *soigné* notabilities of society and I

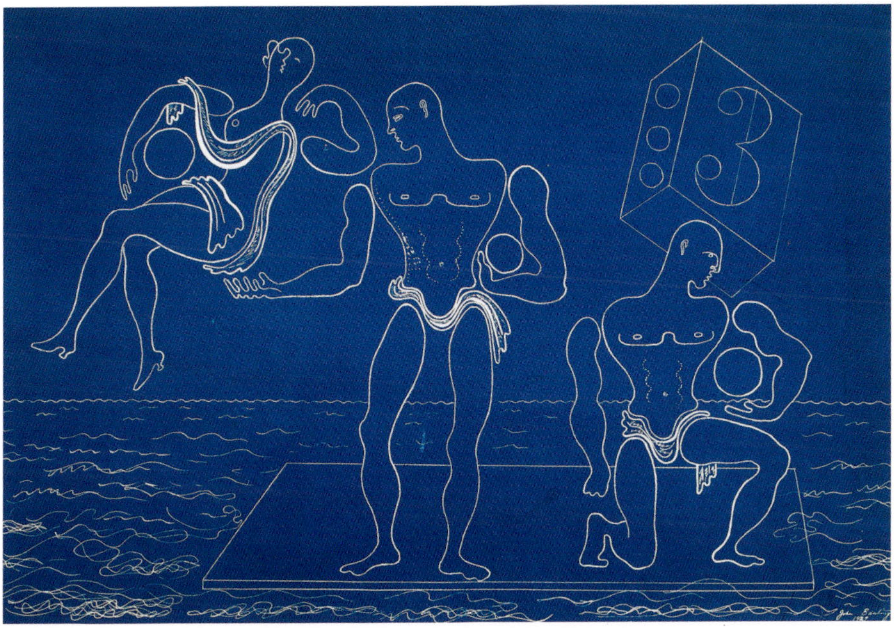

John Banting, *The Bathers*, 1929
Salford Museum & Art Gallery, gift of Lucy Wertheim, 1939

was very content to leave this type in her hands. Especially did she enjoy arranging cocktail parties and helping to receive our guests on private view days. She was an enthusiastic saleswoman and it was a delight to witness her elation when she pulled off a sale. In my mind's eye I still see Ala affixing with childish glee a little red 'sold' spot on a painting or watercolour.

This predilection of hers for a fashionable clientèle left me free to devote my time to the unknown and indigent, with whom I always had more in common.

Henry Stockley

I remember well one morning in those early days of Ala's reign I was sitting at my table discussing some matter with a client when my attention was taken up by an artist at the other end of the gallery. He was a man of about forty who had just unrolled a bundle of paintings and laid them on the floor against the wall. It was to Ala he was displaying them. I could not hear the conversation of these two, but could see from his crestfallen mien that his paintings were not meeting with much appreciation. His efforts were executed on pieces of linoleum and old bits of linen, and though somewhat crude there was a striking quality about them that distracted my attention from the business I had on hand.

When I saw the artist stoop down, collect his paintings and begin to roll them into a bundle again, I asked my client to excuse me for a moment and I went over to the other end of the gallery to have a word with the man himself. He said he was a bus driver who devoted all his spare moments to painting. He had pinched from his wife some old linen pillow slips and ground his own paint, and the results were contained in the bundle! I became interested and told Ala I would deal with him when my interview was concluded.

The upshot of it was that Henry Stockley, bus driver, and myself became friends, and before long he painted at my instigation a series of Illustrations to Bunyan's *Pilgrim's Progress*, which later I exhibited as a one-man show in my gallery.

He used so often to liken himself to Christian that it was this that put the idea into my head. He told me that he had made the round of every gallery in London and could get no one interested in his paintings. He had made a vow the morning he set out to bring his work to me that he would burn everything on his return home if I, too, turned down his efforts.

Stockley had had no art-school training but initiation by his father (who was a sign writer) into the use of pigment gave his paintings a quality that many more 'competent' artists might envy.

That show enchanted me! I still regard it as one of the most exciting exhibitions I ever held, and it created for Stockley himself quite a few admirers. Mr Charles Marriott took a great interest in his paintings and used often to inquire of me, 'And how is your Douanier?' When I asked him if Stockley and I might jointly present him with a painting, he said he made it a rule never to accept pictures that were offered him. Repeating this incident to Frances Hodgkins, she murmured, 'Not without reason do they call him Marriott the Incorruptible.'

No such scruples had Miss Lynda Grier, Warden of Lady Margaret Hall in accepting a painting of Stockley for her Common Rooms.

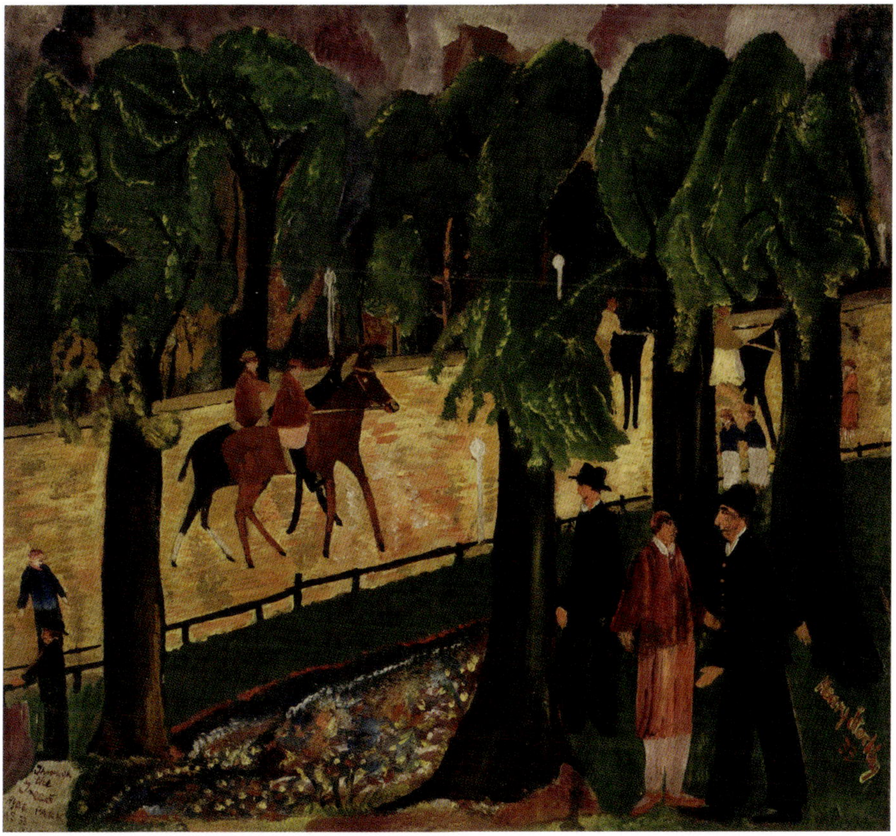

Henry Stockley, *Through the Trees, Hyde Park*, 1933
Towner Eastbourne, The Lucy Wertheim Bequest, 1971

I gave another to Theodore Komisarjevsky, and yet another to Maurice Browne of *Journey's End* fame, who hung it in his private office of the Globe Theatre. In return, Mr Browne presented me with a copy of *Green Pastures*, which I begged him to inscribe from himself to Stockley. This he did and great was Stockley's delight when on opening it he saw the dedication.

We made no sales from this exhibition, apart from a small painting of the Cenotaph, which I sold (nicely framed) for five pounds. The purchaser brought it back the next day, asking if she might return it as none of her friends liked it! But the show gave me so much pleasure that I never regretted the energy, time and expense it cost me. Although Stockley has never become a commercial proposition, his circle of admirers grows. To paint divinely he needs to be inspired – and inspired Stockley was by Bunyan when he painted his *Pilgrim's Progress* pictures.

On one occasion Stockley and I were discussing Shakespeare, and it was only one small step further to infect him with the desire to illustrate some 'Scenes from the Plays of Shakespeare'. These are as lovely as any *décor* I know, and if ever I have the means I will have tapestries woven from them to hand down to posterity.

Nando Manetti

One afternoon during the autumn of 1933, a young school teacher who had been spending her summer holiday in Italy came to me with rapturous accounts of the paintings of a young artist named Nando Manetti. She had 'discovered' him in the little Tuscan town of San Gimignano, where he kept the local inn. Miss Veronica Chambers produced a few canvases which she had brought back from Italy to prove that her faith in her protégé was justified and would not rest until I had agreed to give him an exhibition in my gallery.

Nando Manetti, it seemed, was an entirely self-taught painter, had never had a lesson in his life and Miss Chambers was of the opinion that his work had only to be exhibited for his genius to be recognised.

The dates of the show were fixed. Nando arrived in London. He was a romantic looking young man with clear-cut features and a wealth of dark wavy hair becomingly brushed back from his forehead. I judged him to be rather over thirty years of age.

He was the delight of the press photographers and his show got splendid publicity. Had he been able to speak English, his success might have been even greater still. But my own knowledge of Italian was somewhat fragmentary and that of my 'staff' nil, so we had to depend on Miss Chambers as interpreter in the gallery. This friend of his was indefatigable in her efforts on behalf of the young artist and introduced various friends who bought a number of his paintings. I also persuaded a relation of my own to buy one.

As Miss Chambers was engaged during the day in teaching, it sometimes fell to my lot to entertain Nando over his luncheon hour.

Never shall I forget the sensation my companion and I caused as we walked up Bond Street, the dark, handsome young foreigner attired in a waisted tangerine overcoat that reached almost to his ankles, and shading his uncovered head from the rays of our English sun with an outsize emerald green umbrella. I still see the startled looks of acquaintances as we wound our way towards the restaurant that was our goal. One friend told me later that as she saw us approach she thought we were the vanguard of a circus.

Manetti's paintings had a serenity and charm which grew on one during his show and we were sorry when the gentle stranger took his departure. His thoughtful ways and courtesy endeared him to all in the gallery, and for a couple of years afterwards I got letters from him in which he always addressed me as 'my dear Lady', planning a second exhibition under my auspices. His letters make enchanting reading.

Early Days

When I first opened my gallery I was under the impression that my work would bring me into daily contact with a host of *cognoscenti* (I can't think of a better word), whom I could look up to for a greater knowledge of art than I myself possessed. At the end of a very short time I came to realise that the so-called expert was of no use to me .

In Paris earlier in the year I had been introduced by my friends Christopher Wood and Bertie Jacoby to various owners of modern galleries. The leitmotif of these dealers' conversations was their pleasure in showing work to someone capable of appreciating it on its own merits – someone even more interested in the artist not yet arrived than the artist who had made his reputation. I was told that no London dealer would look at the work of any artist who was not already a commercial proposition and in the light of later experience I can well imagine that this was true. At the time I was prepared to take this statement with a pinch of salt, thinking there was more than a modicum of flattery behind the pretty speeches, but after a few weeks I came to the conclusion that I must rely entirely upon my own judgment and the 'flair' that I had frequently been congratulated on possessing.

Charles Marriott of *The Times* remarked after a few visits to my exhibitions that mine was the most personal gallery in London. I remember wondering exactly what he meant by this statement.

I think Marriott realised that the only work I cared to show had three common factors – sincerity, imagination and the quality of 'putting it across'. Mere competence in painting never interested me much and Mr Marriott and I did not see eye to eye on this matter of technical accomplishment. But I take this opportunity of expressing my deep gratitude to him for his interest in my work and for the many helpful notices he has given me, even when disapproving of my enthusiasms.

From the very beginning the press was interested in my venture and no one was more surprised than myself at the amount of space important papers such as *The Times*, the *New Statesman*, the *Spectator*, the *Daily Telegraph*, the *News Chronicle* and the *New English Weekly*, etc. devoted to my exhibitions.

'Peterborough' gave me a notice in the London Day by Day page of the *Daily Telegraph* every few weeks over that first year, then for some unaccountable reason the notices came to an end. I was told that a confrere in the art world had remarked to a director of the paper that Mrs Wertheim must be paying them pretty hefty sums for the publicity they were giving her, and that that was the reason they had dropped me like a hot coal. Whether there is any truth in this story I am not able to say, but I soon found out that I *had* a number of enemies. A story circulated that after his death I had astutely bought up *all* the work of Christopher Wood, and was making a 'corner' in it. Apropos of this supposed transaction some very unflattering remarks were made to me. Sometimes I was made so unhappy by them that I felt like closing my gallery and saying good-bye to the picture world for ever. But I had not had a Scottish grandmother and Lancashire forebears for nothing. I was not made of the stuff that was easily beaten, but I recognised very soon that I was in for a real fight if I was to win through.

Adverse criticism

At the end of a year I had come to realise to a tragic degree the meaning of the word loneliness. There seemed to be none to whom I could turn who understood *what I wanted to do*. I had no interest in showing merely popular, easily saleable work. I could only enthuse over the artists I really cared for. I became more and more passionately attached to the work of Christopher Wood and Kolle. To me they were the most completely satisfying artists whose work I was familiar with. To me they seemed entirely simple and easy to understand, yet during that first year, when constantly showing examples by them in my gallery, they came in for much adverse criticism. Christopher

Wood's boats were 'badly drawn', his painting was 'crude', he was too 'naïve', his paintings could lay no claim to be 'taken seriously'! Even harsher things were said of the paintings of Kolle. They were regarded as 'weird', 'grotesque', 'without any subtlety', yet to me they were as subtle as Rembrandt at his best and the early Italian Primitives.

'Why can't they *see*?' I felt like crying out when all these stupid visitors to my gallery reduced me to a state of exacerbation by their utter lack of comprehension. It was a disillusioning experience to find that the really good exhibitions I arranged were the least appreciated. Looking back on it, I now see that the crowds who visited my gallery over that first half year did so not so much for love of art but because it was *the thing to do*.

The pages of my visitors' book were scattered with names from the peerage, names of famous novelists, writers, Royal Academicians and the like. On private view days the gossip writers from the daily and weekly journals would besiege my secretary for lists of 'important people present'.

At the weekend my family would chaffingly enquire on my arrival home, 'Well, and how many celebrities have you had in your gallery *this* week?'

I remember one devastating day during the exhibition of the work of Kolle, when I had heard nothing but unkind comments on his work. It was late in the afternoon, not closing time, but I was so tired spiritually and mentally that I was about to put my things on and go home. At this moment women entered the gallery – cosmopolitans evidently – who carried themselves with ease and were obviously entirely at home in their surroundings. After a few moments one of them addressed me, expressing enchantment with the work she was regarding. Oh, the comforting impact of warm, appreciative personalities. I could have hugged them both.

I got out one after another of my beloved Kolle paintings until I had shown them everything I possessed. There was one which especially delighted them, and I, feeling an intense gratitude for their appreciation exclaimed: '*Please* have it – *please* take it away with you. *Do* go on enjoying it!' I can remember the look of amazement and diffidence at accepting the picture as a gift. It was one of my favourite Kolles – and I have wondered often since if the picture continued to give them pleasure, and if they took it round the world with them. (They told me they were travelling.) Or was it perhaps put away in store and never looked at again? If this page should meet their eye will they perhaps write and tell me? One woman had a Dutch name.

I used to be chided by my secretary for tiring myself out showing work with ardour and enthusiasm to visitors who obviously hadn't a bean to spend on a picture. At that time the financial aspect never troubled me. If my protégés met with appreciation, I could dispense with more concrete rewards.

One day, not long before closing time, a slight, simply dressed woman entered the gallery and asked me if she might see all my paintings by Christopher Wood. Now these numbered at that time about thirty, and *half* of them were stored on a shelf that could only be reached by a ladder. My assistant got them down with rather bad grace, the look she gave my secretary saying as clearly as words, 'All this trouble for nothing!'

One after another the pictures were displayed to our visitor. She selected six and asked for them to be put aside temporarily. 'They are not for myself,' she said, 'but I want a friend who lives in Devonshire to see them.' The name of the friend was not disclosed, but even if that friend had not come the following week and bought three of my finest paintings by Christopher Wood, I would like to take this opportunity of telling Miss Fox Strangways that it was a most delightful experience showing her my pictures that afternoon, and I have always felt the warmest gratitude to her for her sensitive appreciation of this artist's work while he was still comparatively unknown.

The General Election of 1931 was followed by a period of depression such as had been hitherto inconceivable. The Economy Campaign – 'Spend less money' – was surely the craziest policy ever launched by short-sighted politicians. The repercussions in the art world were immediate and tragic. Provincial art galleries cut down their grants. Art dealers in London were so badly hit that gallery after gallery closed down and there were many suicides. When I first started, the days were exceptional when I did not make a sale of a painting, or at any rate a watercolour or two. These conditions gradually changed, and days would go by when the gallery was visited by hardly a buyer. I found it increasingly difficult to meet my overhead expenses. Impoverished artists were clamouring all the time to be helped. I helped them with the money that had been provided by my husband for rent and rates.

The bailiffs

In my early twenties I had exclaimed to my husband one day: 'I can't see the use of money in the bank!' and my ideas have not changed much in the meantime.

I remember well one particular morning. Things were more than usually quiet. I had a specially good show on at the time and was feeling rather nerve-racked and disappointed at the non-attendance of the public. Noon had arrived and not a soul had been in. I sat writing at my table in the far corner of the room. Suddenly I looked up and asked Biddy who those two strange-looking men were at the other end of the gallery. They looked entirely detached from the art world and the pictures on the wall, yet there was an air of what I can only describe as permanency about them. Decidedly they looked as if they had come to *stay*! I became more and more intrigued, until at last I said, 'Biddy, *do* go and talk to them and find out something about them.' Biddy obeyed my behest, returning presently with a very long face. 'They're the BUMS, Mrs Wertheim,' she said. 'It is because you haven't paid your rates.'

A personal visit to Mr Budd, our sympathetic rate collector, eased the situation, and my goods and chattels were never actually confiscated. But this episode provided copy for many a ribald jest from my family, and explains various references to 'bailiffs' that occur in my husband's rhymes about the gallery.

Meanwhile I got deeper and deeper into the mire financially. It was impossible to attempt to pay my running expenses by the sales I was making. Two alternatives faced me: either I must give up my lovely room (where I had become exceedingly well-known) or I must change my policy. Hitherto I had made no charge for exhibitions. I decided from this time on to charge a fee to all artists outside my own 'Twenties Group'. I kept the standard as high as possible, and my name having become associated with original and creative work, it was generally not difficult; but occasionally, in order to pay my expenses, I had to arrange an exhibition which was of a popular nature and which accordingly went considerably against the grain.

It is a real vent to my feelings to express the intense resentment I felt towards certain people who adopted a superior attitude of disapproval at this time at my 'letting down the standard of my gallery', as they so kindly put it. What did these people do to help me in practical fashion to maintain my own policy? Nothing.

The financier

About this time when I was growing pretty desperate I was approached by a man who was described to me as a wealthy financier. It seemed his wife (who incidentally also had money) had become bitten with a desire to run an art gallery. The two of them came to my flat in Regent's Park one evening to go fully into the matter. The gist of the talk was that if I would consent to show only popular and saleable pictures they would take over the entire financial responsibility of the gallery. They were both sure they could make it pay.

'Must all my own struggles go for naught?' I asked. 'All these young artists who are slowly but gradually making names for themselves – must I leave *them* entirely in the lurch?' Yes – that was a condition of the financial assistance. With a lump in my throat and heart beating furiously I said good-night and saw them to the door. I was so overwrought that I wept well into the night.

Nearly all the evils of this world can be put down to lack of imagination. I thought there *must* be men who would help me to keep on with my work if they realised exactly *what* I was doing.

At this time I wrote to three men well-known in the art world, whom I knew personally, asking them to help me. In each case they refused, and incidentally none of them ever visited my gallery again.

It has never been easy for me to ask help of other people, and it was only in order to keep my own young group going that I brought myself to write these requests. Personally I have always looked on it as a compliment when my friends have turned to me for help. Is it one of the penalties that riches carry with them, this insensitiveness to suffering? How otherwise dare one be rich? I got sick to death of hearing of 'the rich friend' who might help me. I have not found the rich helpful. I have found them cold, unimaginative, suspicious and callous.

The people who have been most sympathetic to my work are those with very moderate incomes who often have had to make sacrifices in order to purchase a picture or a piece of sculpture they desired. Many of my best clients have been those who have paid in monthly instalments for pictures they have bought.

I should like here to pay a tribute to the late Enoch Lockett, of Nuneaton, who by his understanding sympathy and practical help lightened the task of running a gallery through difficult times. Often when I was feeling pretty desperate and that I could cope with things no longer he would come along and by his quiet attitude of confidence in my work and the certainty that I would pull through in the end made life look quite different again.

Gentle Enoch; kindly, delicate soul, so passionately resentful of the attitude of the authorities and especially of the curators of provincial galleries.

An added complication was my husband's growing hostility to the amount of time the gallery was taking up. Yet my work had become so *personal* that it was difficult to get away from London except at the weekends. More and more artists came to me for encouragement and help, and sometimes exhibitions were arranged as far as six months ahead. I found that I could kindle enthusiasm for their painting and often sell it when my assistants could make no impression on the public.

If I arrived home on a Friday evening looking tired and dispirited, my husband grew angry. 'For God's sake, shut up that damned gallery that is turning you into an old woman before your time,' he would exclaim resentfully, so that I learned after a time to arrive home serene-looking and smiling however heavy-hearted I was feeling inside.

Nannan

I could not have carried on what well might have been described as this 'double life' had it not been for the dependability and devotion of Nannan, our old nurse, who had taken on her shoulders the care of the household in the north when I opened my gallery in London.

She had come to me when my eldest child was a few months old and we had gone through many vicissitudes together. Our relationship was much more that of friends than of mistress and servant. Nannan did not 'hold with' the gallery, and the genus 'artist' was anathema to her. 'A helpless, feckless lot o' folk – why can't they do something *useful* for a living?' she would resentfully exclaim, her Lancashire accent adding venom to her speech. Many of my young painters who have since 'arrived' little suspect that much of the success they have had can be traced to this simple soul. It is certain that had it not been for her complete loyalty and dependability I could never have devoted so much time to my work in London.

Re-reading this last chapter I feel that I may have created a somewhat doleful impression on my reader – as if my life were concerned chiefly with difficulties, hostilities and the like. My art life was a struggle, but fortunately I had a buoyant, optimistic nature. I laughed easily, and I was so much teased by my young family and by my husband on the score of my artists and their (for the most part) unpopular efforts that I was never in danger of taking myself too seriously.

If I wrote that I had had a busy private view, 'lots of people in the gallery' back would come the retort that it must have been a very wet day that so many people had come in to shelter from the rain!

Another evergreen joke was the 'almost customer', the client who was *considering* a picture, who would 'think it over', 'look into his overdraft', or 'bring his wife to see it'.

At Christmas I was invariably presented with a few rhymes, the product of my husband's fertile brain. The gallery became a never-ending source of inspiration for these 'pomes' and fresh ones still appear on Christmas morning. It would be difficult to say whether writer or recipient got more amusement from them.

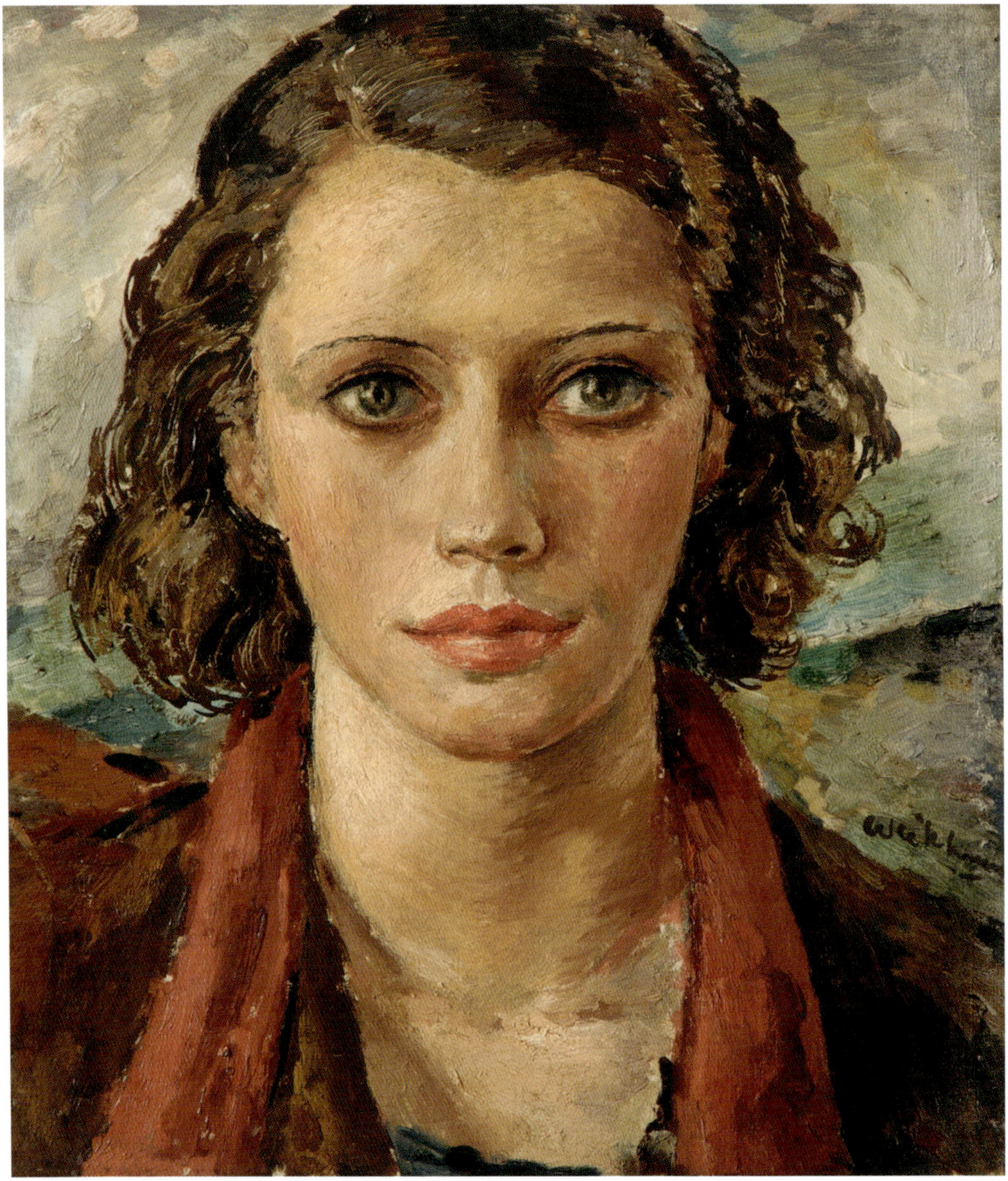

Michael Wickham, *Head of a Girl*, exhibited 1932
Salford Museum & Art Gallery, purchased from Lucy Wertheim, 1934

My Work

What did my work – to which I refer frequently – actually consist of? You will remember that I made it known before I opened my gallery that I was forming a group of young English painters. I called it my 'Twenties Group', as the artists were all in their twenties. There was no subscription and I did not charge a fee for exhibiting. Soon I was inundated by requests to look at work and I made it my job to interview every applicant personally. Artists came to see me from all parts of the British Isles, the Continent and the Colonies.

I was amazed at the amount of talent that I came across and thought I should only have to show it for its worth to be recognised. Alas, as I know now to my cost, this is the last thing to expect in England. An unknown artist's work is *not* appreciated on its merits.

Invitations numbering nearly two thousand to my first 'Twenties Group' exhibition were sent out, with special attention being paid that they should reach curators and heads of art schools. The exhibition had quite a good press but just the people who could have been most helpful held aloof or did not trouble to come, and had my enthusiasm been of the kind that wilts easily, my effort might quite well have come to an end that same spring.

I wrote to many well-known people in the art world, soliciting their interest in this young group. The response was depressing. The *English* artist was not in favour. The chief encouragement I got was strangely enough from the foreigner.

I had a number of visitors from abroad about this time and many of them expressed themselves astonished at the quality of the work I showed. Often the comment was added that it was not known on the Continent that painting of the kind existed in England.

Efforts thwarted and rewarded

It had been Christopher Wood's idea that my gallery should make exchanges of young work in the chief capitals of the world, particularly Paris, Berlin and New York. He actually tried to get a number of young artists in Paris interested in the plan. One painter I remember was Christian Bérard (Bébé Bérard his friends called him) and perhaps if Christopher had lived the scheme might have been put into practice. But I found myself very hampered by the duties that were put on paintings about this time, and though I contacted various galleries and their directors, nothing further came of it.

Herbert Read interested himself in an interchange of German and English work, and I was to have held an exhibition in my gallery of a group of Hamburg artists sponsored by him. I myself arranged an exhibition of the paintings of Paul Klee at this time, but neither of these shows materialised on account of customs difficulties.

I did, however, make headway in one direction. Enterprising schools with an intelligent art policy borrowed selections of paintings, a number of which I always kept in the gallery. Often the art master or art mistress would bring along pupils and allow them to make their own choice. This always pleased me, for children as a rule have good judgement.

Occasionally, I was asked to lecture at schools, colleges, schools of art, clubs and so on.

Miss Grier, Warden of Lady Margaret Hall, Oxford, who borrowed from me a selection of modern paintings to show in their Common Rooms, invited me to give a lecture to the students on the opening day. I had never lectured before, nor spoken in public, and I remember how nervous I was at the prospect, but Miss Grier, with her inimitable tact, turned what might have been an ordeal into a pleasure by calling the lecture a 'talk', and under the informality of it my nervousness vanished.

I also lectured about this time to the Women's Provisional Club in London and I shall always treasure the letter of thanks from the secretary, Miss Leslie.

An exhibition which gave me great pleasure to arrange was the one invited by the Worthing Art Gallery. It consisted entirely of 'Twenties Group' work. I believe I am right in saying that it was the first exhibition

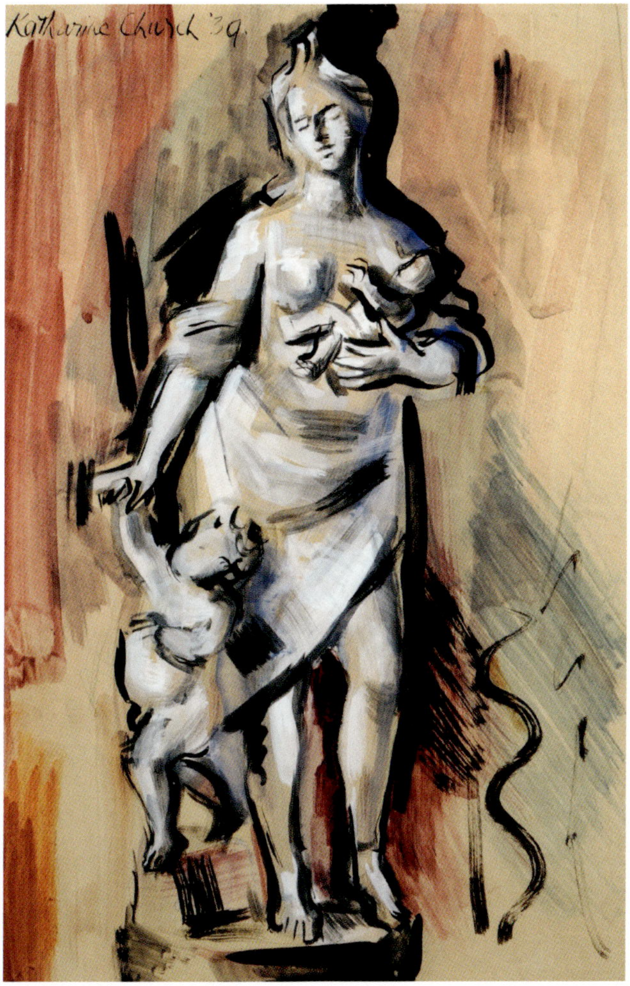

KATHARINE CHURCH, *GARDEN STATUE*, 1939. PRIVATE COLLECTION

of modern art to be held in that charming gallery. There was an excellent attendance and it had a most beneficial effect on local talent.

Another exhibition which I put my back into making a success was the one invited by the City Art Gallery, Salford. Salford adjoins Manchester and has a population of 250,000. I was asked to arrange an exhibition of modern art and the larger gallery, which is immense and well-proportioned, was placed at my disposal. I lent, for the occasion, my best paintings by Christopher Wood, Phelan Gibb, Matthew Smith, Frances Hodgkins, Vivin and Kolle.

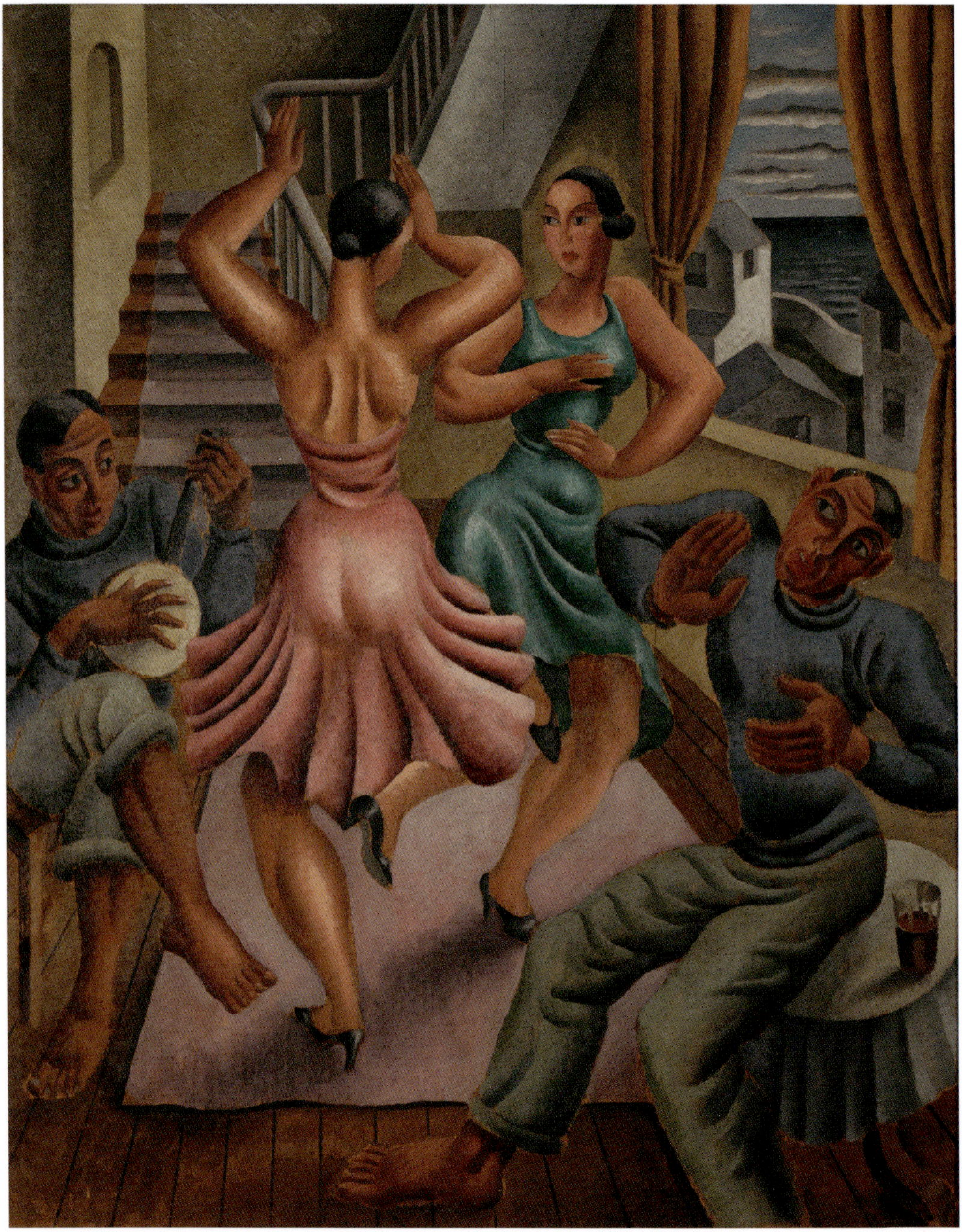

George Branson, *The Dancers* (or *Composition*), 1930
The Lucy Wertheim Estate

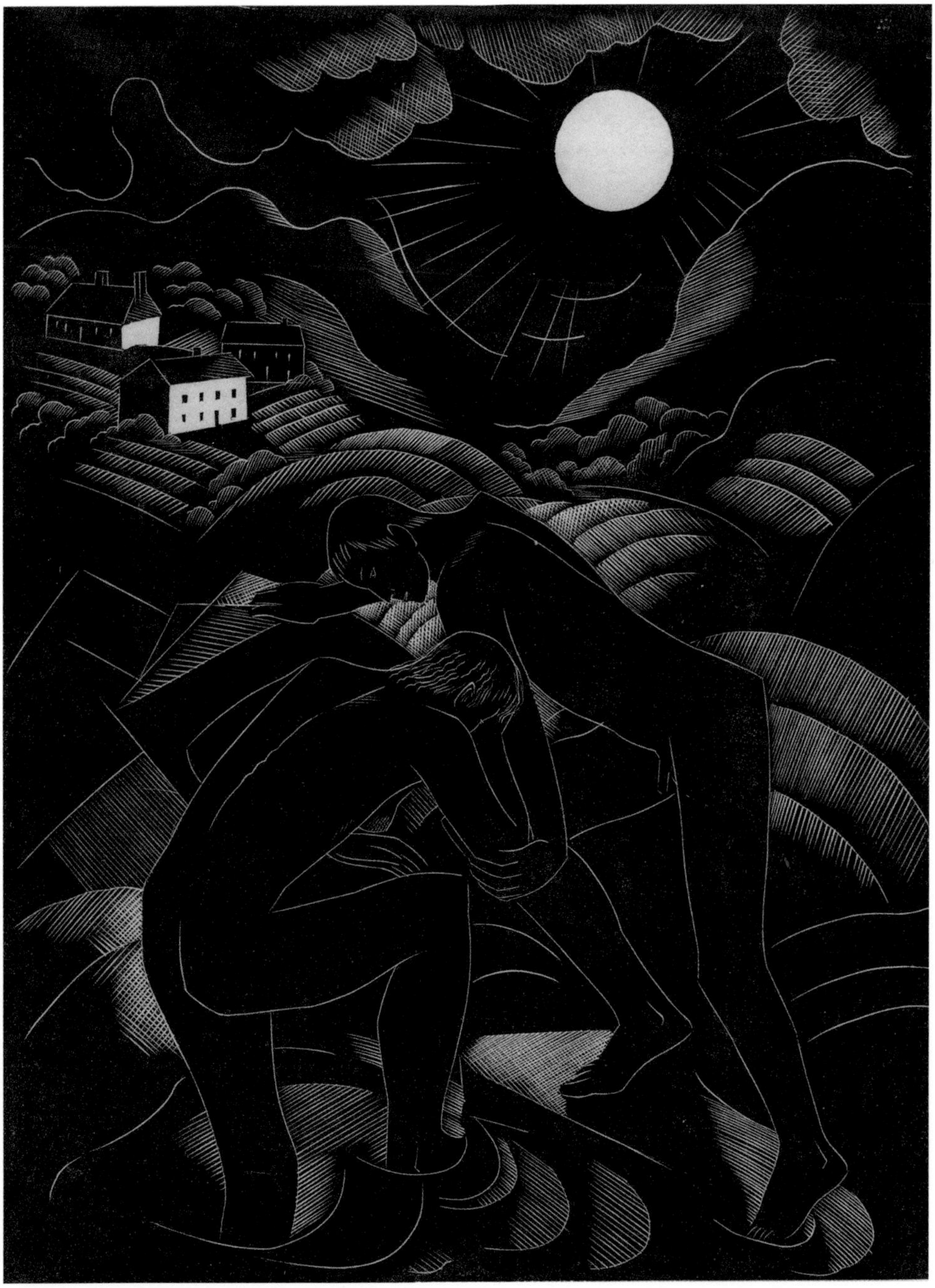

Elizabeth Rivers, *A New Way*, illustration from *This Man*, 1939

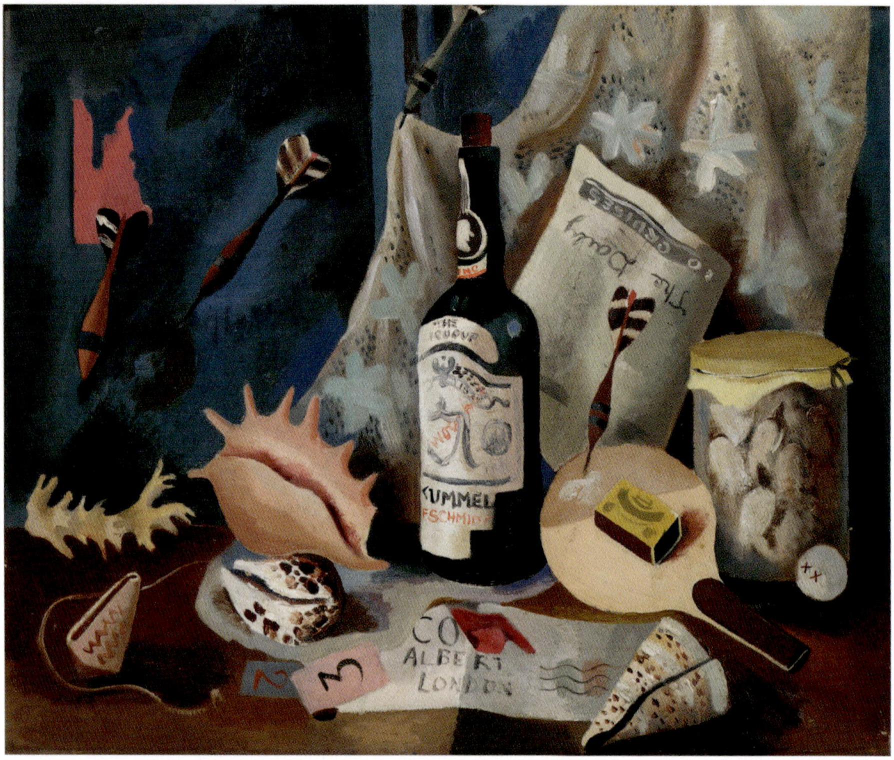

SUZANNE COOPER, *STILL LIFE*, *c*.1938. PRIVATE COLLECTION

The Twenties Group

The 'Twenties Group' was formed by Mrs Wertheim in 1930. It is a group of English artists in their twenties. Past and present members are:

Christopher Wood
Asphodel Fleischmann
Michael Wickham
John Aldridge
Elizabeth Rivers
Rhys Griffiths
Basil Jonzen
Ian White
Clive Branson
Robert Medley
Hooper Rowe
Nan Youngman
Angus McDougall
Anthony Brown
William Townsend
Dorothy Annan
Archibald Ziegler
Norah McGuinness
Maxwell Bates
Irene Furness
Rupert Shephard
Geoffrey Wylde
David Gommon
Paul Godfrey
John Mellon
Elizabeth Briscoe
Dido Applegate
Richard Beck
Anne Clark
John French

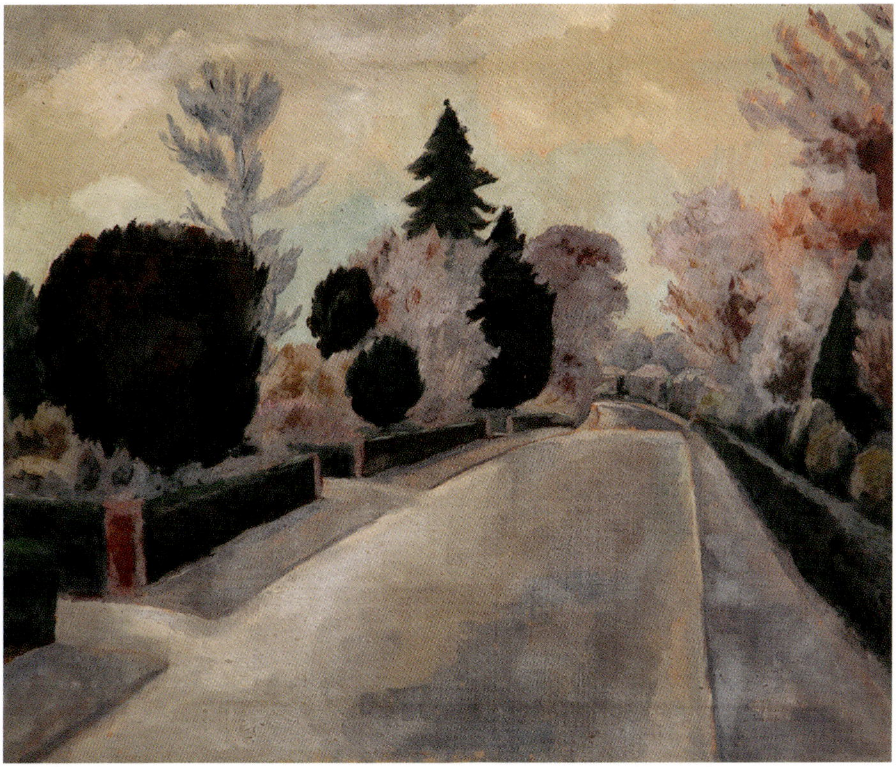

WILLIAM TOWNSEND, *THE WET ROAD* (OR *STRAIGHT ROAD*), EXHIBITED 1933
SALFORD MUSEUM & ART GALLERY, PURCHASED FROM LUCY WERTHEIM

Robert Greenham
E.M. Nelson
Edgar Ritchard
Geoffrey de Selincourt
Jacqueline Squire
Sylvia Bosley
B.G. Hiley
Mervyn Peake
Edna Ginesi
Grahame Mervyn
Anthony Slade
Wogan Phillips
Eunice Simeon
Sylvia Melland
N.S. Walker
Victor Pasmore
Michael Appleton
Aletta Lewis
K.E. Henderson
John Smith
Barbara Hepworth
George Branson
Anthony John
Ann Gimingham
Manus O'Keefe
Lyall Watson
Henning Nyberg
John Melville
Stella Burn
Rex Harris
Roger Hilton
Anthony Bridge
Bainbridge Copnall
Gwen Barnard
Katharine Church
Peg Everington
Doris Haine
Brenda Moore
Robin Pearce
Mariel Russell
Brenda Stretfield
Kenneth Tait
Kanty Cooper
Lulu Jacobsen

The public jeers

In the year 1933 these names were practically unknown to the public and the greater proportion of visitors had never seen a 'modern' painting before. Time and again I was told, sometimes jeeringly, that the crowds who visited the exhibition were only doing so out of curiosity. What if they were? Wasn't it a healthy curiosity? I used to delight in going to the gallery myself on Saturday and Sunday afternoons, mixing with the people and listening to their comments.

One day I overheard the conversation of a young man with an older man. The former, in his middle twenties, rather shabbily dressed, who might have been a clerk or shop assistant, was telling the latter that he lived in Liverpool, that pictures were the breath of life to him and as the Walker Gallery was closed for rebuilding purposes (his usual haunt in his spare hours), he had come over four Saturdays in succession to visit the Salford Gallery. If only for that one tribute I felt repaid for the trouble I had taken.

At the request of one or two officials and various Yorkshire artists, the exhibition was offered to the Wakefield Art Gallery. A refusal came to hand saying the paintings were 'too difficult to understand'. A *Daily Express* reporter, hearing this, called to interview me and the following day the northern edition of that journal carried the caption right across the page, 'Wake up Wakefield', followed by a vituperative article on the art policy of that city. I should like to say in my defence that that reporter had a lively imagination. I was not responsible for quite all the statements he attributed to me.

The exhibition went on to the City Art Gallery, Bradford, for some weeks, and I felt many reverberations later of the interest it aroused. The following incident is typical.

One day, a year or so later, a woman came into my gallery in Burlington Gardens where paintings belonging to my own collection were hanging at the time, and she stopped as if spellbound in front of a large painting by Kolle. 'Oh!' she exclaimed, 'I had never dared hope to see that picture again!' She explained that she and her son, a medical student, had visited the exhibition in Bradford, time after time, and had tried without success to find out from the attendants whence the collection emanated. Her son was now practising

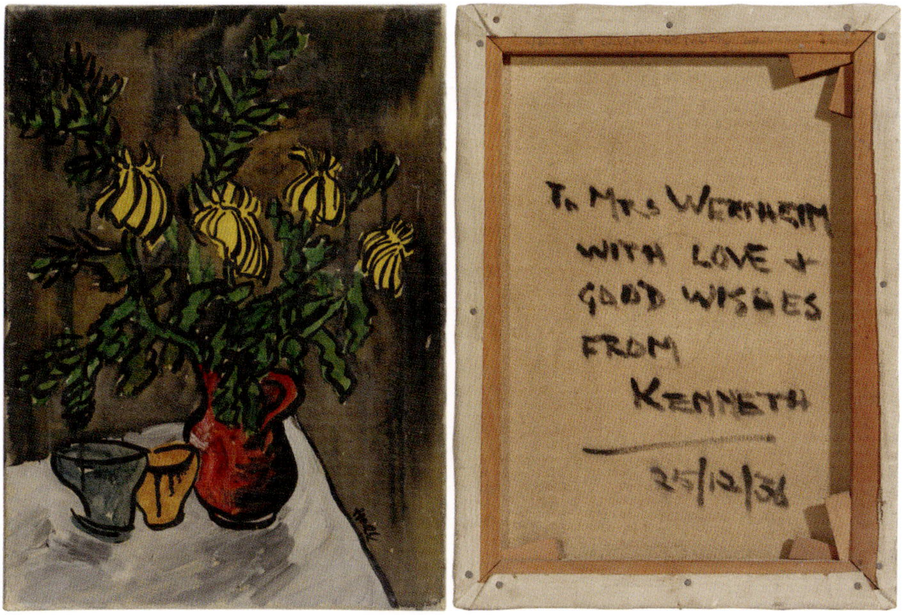

Kenneth Hall, *Red Jug and Yellow Flowers*, 1936 (front and reverse)
The Lucy Wertheim Estate

in London, and as he was passionately interested in modern art, she herself made the round of the galleries as often as she could in order to keep pace with his enthusiasm, and they had many lively discussions. The paintings of Kolle had made a deep impression on them both, and she knew her son would be enchanted at the opportunity of renewing his acquaintance with them.

A curator's enterprise

A beautiful little gallery is the one adjoining the public library at Altrincham, near Manchester. In the midsummer of 1936, Mr Bosworth, its enterprising curator, invited me to arrange an exhibition there of modern English painting. About fifty examples were shown, and the artists represented were Christopher Wood, Frances Hodgkins, Phelan Gibb, Matthew Smith, John Melville, Kenneth Hall, Henry Stockley, David Gommon, Alfred Wallis and Ronald Ossary Dunlop.

Though I say it as shouldn't, this exhibition was one that could have gone to any city in the world and greatly enhanced the reputation of the living English painter.

The curator was insistent on my giving a short lecture at the opening, which reluctantly I agreed to do. I say reluctantly, for speaking in public has always been for me an ordeal – at any rate until I have found the temper of my audience. Ordinarily, in spite of tongue cleaving to roof of mouth, icy hands and a certainty that I am about to faint, I have been pretty well able to disguise my nervousness. But, on this occasion, I felt such an atmosphere of hostility emanating from the gathering that until I had got over the impact (for only by such a word can I describe it), I was powerless to speak.

Some kind person, thinking I was going to faint, brought me sal volatile and perhaps this *did* help me to pull myself together. Anyhow, I realised that the only way to combat it was to take the bull by the horns and I began my lecture by announcing that I was well aware that my audience consisted of three sections: some who had come out of friendliness, some who had come animated by curiosity and a third section who were filled with antagonism for the paintings that surrounded them.

I asked for a show of hands and the third class decidedly had it!

My lecture took the form of proving that almost everything worthwhile throughout the ages, especially in the world of art (Rembrandt being a classic example) had met with the same hostility, and most often it was the work that provoked this antagonism that in the end won through.

Although only on the outskirts of Manchester, this little gallery claimed that the exhibition was visited by 17,000 people.

By a system of balloting, a certain number of paintings might be retained by the gallery. This suburban gallery retained five.

One-track mind

'My mother has a one-track mind. Keep her off the subject of her young artists. If you encourage her to talk about them, she'll never stop,' said my son to a friend of his as the three of us sat down to lunch one day. The friend

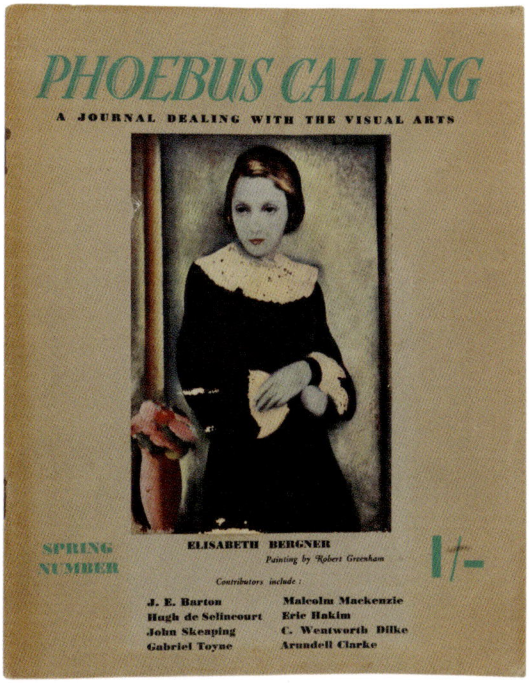

FRONT COVER OF *PHOEBUS CALLING*, SPRING EDITION 1934
THE LUCY WERTHEIM ARCHIVE

was a don at Cambridge, passing through Manchester, who had expressed a desire to make my acquaintance.

'I like one-track minds,' he said and egged me on to talk of this 'mania' of mine, as my family called it, for it was fast becoming an obsession. I was determined that my 'Twenties Group' should achieve fame! The public should be educated to an appreciation of these Masters of Tomorrow! My energy and enthusiasm on their behalf knew no bounds. Talent was surging around me on all sides, demanding recognition. I opened a daughter gallery in Manchester in 1932 and later another on the Brighton front in 1936. Neither paid its way, and each of them survived barely a year. I published a quarterly magazine, *Phoebus Calling*. It only ran into two numbers!

But a survey of the list I append of members of my 'Twenties Group' proves what a galaxy of youthful talent I had gathered round me in the early 1930s.

'Not since Diaghilef's has such a brilliant group existed,' remarked one visitor from Paris.

Nursery for artists

My gallery was often referred to as a 'nursery' for artists. I certainly 'nursed' a large number into recognition and found after a time that having held an exhibition at 'the Wertheim' carried enough prestige to warrant the older established galleries following it up with another a year or two later.

Many artists who were quite unknown when I gave them their first exhibition are now household names in the art world!

I gave Leslie Hurry his first show and was much touched by the gratitude of his mother, who declared that it was through my showing his work that Leslie was given the commission for *Hamlet* and later *Swan Lak*e at Sadler's Wells.

Rowland Suddaby also was one of my protégés. He held his first exhibition in my gallery in the days when a watercolour by him could be acquired for the sum of 2 guineas, yet he wrote me recently in a charming letter which I shall always keep that he considers that that was the best show he has ever held, and he has had nine since!

Kenneth Hall tentatively submitted a portfolio of work to me in 1934 – he had exhibited in no gallery up till then – and I was so thrilled with his paintings and especially his watercolours that I promised him an exhibition then and there as soon as I had a vacant date in the gallery. When his exhibition took place a few months later, I was able to place examples of his work in the hands of a couple of known collectors and he is gradually making his reputation as one of our most distinguished younger painters.

John Melville, the talented Birmingham artist, held his first one-man show with me in 1932. Never shall I forget the effect produced on me by two of the early canvases he brought into the gallery – huge paintings of Picasso-like women of dynamic composition and brilliant hue that took my breath away at first glance but grew on me so much during his exhibition that I acquired them both for my own collection.

Although he never became a 'best-seller', Melville had numerous admirers who appreciated the subtlety of his paint quality and his exquisite draughtsmanship, and examples of his work have gradually found their way into more than one fine collection.

Robert Greenham told me that he was so much influenced by the work

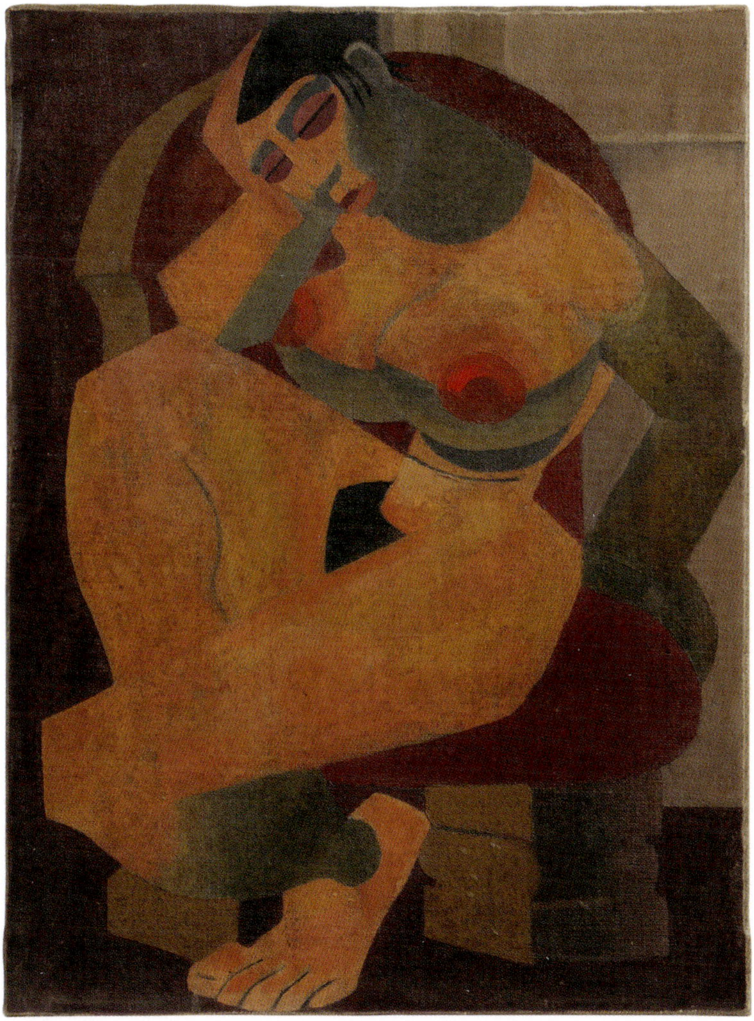

JOHN MELVILLE, *SEATED WOMAN*, *C*.1932. THE LUCY WERTHEIM ESTATE

of Christopher Wood and Helmut Kolle – which I showed in an exhibition at the RBA galleries – that it completely changed his outlook on painting. He held his first exhibition with me in 1933. It got excellent publicity and from being well content at that time with 10 guineas for a portrait, within a couple of years he was refusing 200 guineas for a commission. One of my most delightful pictures is a portrait painted by him of my daughter Hilary. It was once on exhibition in Bath in the Public Gallery, marked in

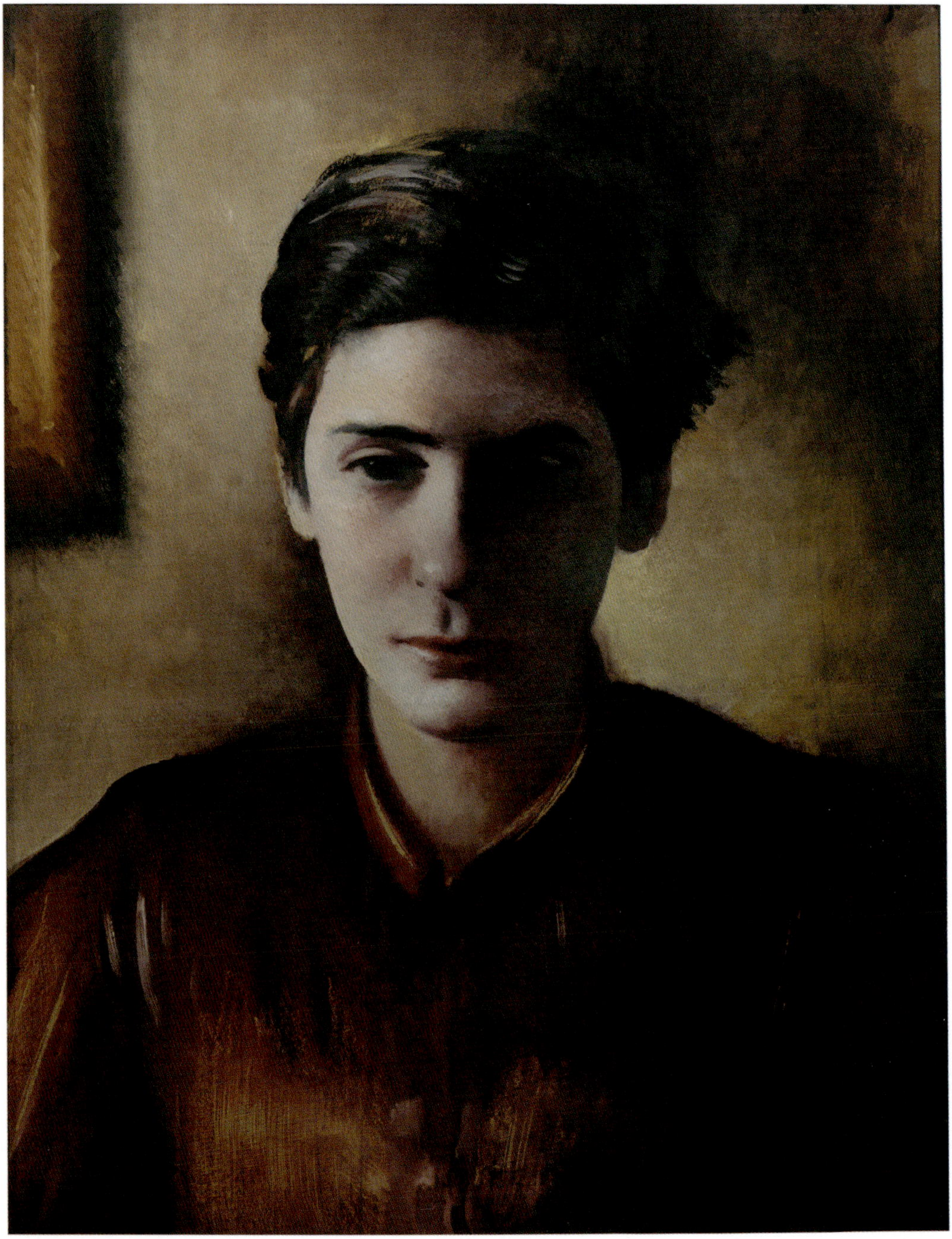

Robert Greenham, *Hilary*, 1934. The Lucy Wertheim Estate

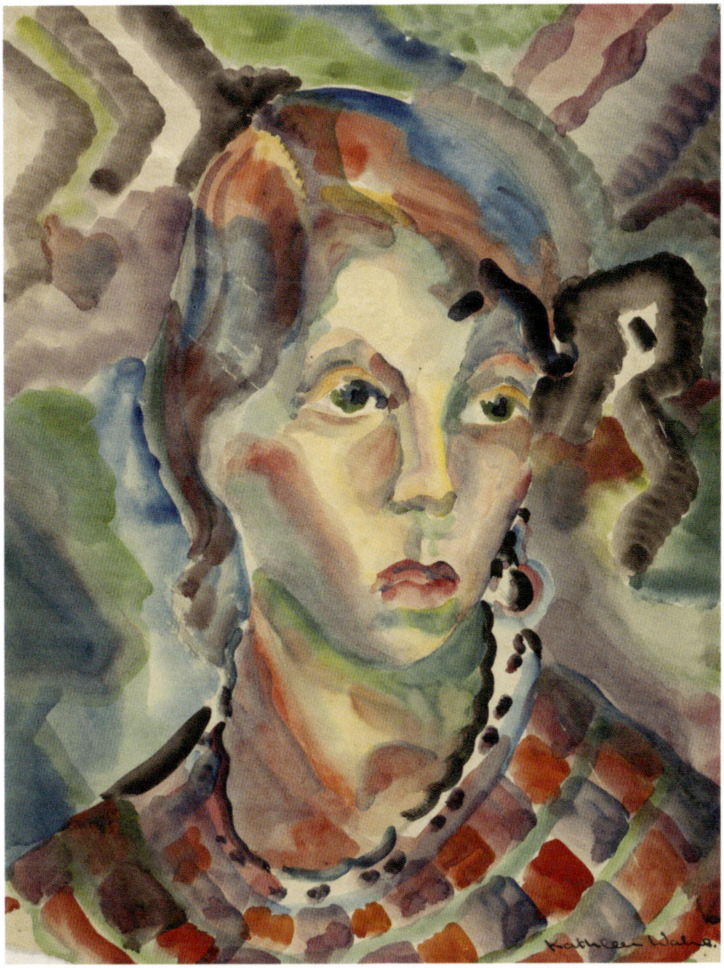

Kathleen Walne, *Self Portrait*, c.1935
Towner Eastbourne, The Lucy Wertheim Bequest, 1971

the catalogue 'Not for Sale'. A man who saw it there and liked it offered me £100 if I should ever care to part with it.

Feliks Topolski is another painter who has achieved fame since he held his first exhibition with me in 1935. His work was outstanding; to my mind far lovelier then than since he has become 'popular'. But I believe I only sold *one* of his drawings, and that to the Polish Ambassador.

Kathleen Walne, a gifted member of my 'Twenties Group', has gradually created for herself a circle of admirers. When she was barely seventeen her mother brought her up from Norfolk to make my acquaintance, wondering what to do with the wayward young artist who seemed incapable of curbing her exuberant and original style. Mrs Walne declared that Kathleen was the despair of her art master, and one glance at her vivid and dynamic paintings made me realise that she would hardly be *persona grata* in the average provincial art school. I showed her watercolours in a portfolio, from that time onwards, and eighteen months later gave her a one-man show, but her work was not easy to sell. The all too rare purchaser complained that his 'Kathleen Walne' made the rest of his pictures appear drab, and on one occasion we were even asked if the painting might be returned to the gallery!

In later years her watercolours have from time to time found their way into the hands of the discerning collector – one man paying her the compliment of furnishing a room round her painting!

Loans to schools

Loans of pictures to schools was a feature of the gallery that increased steadily in importance from its inception in 1931.

Biddy's enthusiastic co-operation was an incalculable asset to the scheme, as it involved much extra secretarial work, a detailed knowledge of the pictures and artists, and often diplomatic handling of the scholastic authorities.

We made no charge for these loans, apart from that of transport and insurance.

Sometimes it was the young art master or art mistress who requested that pictures might be lent, and the head of the school had to be persuaded that even the slight cost of transport and insurance was not 'an unnecessary expense'. Occasionally if the head remained adamant, I let the loan go through and paid the incidental costs out of my own pocket.

A dozen such loans might be in circulation at a time. Not only schools, but colleges, hostels, restaurants and foyers of theatres borrowed our pictures. We had a succession of exhibitions at the Embassy Theatre, Swiss Cottage, and

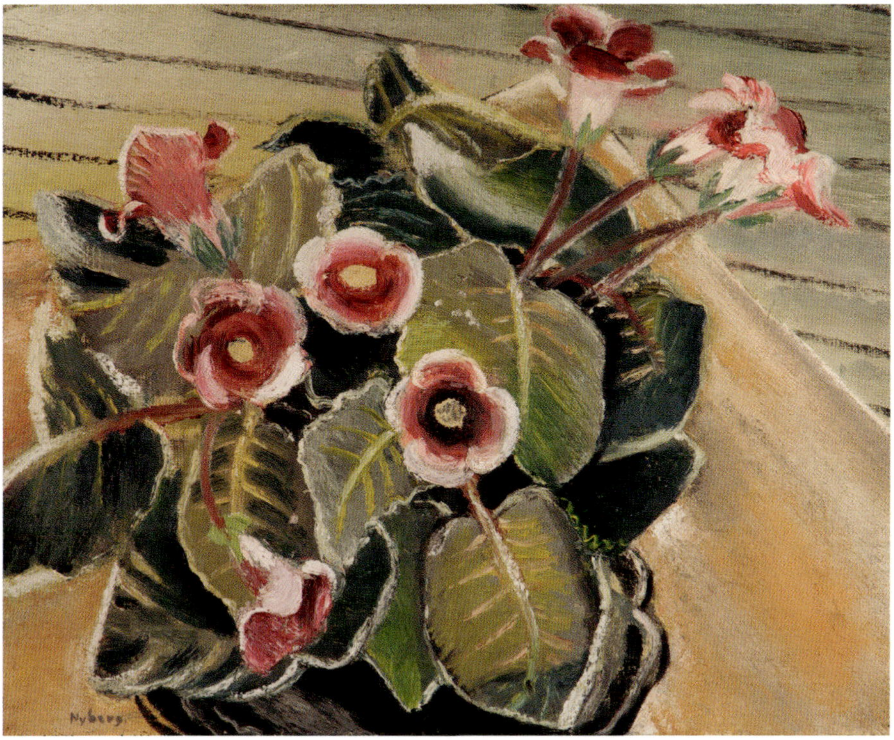

Henning Nyberg, *Gloxinia*, *c.*1932-33
Salford Museum & Art Gallery, purchased from Lucy Wertheim, 1933

one important exhibition in all three foyers of the Little Theatre, Adelphi. The Lombard Restaurant, Chelsea, frequently borrowed a few pictures to hang on their walls, as did a Hungarian restaurant near Piccadilly.

We made regular loans to the Women's Union of Manchester University and to Ashbourne Hall, the women's hostel of the same university, as well as to Bedford College, Regent's Park.

In this way the public became familiar with the work of the (then) little known artists such as Kenneth Hall, Rowland Suddaby, Leslie Hurry, Kenneth Wood, Kathleen Walne, Mervyn Peake and other members of my 'Twenties Group'.

Occasionally an exhibition of higher order was indicated and works by Frances Hodgkins, Christopher Wood, Matthew Smith, Phelan Gibb and Sickert were also included.

Loan exhibitions of selections from the above have been held at:

The Worthing Art Gallery	*Exhibition of Paintings by the 'Twenties Group'*
The Salford Art Gallery	*Exhibition of Six Modern Painters (attendance approx. 27,000)*
	Exhibition of One Hundred Modern English Watercolours
The Cartwright Hall, Bradford	*Exhibition of Six Modern Painters*
The Stretford Art Gallery, Manchester	*Exhibition of Modern Watercolours (attendance over 15,000)*
Astley Cheetham Art Gallery, Stalybridge	*Exhibition of Modern Paintings*
The Women's Union, Manchester University	
Ashbourne Hall, Manchester	*(numerous exhibitions)*
The Lombard Restaurant, Chelsea	
The Print Shop, Cambridge	
The Embassy Theatre, London	*(two exhibitions)*
The Little Theatre, London	

And at many schools and colleges, including:

Bedford College, Regents Park, London	*(two exhibitions)*
Dauntsey's School, Wiltshire	
Mill Bank Demonstration School, London	
Colston School for Boys, Bristol	
Colston School for Girls, Bristol	
St Brandon's School, Bristol	
Abbotsholme School, Staffs	
Hayes Court, Hayes, Kent	
Bryanston School, Dorset	
New Hall, Chelmsford	
Clifton College, Bristol	
The Grammar School, Henley	
The Grammar School, Ilkley	
Sherborne School for Girls, Dorset	
The Guildford School of Art	
St Mary's Calne, Wiltshire	*(several exhibitions)*
Leighton Park School, Reading	
Haileybury College	

There is no charge for these exhibitions, except for transport and insurance

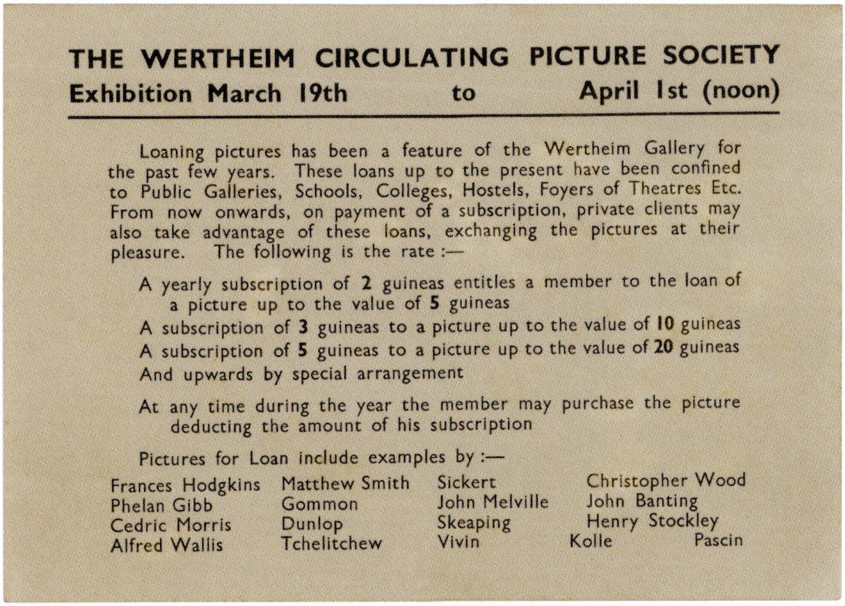

THE WERTHEIM CIRCULATING PICTURE SOCIETY
Exhibition March 19th to April 1st (noon)

Loaning pictures has been a feature of the Wertheim Gallery for the past few years. These loans up to the present have been confined to Public Galleries, Schools, Colleges, Hostels, Foyers of Theatres Etc. From now onwards, on payment of a subscription, private clients may also take advantage of these loans, exchanging the pictures at their pleasure. The following is the rate :—

A yearly subscription of **2** guineas entitles a member to the loan of a picture up to the value of **5** guineas
A subscription of **3** guineas to a picture up to the value of **10** guineas
A subscription of **5** guineas to a picture up to the value of **20** guineas
And upwards by special arrangement

At any time during the year the member may purchase the picture deducting the amount of his subscription

Pictures for Loan include examples by :—

Frances Hodgkins	Matthew Smith	Sickert	Christopher Wood
Phelan Gibb	Gommon	John Melville	John Banting
Cedric Morris	Dunlop	Skeaping	Henry Stockley
Alfred Wallis	Tchelitchew	Vivin	Kolle Pascin

ANNOUNCEMENT CARD FOR THE WERTHEIM LOAN COLLECTION
THE LUCY WERTHEIM ARCHIVE

Paintings by

Christopher Wood
George Bissill
David Gommon
Matthew Smith
John Melville
Moshe Castel
Walter Sickert
Alfred Wallis
Helmut Kolle
Frances Hodgkins
Henry Stockley
Louis Vivin
Cedric Morris
Rowland Suddaby
Van Hengelaar
Ronald Ossary Dunlop
Maxwell Bates
Pavel Tchelitchew
Phelan Gibb
Roland Vivian Pitchforth
Humphrey Slater

Watercolours and drawings by

Sickert
Rowland Suddaby
John Deakin
Frances Hodgkins
C.R. Humberstone
Henrik Ripszam
Phelan Gibb
Justin Pieris
Edward Wadsworth
David Gommon
Doris Vaughan
Stella Burford
Kathleen Walne
Anthony Brown
George Bissill
Lancelot D. Rust
John Hilliard
John Melville
Rex Harris
Maxwell Bates
Jules Pascin

I have reason to believe that the loans did much to create a taste for good pictures in the younger generation.

It even happened from time to time that a pupil made a purchase of a painting. I remember in a selection lent to a public school a picture by the artist Henning Nyberg, which carried an insurance of 35 guineas. The artist received (via the gallery) a letter from one of the boys asking if the painting could be acquired for £5, the sum total of his pocket money. Nyberg was so touched at the lad's appreciation that he concluded the deal.

It was a pity that the 'authorities' did not recognise the value of this excellent scheme that ran so smoothly and that was so efficiently organised. I process scores of letters from heads of schools, art master and mistresses, expressing their gratitude for the loans.

Dreams Come True

An old friend staying with me recently reminded me of childish ambitions I had confided to her in my school days.

I had played with my dolls until I was almost grown up. On my fifteenth birthday my spartan mother thought it was high time I gave up 'toys' and handed to our 'char' for her own small daughter my doll Mildred, the last of my family. This parting was a great wrench, for Mildred was always ailing and I felt that her foster mother would never bestow on her the loving care and understanding she needed.

My friend recalled this confidence and a prayer I had confessed to offering up when very small. 'Please God, when I'm grown-up let me have *lots* of children *and please let them all be delicate*.' Happily, God did not hear my prayer, for I reared a normal, healthy family of two sons and a daughter without any ailments apart from the ordinary nursery ones.

Later, at school in France pacing the *cour* after study hours, this same friend and a couple of other English girls joined me in voicing freely our ambitions for the future.

'I want to be a great singer,' said my friend.

'I want to be rich and a social success,' said another.

'I want to marry George, have a family and live happily ever after,' said the third.

'I want to know Interesting People who do Interesting Things,' said I.

'And my goodness,' exclaimed my friend, reminding me of this conversation, 'of the four of us *you* most surely have realised your ambition.'

It is certain that running a gallery for modern art brings one into contact with a class that possibly can lay the best claim to be labelled 'interesting'.

By 'interesting' I do not mean necessarily those who have 'arrived'. Personally, I have found obscure people with their name yet to make often the most exhilarating to know. Lions (and lionesses) so often grow self-conscious or 'play up' to the gallery.

Being in the limelight may lend a certain glamour but it does not give the quality that I call 'interesting'.

Perhaps here I had better make it clear that I was born without any social aspirations, and possibly for my gallery work this was unfortunate. But it so happens that I am only at my ease with simple people, people who are their natural selves. Royalty and many members of our true aristocracy come into this class, but with the typical product of society I confess I don't make much headway. What have we in common? I was never presented at Court; I was never at Ascot; the hunting field knows me not; social functions I abhor; cocktail parties are my pet abomination; small talk bores me and I have no use for scandal.

The 'cultured' classes also fill me with dread. I should be worsted in the first round in a discussion with Aldous Huxley, or arguing 'technically' with Wilenski.

Parties

An odd sort of person I, then, to be running a gallery in the most expensive and fashionable quarter of London. A square peg in a round hole?

But every kind of artist – painter, sculptor, theatre designer, dancer, actor, novelist, journalist, many poor and unsuccessful, others rich and famous – became regular visitors to the exhibitions in my lovely room and to the parties I gave once a month over the first year of my venture.

The latter were not 'grand' affairs in any meaning of the word. Everyone dressed as they liked; an impecunious painter in not over-clean bags feeling as much at ease as a countess in full war-paint going on later to a reception.

I began now to make acquaintance in the flesh of many people in the public eye who had only been names to me in the past.

One whom I knew by sight and whom I felt I knew already as a friend through her 'autobiography' (had I not felt exactly the same emotion over the birth of my first-born as she so tellingly described?) was Margot Asquith. She came in one morning in the company of Princess Bibesco and in that voice of hers, so full of charm and allure, roundly denounced my taste in pictures, but so warmly admired my room and certain pieces of furniture which she said she would have liked to acquire had they been for sale, that her denunciation left no sting.

Another early visitor was Lord Sandwich, whose identity I did not know and which I only discovered later from my visitors' book. I remember how he sat quiet and detached-looking in a far corner of the gallery, and I, feeling rather sorry for him, went and talked to him about the artists whose work I was showing at the time. There was no thought at the back of my mind of selling him a picture. Somehow he didn't look like what then was my notion of a buyer. It was during this conversation that he let fall a remark that was to become classic in the annals of the gallery. Mentioning that there was more than one picture there that he would like to possess, he sighed regretfully, 'Alas, I'll have to wait until I've paid my Income Tax!'

Lord Berners was also a visitor to the gallery about this time, though not as yet a purchaser, and my description to my husband of their visits brought forth the 'pome': 'We're Sandwich and Berners'.

It is sometimes a drawback to possess too vivid a faculty of visualisation. There were certain people whom, though I had never set eyes on, I believed I should recognise immediately if I met them in the flesh. Occasionally I was mistaken.

It was the morning of a private view, and I was showing a collection of works by English woodcarvers. From a stand close to the table where I was sitting, a man lifted lovingly a piece of carving, handling it with caressing touch and with a glint in his eye that bespoke the expert. As he stood there hatless in his bright blue shirt open at the neck, ARTIST was written all over him.

'Are *you* a sculptor?' I asked him. A look of incredulous amazement overspread his features as he replied, 'There are many who think so.'

I had an uncomfortable feeling that somehow I'd put my foot in it.

Swiftly my secretary came to the rescue, saying : 'Mrs Wertheim, have you not met Mr Epstein?' and the introduction effected, we spent some pleasant moments chatting.

Another 'lion' whom I imagined I should recognise was James Agate. But I was far from associating the affluent-looking individual stepping from a trim chauffeur-driven car and smoking an expensive cigar with the lanky, possibly hungry-looking creature I had visualised.

Agate bought a clever caricature of George Bernard Shaw, by Coia, from me, and on a subsequent visit was full of glee when he heard that G.B.S. had exclaimed on being told of the purchase, 'Damn him for getting in first.'

Apropos of the latter's visit during the same exhibition, I returned from my lunch one day and glancing at my visitors' book as I came in saw in large letters scrawled across the page 'George Bernard Shaw'.

'I see you have had Mr Shaw in, Biddy,' I said.

'Yes, and you're jolly lucky to have his autograph,' remarked a visitor standing near. 'How did you manage to get it ?'

'Och, shure,' replied Biddy in her attractive Irish brogue. 'Oi just said to him "Put your name in the visitors' book, Mr Shaw," and he put it in.'

I can imagine that Biddy's tone was so authoritative that Mr Shaw did not dare say nay.

I think I might be excused for not recognising Mr H.G. Wells when he came to one of my exhibitions. He was wearing extremely unconventional garb for an afternoon visit to a gallery: a loose white shirt and shorts, and on his somewhat tousled head a beret. He said he was on his way from a game of squash.

The rebuff

It was my natural instinct to greet visitors to my gallery in the same way that a hostess would be attentive to her guests, not with any idea of pressing them to buy but to make them feel welcome and at their ease. I think this instinct of hospitality is more inherent in Lancashire folk than in those born and bred in the south.

After a time I found that there were occasionally people who resented being spoken to. The first rebuff was administered to me by Mr William Somerset Maugham.

I had read many of his novels and seen practically every one of his plays, some of them two or three times, and to me he was not a stranger but a very real person. After reading *The Moon and Sixpence*, which a friend had given me at my own request when it first appeared, I thought he and I would have many things in common, especially in our taste in art.

When I got my 'Twenties Group' thoroughly going, I wrote personally, inviting him to the first exhibition. An out of date address must have been given to me, for the letter came back with the envelope marked 'gone away'.

One afternoon I was sitting at my table writing when Biddy said to me, 'Mrs Wertheim, that is Somerset Maugham who has just come in.' My heart gave a little leap of delight and I immediately got up and went towards him, prepared to tell him of my pleasure at making his personal acquaintance and about to ask him if sometime he would allow me to show him examples of my 'Twenties Group', which I thought would interest him.

I cannot remember how far I got with my little speech for I received such a cold look from him that my blood seemed to congeal in my veins and I retired to my corner of the room feeling more snubbed than I had felt in all my life.

'Gushing, unpleasant female,' he might have been saying to himself (and quite probably was).

For a while this incident made me very self-conscious and chary of speaking to strangers when they entered the gallery, but after a time I had to remind myself of the fable of the Man, the Boy and the Donkey, for it was not long afterwards that an artist told me resentfully of a friend of hers who had come to an exhibition and 'though Mrs Wertheim was in the gallery at the time she had not addressed a word to her!'

I began to say to myself: 'Well, evidently I can't please everybody so I'll just go my own way and do as I feel' – which I did.

Most writers I have found easy to talk to about pictures.

Professor Malinowski was a particularly congenial visitor with a sensitive appreciation of original work.

A writer whom I was very thrilled to meet in the flesh was Paul Selver, whose novel *Private Life* had made a great impression on me.

Igor Schwezoff (author of *Borzoi*) and I became good friends through his visits to my exhibitions. At that time he had a school of dancing in London. He knew that I was intensely interested in palmistry and I remember being amused when one day we were discussing this fascinating subject at his telling me that *he* could always tell his pupils' characters *by their feet.*

Aldous Huxley was another of my visitors but I always felt rather shy with him, perhaps because I find his books difficult to read.

I made the acquaintance of Edith Sitwell through my gallery, also of Beverley Nichols, Alan Patrick Herbert, Edward Verrall Lucas, John Drinkwater, Sir Philip Gibbs, William Gerhardi and Hugh de Sélincourt, all of whom were interested in my policy.

Howard Spring and Dorothy Gladys 'Dodie' Smith bought pictures from me.

Mark Benney, who wrote *Low Company*, I hope will come to see me again sometime. The afternoon he came there was such a crowd present that it was impossible to have more than a few minutes' conversation. If I could emulate his gift of vivid word-painting what a happy person I should be.

Indirectly through the gallery I also met Wilfred Macartney, whose *Walls have Mouths* was such a terrible indictment of our prison system.

Sometimes an artist still unknown to the public would think it expedient to get a notability to open his exhibition. Then Biddy and I would set our wits to work, wondering whom we might approach.

If the artist was a foreigner, sometimes it was possible to persuade the ambassador of his country to do him that honour.

Signor Grandi, Monsieur Corbin, Jan Masaiyk, Lord Rennell, and the Polish Ambassador all sponsored shows for me at one time or another.

Or occasionally a famous actress was invited. Cicely Courtneidge allowed her name to appear in an invitation to a private view, with the condition attached that she need not make a speech! I got the impression that she was dithering with nerves when the moment arrived for the actual opening. But I have noticed frequently that great artistes used to holding vast audiences in the hollow of their hand are often extremely shy when deprived of the sense of security that footlights afford.

On another occasion Viola Tree declared open an exhibition of the work of fellow Thespians, making her little 'impromptu' speech somewhat nervously, I thought. But her presence lent a warm, delightful note to the ceremony and everyone declared the afternoon a great success,

The following day, I got a letter from Viola herself, paying a charming tribute to the gallery and congratulating me on its 'wonderful organisation'. Among others present that day, all of them exhibitors, were Ernest Thesiger, Peggy O'Neil, Ethel Warwick and Margaret Rawlings.

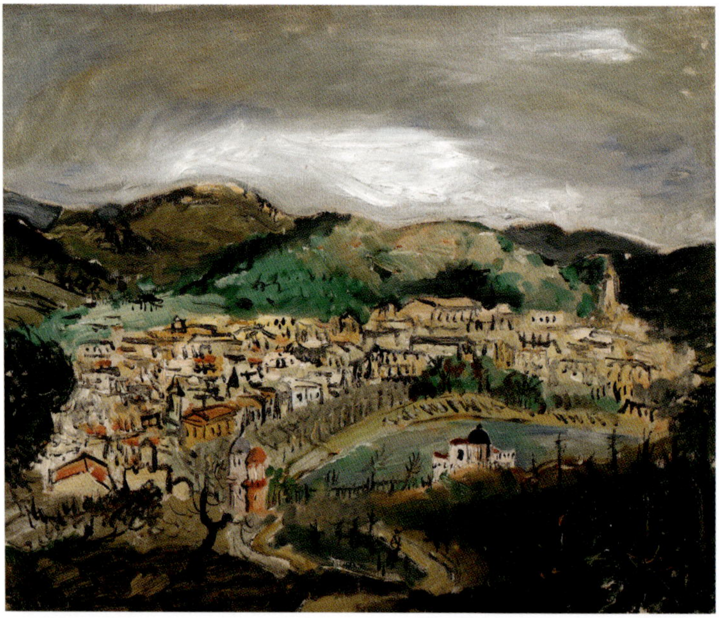

Kenneth Hall, *Mediterranean Cove*, 1938. Private Collection

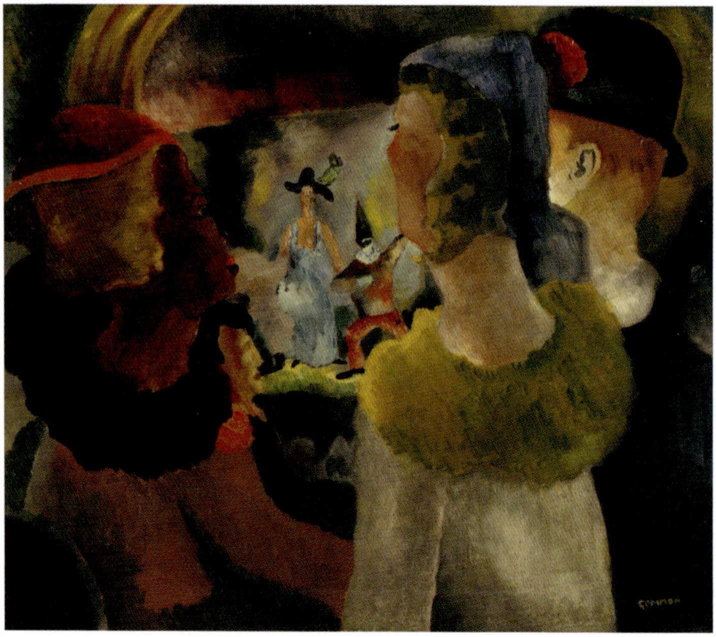

David Gommon, *Music Hall*, *c.*1934
Towner Eastbourne, The Lucy Wertheim Bequest, 1971

F.I. Albany

'"Il faut toujours risquer dans la vie" or "live dangerously" is my motto,' wrote Christopher Wood in one of his letters to me.

In the summer of 1934 the chance came my way of leasing the ground floor chambers of F.I. Albany (Piccadilly), just across the way from where I was established in the entresol at 3-5 Burlington Gardens.

I knew the advantages would be immense of having a ground floor gallery. So many people thought twice before climbing steps or entering a lift to attend an exhibition. But dare I take the risk? My signature was hardly dry on a document committing myself to a continuation of my present tenancy. My finances were at the lowest possible ebb. I was overdrawn to the last penny of the overdraft guaranteed by my husband. I didn't want to ask him for further help. All too well he was aware that earlier in the year I had been offered £500 for my lovely *Dieppe* by Christopher Wood, but could not bring myself to part with it. ('I thought the purpose of your gallery was *to sell* pictures,' was his slightly caustic remark, when he heard that I had refused this offer.)

That heavenly white Adam door across the road continued to haunt my dreams, and I saw those gracious rooms with their Adam fireplaces and harmonious proportions as the perfect setting for my pictures. The temptation was great. I fell. The lease was signed. My husband guaranteed my rent for a further term, and I became the happy possessor of a gallery in Albany.

Had I been out to secure a merely fashionable clientèle I could have made my expenses hand over fist by consistently 'letting' the rooms for exhibitions. But I was determined as far as possible to continue my own

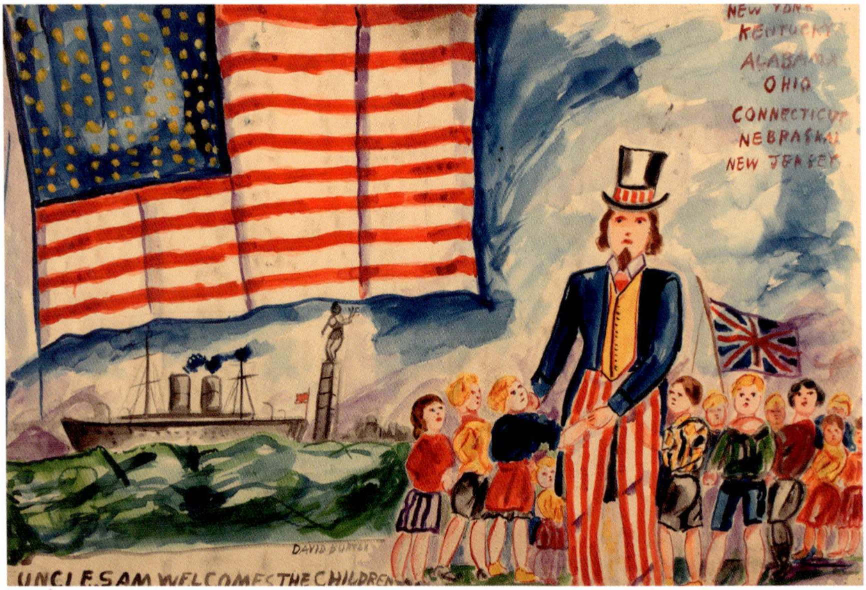

DAVID BURTON, *UNCLE SAM*, 1938-45. PRIVATE COLLECTION

policy, and within a year refused on more than one occasion fees of a 100 guineas for a three-week show in the Large Gallery, in order to give such protégés as David Burton, David Gommon and Kenneth Hall exhibitions I had promised them.

David Burton

The exhibition of David Burton's watercolours I look back on as one of the most exciting I ever held. Through it I made a number of delightful new friends who shared my enthusiasm for his work: among others two Greek women Speranza and Irene Poulopoulo, who were on holiday in London at the time, and who having seen a notice of the Pavement Artist's Show dropped in out of curiosity. Both were enraptured with it and came many times again. I gave them one of his paintings, and they in turn presented Burton with a flask of whiskey, a little kindness he never forgot.

An American who came to the private view told me he was sailing for New York the following day and prevailed on me to let him take back with

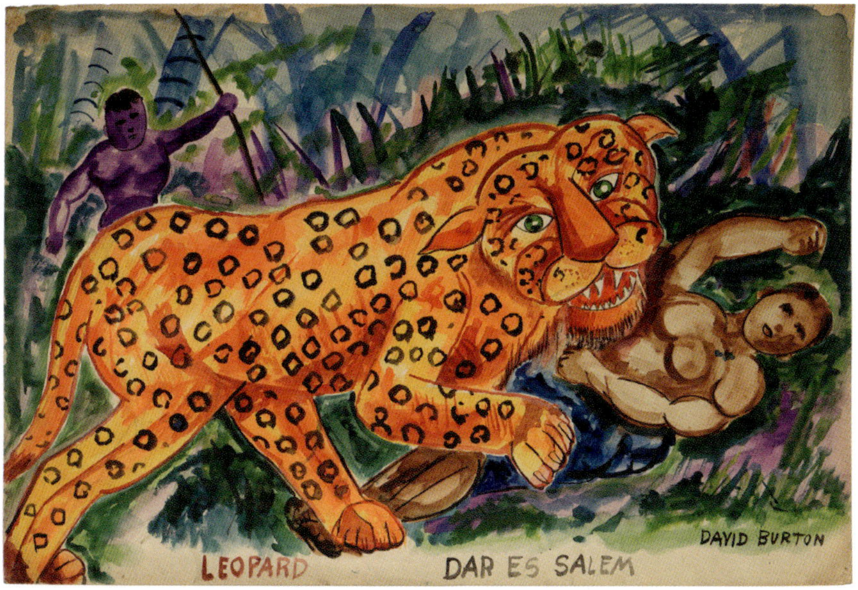

David Burton, *Leopard Dar es Salem* [sic], 1938-45. The Lucy Wertheim Estate

him one of the most outstanding pictures in the show to give to a friend in the States who had a collection of naïve paintings. He added that if I would arrange an exhibition of Burton's work in New York, he was convinced it would have a *succès fou*.

Eric Newton bought from me one of his *Jungle* paintings – an *Elephant* that I had earmarked for my own collection. Lord Hastings was another enthusiast, and somewhat later 'Klara', who illustrates children's books so enchantingly, and who herself has much in common with Burton.

Burton and I became great friends through my appreciation of his work. He had a 'pitch' at Hampstead and told me how he came in the first place to make my acquaintance. It seemed more than one passer-by had told him he should take his paintings to Mrs Wertheim. '*She* would like them,' they had said. And finally he plucked up courage and brought them to my gallery. From that time onwards I paid him a weekly sum, and promised him a show as soon as it could conveniently be arranged.

I possess a most entertaining correspondence from him which one day I hope to publish. In spite of his numerous admirers, David Burton remains an artist's artist, and I have given away far more of his paintings than I have sold.

The Yellow Man

Pursuing my set policy I gave many shows at this time to young and unknown artists: to Kenneth Hall and David Gommon among others. Both exhibitions were outstanding and gave me enormous pleasure personally. But both shows were disastrous as commercial propositions. I sold two pictures by Kenneth Hall and not one by Gommon.

The following summer my 'pig-headed policy', as an unsympathetic relation called it, cost me my precious *Yellow Man*. I was in such low water that I was prevailed upon to sell this well-loved painting by Christopher Wood. It was July and I was staying with my children at our little seaside house in Sussex. I had left Biddy in charge of the gallery.

One morning I got a communication from her to the effect that a client had seen *The Yellow Man* in my sitting room in Albany and expressed a wish to buy it. He had offered £350 for it. The matter was urgent. Would I wire my decision? I telegraphed that the painting was not for sale. I could not bring myself to part with it.

A young member of my family despatched the telegram, returning from the post office (we were not on the telephone) with crestfallen mien. There were so many pleasures I had had to deny him that summer! I began to waver. The following morning I got a cajoling letter from Brinsley Ford himself, the would-be purchaser (and a regular client from early days). I yielded.

The Yellow Man changed hands.

When Mr Ford wrote me that he had surrendered his long-booked air reservation to Switzerland in order to enjoy his painting for a few days longer, it took the edge off my regret at parting with my treasure.

Tea and turps

My move to Albany and ground-floor premises proved a wise one. Every month saw me busier and busier. I had many foreign visitors and the gallery became especially popular with Americans. There was an air about my rooms that made them extremely attractive for exhibitions and had I had

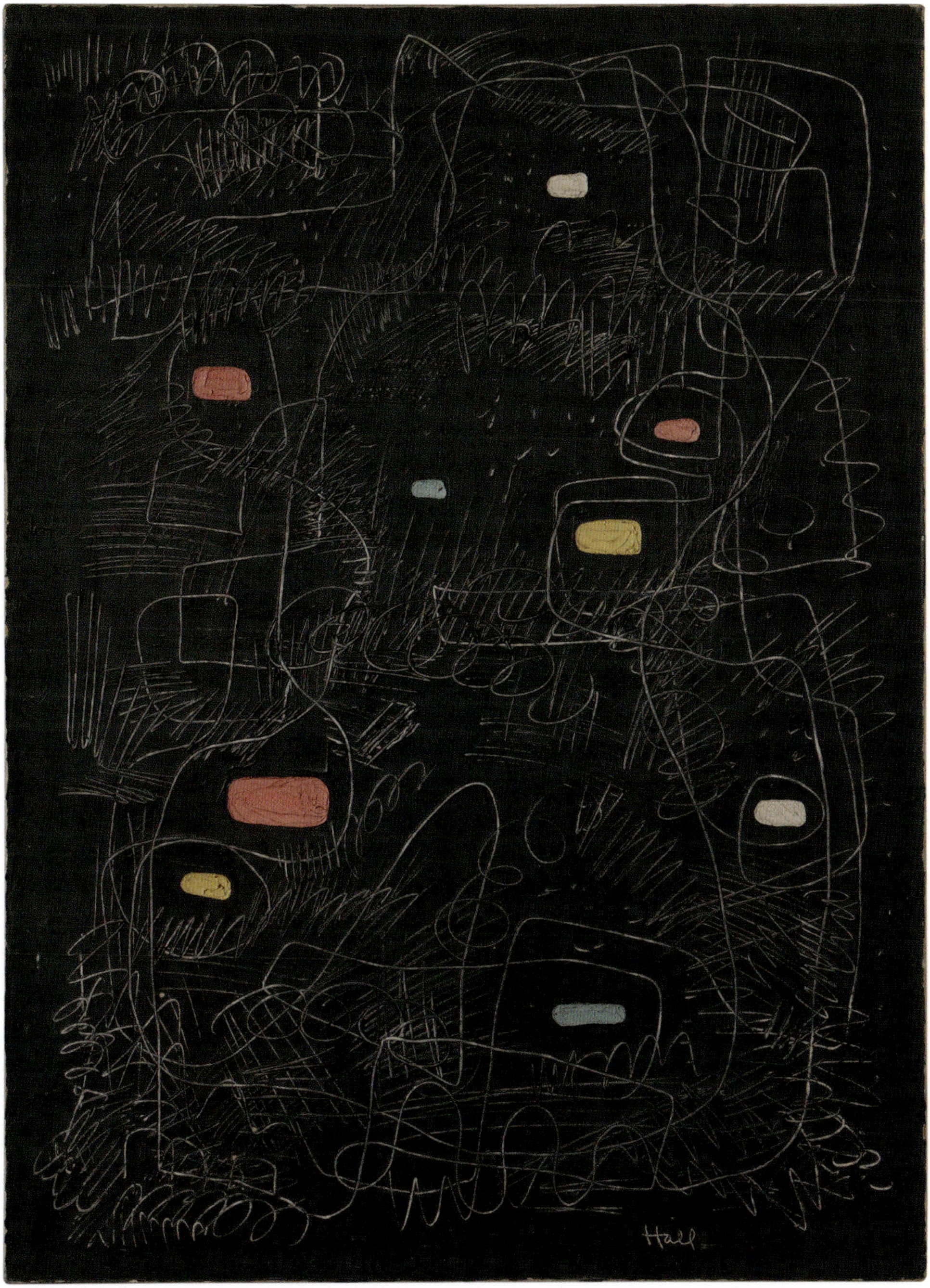

KENNETH HALL, *UNTITLED*, EARLY 1940S. THE LUCY WERTHEIM ESTATE

a commercially minded and really practical partner my experiment might have become self-supporting.

At the time I left 3-5 Burlington Gardens, Mrs Story had gone into partnership with an art dealer in Kensington and I determined until I could get on the right side of my overdraft, to make do with only Biddy and another young helper.

The drain on my financial resources was increased by sums I was paying out at this time to various artists to enable them to keep going. Five had come to depend on me for regular help.

'The back is made for the burden,' was one of Nannan's favourite little sayings, and I was never one given to self-pity. But at times I used to wonder if England was the only country which was so indifferent to the fate of her artists.

Americans interested in my venture used often to tell me that if I transferred my headquarters to New York my work would meet with much greater encouragement from the authorities there. An American woman with many contacts in the art world invited me to go into partnership with her in Boston, continuing my policy of sponsoring the young artist. A literary agent asked me to let him fix a lecture tour for me in the States.

Family claims and gallery commitments made such propositions appear fantastic. I turned them all down.

By the late spring of 1935 my husband became impatient at my reluctance to make plans for the summer. He reminded me that it was five years since I had taken a real holiday; that even if I had gone away I had remained in touch by telephone or correspondence with my secretary. Affirming that the gallery could jolly well look after itself for a fortnight, he booked reservations for a cruise to Scandinavia, in June. Thus the matter was taken out of my own hands.

Biddy assured me that all should go smoothly in my absence and Evelyn Weil, the young artist whose exhibition was imminent, begged me not to worry but to go away with an easy mind, adding that she herself would help in the gallery during the weeks her work was on show.

I had become so inured to my responsibilities – to my Friday journey to Manchester, my weekend housekeeping and Sunday entertaining at home,

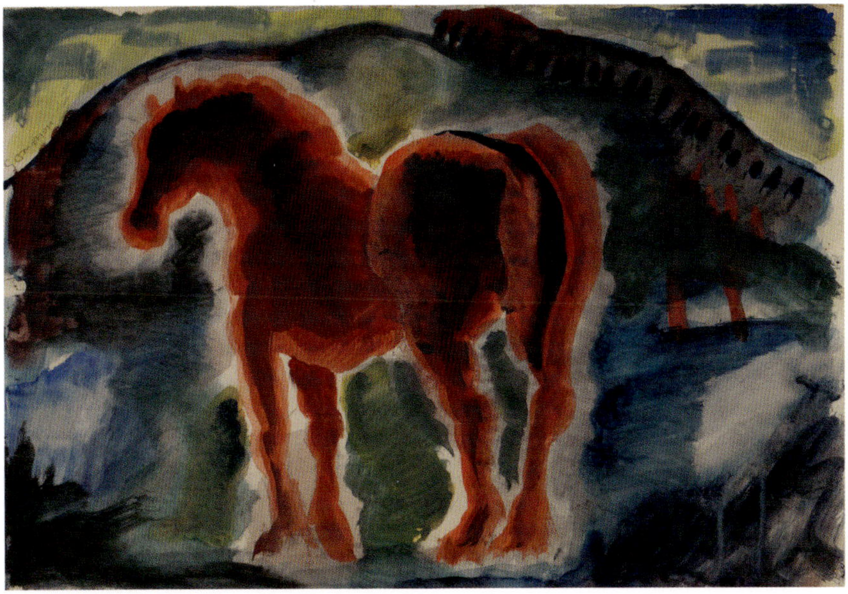

DAVID GOMMON, *RED HORSE,* EXHIBITED 1935. THE LUCY WERTHEIM ESTATE

to travelling back to London by the breakfast train on Monday morning (which meant rising at 6:00 am) to appointments every moment of the day, appointments that kept me on my feet from 10:00 am till 6:00 pm, with often only a snatched sandwich and cup of coffee at midday in my room overlooking the Rope Walk, that I was completely disorientated those first days. I could not get used to my enforced leisure, and felt miserable cut adrift from my usual routine. But after a week of sea and sunshine, the gallery assumed a truer perspective. It could go on without me.

I returned refreshed and invigorated. Biddy reported that nothing had gone amiss during my absence, save that the private view had been something of a fiasco.

My other young helper was Kathleen Walne, an artist given to enthusiastic bouts of painting at odd hours of the day regardless of the task she might be engaged on.

It was our custom to serve tea on private view days. We possessed perhaps two to three dozen cups and saucers and sometimes had twice that number of guests, which meant a hurried washing up in the kitchen to make available a fresh relay.

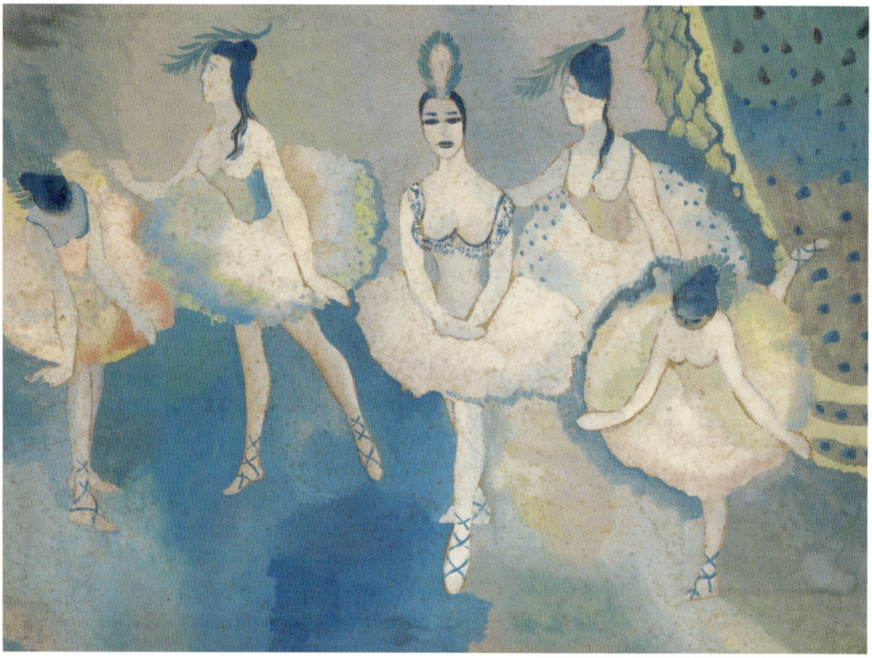

KATHLEEN WALNE, *BALLET DANCERS,* EXHIBITED 1938
TOWNER EASTBOURNE, GIFT OF HILARY WARD, DAUGHTER OF KATHLEEN WALNE
IN MEMORY OF KATHLEEN'S FRIENDSHIP WITH LUCY WERTHEIM, 2019

The attendance was large at Evelyn Weil's opening, and Kathleen offered to help in the kitchen. During a lull in the tea party she was seized with a desire to do a still life of objects on the kitchen dresser. The result was disaster. Somehow she mistook her paint rag for her dishcloth, and Biddy recounts peculiar looks of consternation on the faces of all to whom she handed a second cup of tea. One guest after another pushed her cup away exclaiming, 'What vile stuff – it tastes more like turpentine than tea!'

Captions

My readers may have gathered that my gallery was run on somewhat original lines. Even the cards we sent out every three weeks announcing various shows had their individual character.

Christopher Wood gave me the idea, borrowed from Paris, of invitations

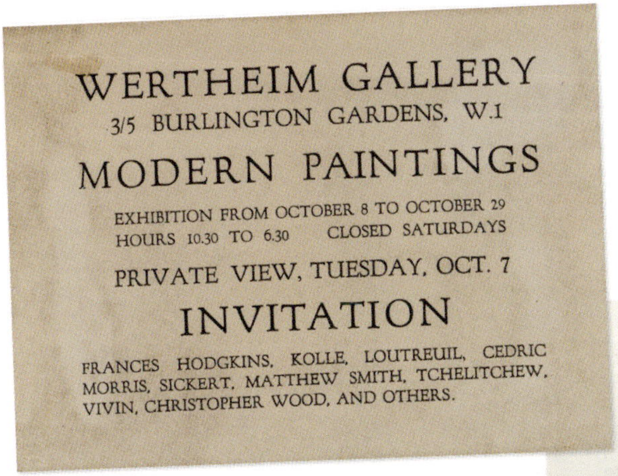

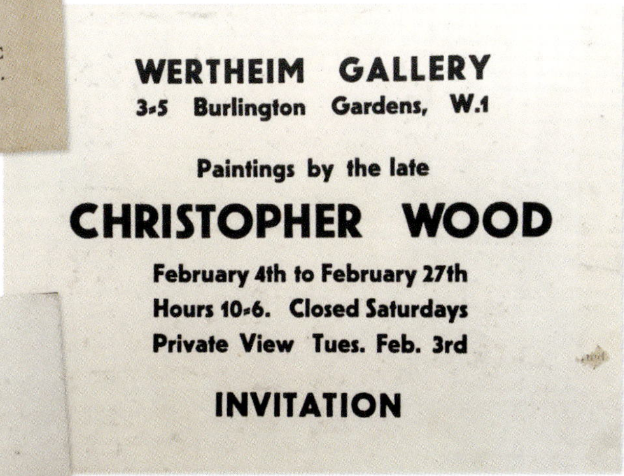

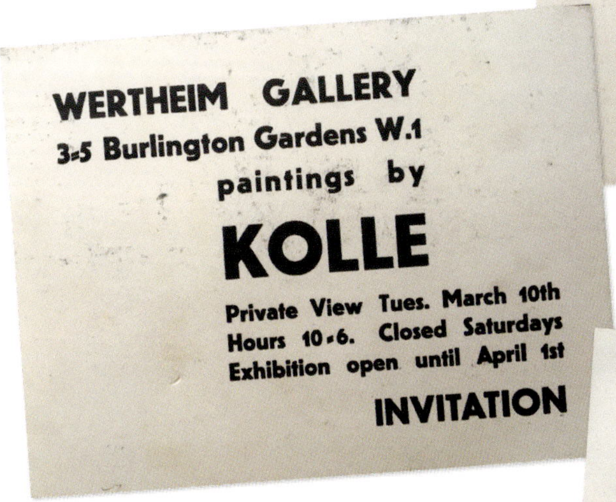

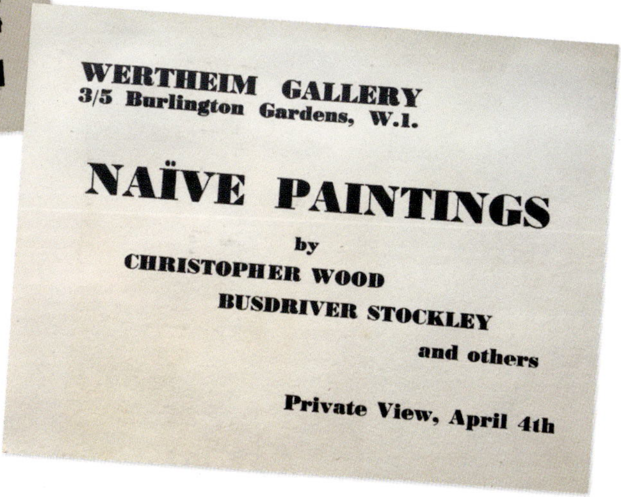

Exhibitions Invitations:
Modern Paintings – October 1930
Christopher Wood – February 1931
Kolle – March 1931
Naïve Paintings – April 1934
The Lucy Wertheim Archive

sans envelope, with the name of the artist in heavy block lettering. Before he died we had discussed the card for his coming exhibition with me in the autumn. The card was to resemble in essential the one sent out by Georges Bernheim for his show earlier in the year. The fashion took on in London.

Proving how personal to my gallery this type of invitation had become, we noticed at one time many visitors dropping in to our current exhibition expecting to find on the walls paintings by another artist. We discovered the reason. A Bond Street dealer had adopted identically the same type of invitation!

I wrote courteously, suggesting that in their own interest as well as ours this firm should refrain from using a card that had come to be regarded as peculiar to ourselves. The request was acceded to.

I confess I got a kick thinking out captions for our various shows.

I quote a few that gave me special pleasure. We were considering an exhibition of portraits of women in the public eye. A telling caption was needed: something crisp and short and striking. I had it! 'Mrs and Miss 1933'. The press was intrigued when the cards arrived, and gave the show excellent publicity. Crowds visited the gallery and the exhibition was a great success. On the opening day the *Daily Mail* splashed the caption across the page, at the same time reproducing three of the portraits. The weekly *Sketch* gave us two full-page illustrations, including the frontispiece (Douglas Byng in the role of Flora Macdonald, by Lesley Blanch.) Other papers vied with one another in giving us notices. Gertrude Lawrence, Valerie Taylor, Beatrix Lehmann, Lydia Sherwood, Catherine Lacey and Elisabeth Bergner were among the women represented.

'Twelve Free Thinkers in Painting', was another caption I gave myself a pat on the back for!

But I can claim no credit for the title 'Forgotten Beauty for Eye and Ear', which Miss Constance Jenkins chose for her exhibition of early brass rubbings – one of the most unusual shows I ever held. These reproductions of treasures, some as early as the thirteenth century, came as a revelation to many, with quite a number of visitors not even having known of their existence.

Miss Jenkins entranced our ears as well as our eyes by playing each day from 5:00 till 6:00 o'clock on her piano little-known melodies by Purcell, Field and Byrd. Even 'specialists' of that period (of music) enquired of her whence she had unearthed these unfamiliar delights!

'Military Tattoo', was another original title, chosen by William Farley for an exhibition of war paintings (1914–18). These had a harrowing effect on those who lived with them in the spring of 1935 for three whole weeks. In spite of their lovely paint quality (and the artist knew his business as a craftsman), I was glad when the time came to hang more cheerful pictures on the walls.

Puppets

In the autumn of 1937 I was introduced by an artist friend to Stanley Maile, maker of marionettes. In spite of his shy, unobtrusive personality, it took a very few moments to recognise in him an enthusiast – and an enthusiast who was no mere amateur.

I enquired tentatively if it were possible to see some of his work, and a day or two later he brought to the gallery one of his puppets to show me. I became a puppet fan.

This introduction to the art of Stanley Maile opened up a new world for me and it was not long before I had agreed to lend the gallery for a month for an exhibition of marionettes.

The idea was a novel one for a gallery, and the little late afternoon entertainments staged by the various exhibitors gave infinite delight to many visitors.

I often said to myself that if ever I came into a fortune I would build and equip a theatre for marionettes.

Some Women Painters

I held several exhibitions of women painters in the Albany gallery between 1934 and 1939, perhaps the most remarkable being a collection of paintings of Polynesian women by Madge Tennent, a New Zealander born in England, then living in Honolulu. These forceful pictures were shown to great advantage in the lofty room we called the 'Gallery'.

If charm is the quality of making the other fellow feel pleased with himself, as I once heard it defined, then Madge Tennent possessed 'charm' in abundance. She positively radiated approbation of the gallery and its personnel and all of us felt sorry when her show came to an end. Her little inaugural luncheon party at The Ivy was also an occasion to look back on with pleasure.

Gwen Gallienne held a one-man show with me in the spring of 1936, which attracted a large number of visitors and increased her reputation as a painter. She had an enormously successful private view, at which many people in the public eye were present, among others Emlyn Williams the actor, J.B. Manson, Director of the Tate, and Amelia Earhart, the American airwoman, of whom she had done portraits.

The exhibition had been originally fixed for the previous autumn, but in Paris she had had a warning from some occult source that the date decided on for the opening would be an unlucky one for her, and she was advised to postpone her show till later. Sure enough, just at the time the exhibition should have opened the artist broke her arm and was completely incapacitated.

She was a picturesque and endearing person, and we missed her when she returned to Paris and no longer frequented the gallery.

Lord Dunsany

A very appreciative exhibitor about this time (1936) was Lord Dunsany. He held an amusing show of his little clay figures, each of which carried a witty caption and caused great merriment in the gallery.

It was very gratifying to receive his charming letter of thanks at the close of the exhibition. I still treasure the little figure he bestowed on me as a memento of its sojourn in my gallery.

When a child at a convent school abroad I remember our Mother Superior saying in one of her homilies to the girls that a sense of appreciation or gratitude ('reconnaissance' was the actual word she used) was the mark of true breeding.

How often in the years I ran my gallery did her words come back to me.

As others see us

I know no more revealing test of character than the way 'the great ones' stand up to being caricatured.

During the numerous exhibitions of caricatures, cartoons, etc., I have held it has been interesting to see their reaction to the artist's conception of themselves.

George Belcher gives an indefinable air of the char to even the most erudite of his sitters. Lilian Baylis, though not flattered by his drawing of her, stood up to hers remarkably well .

I think women are less vain in this respect than men.

When George Scott had a show of his caricatures with me in 1934, irate professors frequently popped in and out of the gallery protesting at 'the impudence of this young puppy'.

Rebecca West and Storm Jameson are two women writers who went up in my estimation after appearing in an exhibition of caricatures by Emilio Coia. Both drawings were so cruel that it was a *tour de force* not to wince visibly when they came face to face with them for the first time in public. My admiration for these two, which had been great before, went up by leaps and bounds. That was a display of real grit. Bravo!

Edmond Kapp held an exhibition with me in 1935 of cartoons of the principal delegates to the League of Nations at Geneva. These were more or less straightforward likenesses and it was not so intriguing to watch the reaction of the sitters. It *was* interesting, though, to listen to Kapp's many anecdotes of the sittings. He told me that the most famous had almost invariably been the easiest of approach.

Ivan Opffer appears to have drawn more well-known people than any artist I know. He had a show with me in 1938 and a great number of his sitters came along to see themselves.

He has a devilish way of picking out salient, not always enviable characteristics. Nevertheless, most of his visitors were quite good tempered and laughed off their discomfiture when they felt they had been the reverse of flattered. A notable exception was Jacob Epstein, who protested in no measured terms at the liberty the artist had taken with him. He angrily refused to stay in the gallery as long as Opffer himself was there.

Through Opffer I made the acquaintance of Eric Muspratt, the author of *My South Sea Island*, and a quick, spontaneous friendship was the outcome of the introduction. I felt at the end of a few hours that I had known him for as many years.

Paint or Perish

I have referred to appointments that kept me busy in the gallery. A task I never delegated to my helpers was that of 'criticism' of work brought to me, especially by the younger artist. On my arriving at the gallery, Biddy would tell me of half a dozen such appointments she had arranged for me during the day.

Not only did painters, sculptors, woodcarvers, potters, theatre, textile and other designers bring their work to show me, but often a budding artist would be accompanied by parent or guardian seeking my opinion or advice. Were the sketches in the portfolio or these attempts on canvas promising enough to justify an expensive art school training? Often a training that meant considerable sacrifice on the part of the parent? Could I hold out hope that at the end of three years the artist would be able to support himself or herself, as the case might be?

What a delicate problem this! How well I knew that the more original the vision and the greater the individuality of the artist, the less chance he had for years to come of turning his work into a commercial proposition. How I hated to seem discouraging. Those imploring young eyes that looked to me perhaps as their last resort: would I not put in the word that would weight the scales in their favour? But it was no use holding out false hopes. I had too many examples of brilliant young people on my hands struggling to make ends meet. Unless the artist was prepared for years of lean living and gruelling toil, I advised against taking up art as a career.

I knew that nothing I could say would quench the fire of the genius who would create or starve, paint or perish, but oh for a deeper pocket that I might have helped more of those fledglings who with their enthusiasm and even moderate gifts had it in them to create a fairer, finer world if timely support had been forthcoming.

To me it is a very terrible thing to see England neglecting her artists the way she does. We are much less civilised in our attitude towards art than the French, the Dutch and the Scandinavians.

Consider, for example, the infinitesimal space accorded in our daily papers to art criticism. A really serious Dutch painter holding his first exhibition in his own country is treated with the respect he deserves, and whole columns will be devoted to him by the chief newspapers. A Norwegian friend tells me that the same conditions obtain in Norway. This attitude of the press naturally tends to raise the prestige of the artist, and public taste benefits accordingly.

Whilst possessing what one of my friends describes as 'very Jingoistic leanings', I have led a sufficiently cosmopolitan existence to recognise that England lags sadly behind other countries in an appreciation of creative art.

Take the two foreign countries I know best: France, where I was partly educated ('partly' is the word I hear my husband murmur) and Holland, where I have spent chunks of my life since I was twenty. Ask any artist who has had the chance of painting in France if he has not found it a thousand times easier to work there. Why? Because there is a something in the air, an *interest* that stimulates one to one's best effort. The artist *matters*. Even the *ouvrier* passing by and glancing at the sketch in progress exclaims heartily: '*Courage, Monsieur! Ce n'est pas mal, ça. Courage!*'

Why do Americans, Canadians, New Zealanders, South Africans, Dutchmen, Scandinavians and the rest of them flock to Paris to study? There are numerous art schools in London, efficient ones too. But where one foreigner comes to London to study art, probably ninety-nine go to Paris. What is the reason for this? I would put it down to our backward attitude to art in the immediate past and the fact that men who have now reached middle age and *positions of authority* relegate art to a place of third-rate importance. The result is seen in the chilling indifference of the public, from the man-in-the-street to the Lord Mayor of his city, to the fate of the artist in the scheme of things.

Tin Gods

How often have I suffered at the hands of these little tin gods (I refer to men who have reached positions of authority). The following incident is typical. A few years ago I arranged an exhibition of modern paintings in a municipal gallery of an important city in Lancashire. I offered to present a number of these paintings to their permanent collection if they were selected by ballot and school children were also allowed to record their votes. I had the wholehearted co-operation of the curator.

The local Director of Education vetoed the scheme because 'personally he did not approve of modern art'. I wrote to him, begging for an interview that I might better understand his point of view. He confessed that he had never even visited an exhibition of modern art. His prejudice was based on reproductions he had seen from time to time in the press! As a protest to this unenlightened attitude of the educational authorities, I withdrew the example of Christopher Wood in my offer.

Sometimes I think England might do well to take a leaf out of the book of Dutch education authorities.

Throughout my married years I have been thrown frequently into the company of young Dutchmen, mostly boys in their late teens who came to study the Lancashire export trade of cotton textiles for Java. It was usual for these young men to make a sojourn of six months in Manchester before proceeding east. Many of them regarded our house as their second home and I got to understand unusually well the mentality of these young Dutchmen. One thing always struck me very forcibly – their interest in current art and their pride in the achievements of their own living artists and architects. Town planning was for them a topic of vital interest. Had I seen the new part of Amsterdam yet? Did I like the new type of school that was being designed by Willem Dudok? Or did I prefer the more traditional Pierre Cuypers? Where in Manchester could be seen examples of young *English* architecture? How were we tackling in our country the problem of ribbon development?

Now these questions were asked by young athletes whose minds had been trained as intelligently as their bodies, a type that could not be cursorily dismissed as 'sloppy' or 'sissy' by their English counterpart, the public schoolboy. These men, twenty years hence would be making important decisions for their country as mayors, councillors, members of committees, and their education and training had fitted them for the job.

I used to think one of the pleasantest sights in Holland was watching fathers taking their young families round the public galleries on a Sunday, instilling pride of their national treasures in the minds of the young generation.

The Critic

'There always seems more "*mouvement*" in your gallery than any other in London,' once observed a Frenchman to me, and quite often again the same remark was made to me.

As the Leicester Galleries and others had a larger attendance, it was perhaps the preponderating element of youth that created this impression. But it was also known that my exhibitions got excellent publicity.

Many of our foremost newspaper editors interested themselves in my policy.

Robert Tatlock of the *Daily Telegraph* used to look in at many of my shows. He was a delightful visitor.

Edgar W. Record of the *Birmingham Post* sent his gifted reporter, Mrs Hill, to write up my exhibitions. Later I got to know him personally and he encouraged me to write this 'adventure'.

Ralph David Blumenfeld of the *Daily Express* called upon me personally, creating the pleasant impression that making the acquaintance of my gallery was for him a memorable occasion!

James Drawbell of the *Sunday Chronicle* bought a picture from me, a clever caricature of himself by the artist Emilio Coia, and give me a notice from time to time.

The London Editor of the *Manchester Guardian* reproduced a painting in that paper when there was a Manchester angle to one of my exhibitions.

Harry Ainsworth of the *People*, with whom I once travelled to Manchester, sent in a reporter who wrote up my current show. It happened this way. A seat had been booked for him at the last moment on the diner of the 06:25 from St Pancras. Biddy had also booked a seat for me.

They were the last two seats available and there was some confusion as to which was whose. We began to talk. I remember our conversation almost word for word. He had been interviewing Charlie Chaplin and gave me a lively description of his afternoon. I remember, too, how ravenously hungry we both were and that we had to wait a good hour before our meal was served. Ainsworth did not reveal his identity until just as we were leaving the train, when he handed me his card, saying that I should hear from him.

Of the weekly journals, the following distinguished critics are among many who helped to make my protégés known: Clive Bell, Raymond Mortimer, Philip Hendy, Cyril Connolly, Hugh Gordon Porteous.

I have earlier acknowledged my debt to Mr Charles Marriott of *The Times*, who not only wrote *about* the artists but often followed their careers with interest and helped them in practical fashion by many a kindly act.

Thomas Earp, of whom Christopher Wood had written me, 'he has the wittiest tongue in London', came regularly to my exhibitions and was instrumental in putting many of my artists on the map.

Reginald Wilenski was another helpful critic, also Pierre Jeannerat of the *Daily Mail*, and Gui St Bernard of the *News Chronicle*.

Frank Rutter, Philip Konody and Walter Greg all noticed my shows at length. But in the early days of running my gallery I learnt often to dread their comments. I remember a whole column in the *Sunday Times*, by Rutter, devoted to a show on Henry Stockley, my bus driver painter, which he headed: 'This Craze for Simplicity'.

It was only for the artists' sake that I dreaded these notices. I was becoming so used to vituperation that most of it fell like water on a duck's back and made no impression on me personally.

Patrick Balfour from time to time gave me a paragraph in the 'Londoner's Diary' of the *Evening Standard*. 'The most coveted publicity space of any London paper', remarked a journalist friend when he was turning over the leaves of my press cuttings book.

Percy Cater was another journalist who could always be relied upon to give my current show a sympathetic notice.

Tom Driberg also proved a kind friend. He lunched with me at my flat in the early days of my venture and I recall my pleasure at his saying and feeling all the things I wanted him to say and feel about my pictures.

Prophet without Honour

I encountered outstanding examples of the friendliness of journalists when opening my little daughter gallery in Manchester, in the year 1932. It was by no means the fault of the press that the venture failed and that I had to give it up at the end of a year. The *Manchester Guardian* was consistently kind. Eric Newton, then on its staff, noticed most of my important shows and gave me one of the most sympathetic notices I have ever received when I showed a selection of my paintings by Christopher Wood.

George Grafton-Green of the *Manchester Evening News* was also very helpful, as were also the northern editors of the *Daily Herald*, *Daily Mail*, *Daily Express*, *Daily Dispatch* and the *Manchester Evening Chronicle*.

I had hoped for some measure of co-operation from the powers that be at the Manchester City Art Gallery. But William Batho, Assistant Curator, and S.D. Cleveland were the only officials whose attitude was encouraging.

It was soon made clear to me that I was not *persona grata* either to curator or his committee. My little gallery for some reason or another was not in favour with the authorities. I am ignorant of the reason to this day. But that this antagonism existed was soon made clear to me. Therefore it did not come as much of a surprise when (putting my pride in my pocket) a request I made to them was turned down.

The first year nearing an end, my accountant urged me to give up the venture, as he said it was proving too great a drain on my resources, but the little place had become such a centre of interest that I wanted to try out the experiment for a further twelve months.

With this in mind, I wrote asking if the committee of the City Art Gallery could see its way to buying from me three paintings of the first order by Christopher Wood, Phelan Gibb and Frances Hodgkins for £150, which sum would cover my *rates* for a further twelve months. The answer was an uncompromising refusal.

Later I sold the painting I had offered them by Christopher Wood for £350.

Some years earlier (before I had even thought of running a gallery), I had offered this same committee *as a gift* a fine painting by Roland Pitchforth, which they refused on the score (I understood later) of it being a nude.

Although the Whitworth Gallery, Manchester, had bought from me and various municipal galleries in the north, including Liverpool, Hull, Newcastle upon Tyne and Salford, I have not had the honour of placing a painting in Manchester, where I was a citizen for over twenty years.

Although it proved an expensive experiment from the financial point of view, I never regret the enthusiasm and energy I put into that venture in Manchester. I took premises with three good windows close to the Royal Exchange. Willy-Nilly, the man in the street, should be educated to an appreciation of modern art! It often happened that as many as thirty to forty people would be clustering round the little gallery, and sometimes overhearing an argument or lively discussion I have gone out and held forth in the street trying to *explain* what was baffling them.

Distortions were very difficult for them to accept in those early days, and abstract work was quite beyond the comprehension of the average window-gazer.

An old friend, calling to see me one day, told me he thought there was a Salvation Army meeting in progress as he neared my premises!

What I found particularly interesting was that the so-called *un*educated man often had a much surer judgment than the man who prided himself on his knowledge of art, and I made many friends among this class. Also errand boys, telegraph boys, apprentices, typists and the like paid me the compliment of taking a lively interest in the pictures in the windows.

Many artists came to see me, bringing me their work to criticise, some from as far away as Yorkshire and Liverpool. I received scores of kind and encouraging letters. It was a real grief to many, I have good reason to believe, when I had to give up my little gallery in Manchester.

Links with Lancashire

In my story I have made many references to Manchester, for it is the city I am most interested in, my forbears for generations past having gained their living in the cotton industry, and also because it is also the city of my husband's adoption, he being of Dutch extraction and the Consul for the Netherlands in Manchester.

I was brought up from a child to believe that Manchester was a wonderful city! My father, William Pearson, Hon. M.Sc. of Manchester University, was connected with many of its institutions, and obituary notices in the *Manchester Guardian* and in the *Manchester City News* testify to his public spirit and the respect and affection in which he was held. Although a cotton merchant, he was chiefly known for his climbing, literary and botanical activities.

He was a dynamic member of the Rucksack Club, he belonged to various literary societies, he wrote a standard book on British Hepaticae, and when he died his valuable collection of mosses was left to the Museum of the Manchester University.

What more natural than that I, his daughter who idolised him, should imbibe much of his own passionate loyalty to this city of grime and squalor? To this day the sight of approaching chimney stacks gives me a thrill reminiscent of the days when my father would take me to some 'treat' in Manchester from Knutsford, where we lived from my being a child until I was nearly twenty.

The treat I first remember was a lecture on spiders by Dr Dallinger, illustrated by lantern slides. I cannot have been much more than a baby, yet I recall some of those illustrations as clearly now as if I had seen them this morning. The lecturer must have had an enchanting way of presenting his subject, for I have loved spiders ever afterwards.

It was from my father that I inherited my passion for pictures.

Another early joy was being taken by him to the Manchester City Gallery, and I remember the impression of a painting by Tom Mostyn, a Lancashire painter – some brilliant effect of firelight, if my memory serves me right, from the brazier of a road-mender. It would intrigue me to see that picture again. Whatever its intrinsic merits as a painting, I am almost sure I could recapture part of that early thrill.

As well as for pictures, my father had a passion for a good sermon, and no orthodox religion. This predilection led to many an argument with my mother, who did not hold with (I *must* use this north country expression) his attending Roman Catholic, Wesleyan, Unitarian, Presbyterian and Church of England services indiscriminately.

Nevertheless, my education was furthered by this enthusiasm of his and at a tender age I had heard Annie Besant preach, also Stopford Brooke, Father Bernard Vaughan, Ian McLaren, R.J. Campbell and a Welsh orator named Lewis.

I suppose I must have been a very impressionable and emotional child, for all these years later I can distinctly recall the reaction I had to each of these preachers.

Annie Besant in her white robe, calm yet impassioned, speaking for over an hour without recourse to a single note, holding her audience in the vast Free Trade Hall, Manchester, in such tense silence that at any moment you might have heard the proverbial pin drop.

Lastly Lewis, the little Welsh revivalist, who in the Wesleyan chapel at Eccles, Lancashire, besought his hearers to give themselves to God.

It seemed terrible to me that his impassioned appeal should meet with so cold a response. I visualised a hurt and disappointed deity, and making a superhuman effort to overcome my shyness I rose in the midst of that crowded congregation and a solitary figure made my way to the vestry, there solemnly to dedicate myself to Him for the rest of my days. I think I was nine years old.

The understanding between my father and myself was so great that he was wise enough to take this dedication seriously, and though he followed me to the vestry at the close of the service (where other 'revivalists' had gathered), he refrained from any comment. He kissed me good-night silently with great tenderness on our return home. I was so worn out with emotion that I fell asleep on my knees, repeating mechanically my obligatory prayer 'Gentle Jesus' and woke in the early hours cold as ice, crumpled up on the floor.

Until I was eleven or twelve years of age, my father's was the most dominating influence in my life. His genial personality and wide interests attracted to him a large acquaintance and his friends numbered many young people of both sexes.

Among those who came often to our house was a young person of the name of Mabel Lenny-Smith, an artist who divided her time between the Latin Quarter in Paris and her parents' home at Knutsford.

Did I say, 'young person'? Should I not rather have written 'goddess', for I was held in thrall by this divine creature from the moment I met her.

Her grace, her wit, her merry laugh, the twinkle in her eye, her chic French clothes all combined to make me, impressionable child that I was, her abject slave. And her enthralling tales of student life in Paris! I was never tired of listening to descriptions of this world peopled with painters, sculptors, models, impecunious artists and a curious being called a concierge, whom I conceived at that time to be a creature who rocked babies to sleep!

In those days my divinity would appear from Paris laden with a mass of art journals and illustrated catalogues of current exhibitions, and encourage me to air my views on these strange paintings, possibly my first introduction to MODERN ART. When the delight of these began to pall, forth would come reproductions of the Old Masters: Dürer, Holbein, Rembrandt, and the early Italian Primitives over which we would pore for another hour or more.

'Luce dear, which means more to you, *Colour or Form*?' she enquired on one occasion. 'I think Colour,' I replied.

Equally provocative questions still crop up in our letters to one another.

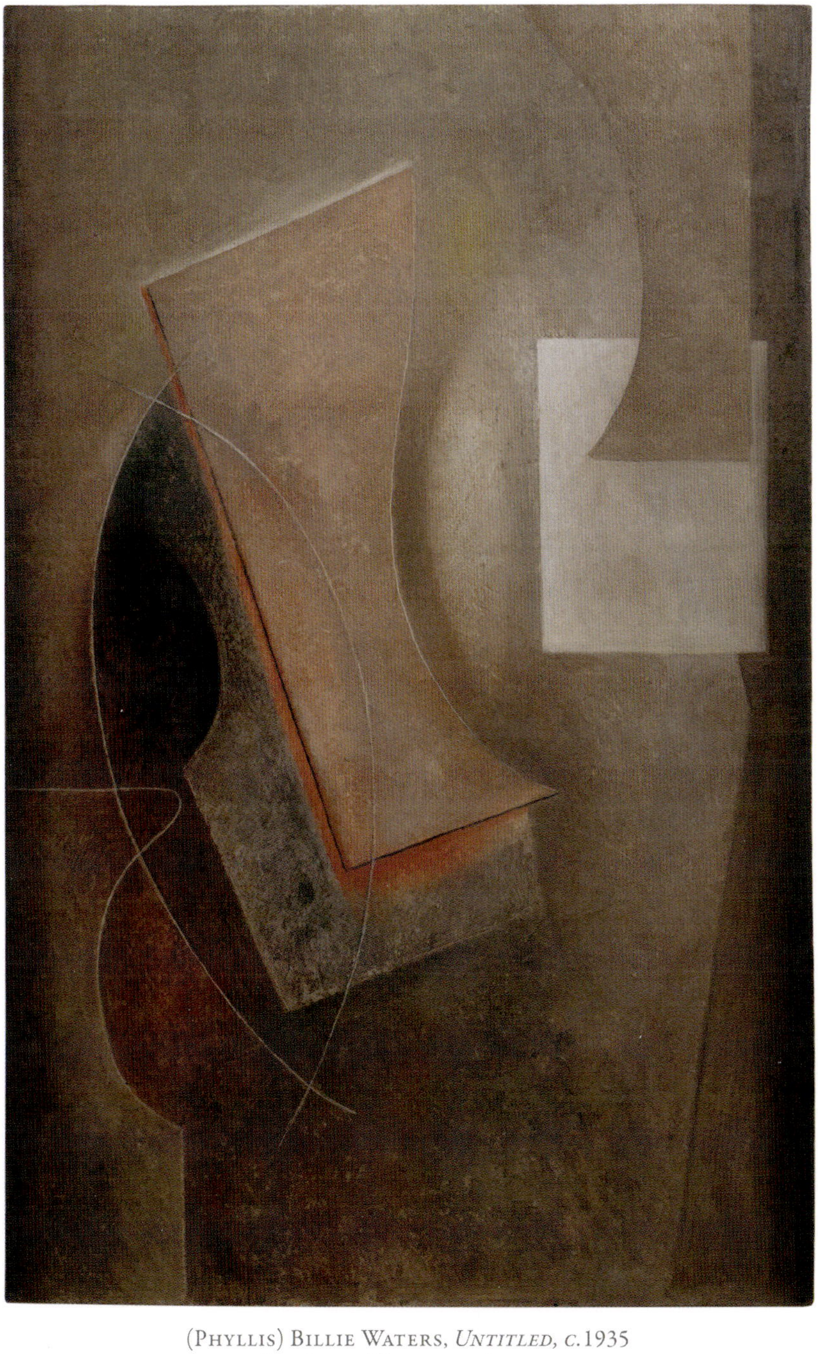

(Phyllis) Billie Waters, *Untitled*, c.1935
The Lucy Wertheim Estate

The Curator

What is the true function of the curator? In England it consists as often as not in acting as custodian of relics of the past.

The curators capable of selecting works of art produced during the past decade that are likely to be of permanent value are probably to be counted on the fingers of one hand. And even these four or five live in such fear and dread of losing their jobs through any determined stand they might take in support of creative work that frequently their attempts to bring their galleries into line with modern ideas are abortive.

How often have these rather tremulous gentlemen entered my gallery and, surrounded by paintings of *unknown* artists, stood tongue-tied and wondering, at a loss what to say if invited to express an opinion.

How could they be expected to *know* if the work was good when they had still to learn what Charles Marriott, Thomas Earp, Eric Newton and Co. had to say about it?

I was so foolish as to imagine in the early days of running my gallery that curators would welcome my co-operation in bringing to their notice outstanding talent, and especially talent of local interest.

I was mistaken.

I could name a dozen or more artists whose paintings might have been bought from me for a nominal sum before they were written up by the critics and taken up by picture dealers as a commercial proposition. Invariably, the curator and his committee would wait until this work could only be acquired at five times the sum I had offered it.

The trouble is that most of these functionaries are completely out of touch with the younger generation and their needs.

In Britain, all too often a town or city has no art policy at all. The curator of the local art gallery has frequently been appointed because he is the son of or the nephew of, or the friend of, so and so, and 'I'd like to do him a good turn, don't you know,' says the man with the most influence on the local council. Sometimes the local librarian assumes the office of curator as the demand for a gallery (of sorts) becomes manifest in his town.

All this implies an incredibly casual attitude towards art in Britain.

Why should not our public galleries be brought under some scheme of administration by which the director or curator must possess at least as strong qualifications in *his* line as the municipality would demand in the case of say the borough surveyor or the medical officer of health? Why, for example, should a city whose artistic reputation has rested only on music appoint for the care of its art gallery a man whose qualifications are solely musical?

I have had much to do with these gentlemen in the course of arranging numerous art exhibitions in provincial art galleries and I have learnt to place them in two categories: the complacent and the apologetic. The complacent ones continue in the same old groove, taking the line of least resistance, impervious to the forces now at work that will presently force them out of their aloof indifference. The apologetic resort to all sorts of unworthy ruses in order to acquire for their gallery a work of art, the purchase of which does not meet with the approval of the city fathers. Even if a curator knows his job, he is often so frustrated by the ignorance of his local committee that he has a very small chance of forming in his gallery a collection of lasting value.

British Art Spurned

How ironical, not to say tragic, are the announcements from time to time in the Civil List of puny grants and miserly pensions meted out to artists, often when they have reached their dotage and are incapable of sustained creative effort. If the artist received adequate reward for his efforts, such grants would be unnecessary. Which boils down to the conclusion that as a nation we need to alter our entire attitude towards art.

I found it galling during frequent sojourns in Holland in pre-war days

YOU ARE INVITED TO THE PRIVATE VIEW

of the

FRANCO-ITALIAN EXHIBITION

organized by the

SOCIETY "L'ARTE D'OGGI"

under the patronage of H.R.H. THE PRINCESS OF PIEDMONT

and the

"SOCIÉTE DE L'ART PRÉSENT"

under the patronage of His Excellency Henry de Jouvenal and the Prince de Beauvau-Craon

to be held at the

WERTHEIM GALLERY

8 BURLINGTON GARDENS, W.1

PRIVATE VIEW · JUNE 25

1935

COMMITTEE:

Honorary Presidents :

His Excellency Dino Grandi, *The Italian Ambassador*

His Excellency Charles Corbin, *The French Ambassador*

President : Lord Balniel, M.P.

The Rt. Hon. Viscount D'Abernon, G.C.B., G.C.M.G.

Beddington Behrens, Esq., M.C.

Clive Bell, Esq.

Lady Henry Bentinck

Lord Berners

Lady Austen Chamberlain

Lord Ivor Spencer Churchill

Kenneth M. Clark, Esq.
Director National Gallery

Lady Colefax

Samuel Courtauld, Esq., LL.D.

The Lord Duveen

H. S. Ede, Esq.
Assistant Director of the Tate Gallery

The Viscount Esher, M.B.E.

Augustus John, Esq., R.A.

J. B. Manson, Esq.
Director of the Tate Gallery

Edward Marsh, Esq., C.B.

Raymond Mortimer, Esq.

The Rt. Hon. Lord Rennell, G.C.B., G.C.M.G., G.C.V.O.

Sir William Rothenstein

The Earl of Sandwich

Montagu Shearman, O.B.E.

Mrs. Arthur Strong, C.B.E., LL.D., Litt.D.

Lord Howard de Walden

Franco-Italian exhibition private view invitation, June 1935
The Lucy Wertheim Archive

when I visited exhibitions of contemporary art in the municipal galleries, to see almost every other country represented except Britain.

When I enquired why no British artist was included, all sorts of curious reasons were given to me, the most frequent being that British art did not 'fit in' with the rest, that it was too 'old-fashioned'.

One such exhibition was on at the Municipal Gallery in Amsterdam, in the summer of 1935. It was an exceedingly interesting collection of paintings by artists as well-known as Gauguin and as little known as Herman Kruyder, a Dutchman then living, alas up to his death not sufficiently appreciated.

Given the chance, I could offer Holland an exhibition of modern English paintings that would hold their own with examples she could gather from other countries. But such an exhibition would need the patronage of officialdom, and how am I to obtain that?

If I were proposing to sponsor a collection of paintings by Jewish refugees, or by young French and Italian painters, probably the funds would be forthcoming, also the enthusiasm.

I print on the opposite page the invitation card of an exhibition held in my own gallery in Burlington Gardens, in the summer of 1935, arranged by the Princess de Bassiano, an American married to an Italian. Was ever a more formidable array of names brought together to ensure the success of an exhibition?

The artists were French and Italian. Can you imagine in Italy, France, Holland – and for that matter England – an equally imposing list compiled to sponsor an English group of painters? No. Definitely no. Yet the exhibition was not an outstanding one. I could have got together a collection of living English painters that would have surpassed it in merit, and many unbiased judges made this remark during the weeks that the Princess de Bassiano showed her work.

Lord Duveen came to the exhibition and made the error of selecting in an adjoining room a painting of one of my 'Twenties Group'. 'That is the most interesting thing here,' he said, enquiring the price of it, and the name of the artist. It was tantalising to have to reply: 'Lord Duveen, you have been invited here as a patron of the exhibition in the Large Gallery, where are hung French and Italian paintings. Much as I am tempted, it would hardly be playing the game to let you buy this one in its place.' Incidentally, the price of the English painting was 5 guineas, and the foreign one he finally selected several times as much.

During this exhibition of French and Italian paintings, Mr Kenneth Clark, Director of our National Gallery, was a frequent visitor to my gallery, yet when I sent him a personal invitation begging him to see the work of my 'Twenties Group', he could not find the time to come.

Years later, when he – Sir Kenneth Clark by this time – wrote asking me to lend my *Yellow Horse* by Christopher Wood to the Biennale Exhibition in Venice, in addition to the six other paintings already borrowed from me, I replied by asking if he was going to wait until Phelan Gibb, Frances Hodgkins and other English artists worthy of being represented at Venice had been dead eight years before he took notice of them.

As long, however, as modern art in our National Gallery in Trafalgar Square is represented only by French painters (Manet, Renoir, etc.), and our living artists allowed to starve (or commit suicide), so long will this attitude towards English art persist.

We bring it on ourselves by our 'snobbery'.

Recognition

It might relevantly be asked at this point by what right I criticise my 'betters'.

I have explained earlier in my story that in the opening days of my venture no one could have sought advice and help more eagerly than I. I have also stated that mere competence in painting never interested me much. It was the quality of imagination, vision, or what our friend Collie Knox aptly describes as 'that undefinable blessing personality', that I sought in work brought to me.

This quality I found all too rarely in the artists recommended to my notice. James Manson, Director of the Tate, and his Assistant Director, H.S. [Jim] Ede, had their pet protégés and made eulogistic supplication to me on their behalf, as did also certain art patrons and principals of art schools. The work in each case was distinguished for its *skill*, but none of the painters thus brought

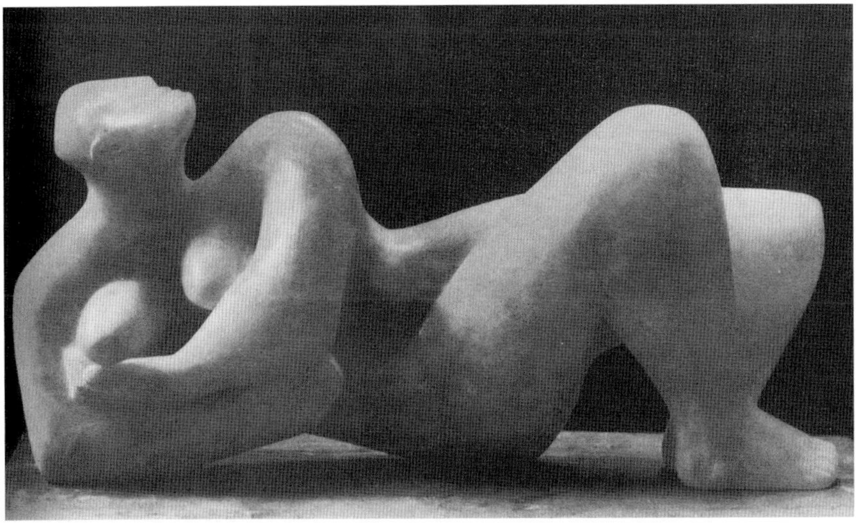

HENRY MOORE, *RECLINING FIGURE*, 1929
REPRODUCED FROM AN ORIGINAL PHOTOGRAPH

to my notice have achieved more than mediocrity in the intervening years.

Contrariwise, artists whom I (in vulgar parlance) put my shirt on have justified or are justifying my early confidence in their permanent value.

Henry Moore

Foremost I would place the sculptor Henry Moore. I fell under the spell of his work in 1928 and within a year had acquired from him *The Reclining Nude* in alabaster, *Head of a Girl* and two smaller carvings, in addition to numerous drawings.

Yet I was constantly asked over those early years of running my gallery what *beauty* I could see in this sculptor's work, and truly I found it difficult to explain its fascination. Personal vision, balance of form and rhythm are difficult qualities to communicate to another.

Visitors would sometimes ask me to help them to see what *I* could see. They knew that I was sincere in my own feeling, that it was no pose on my part when I confessed to the thrill I got from Moore's work. Others would impatiently dismiss *The Reclining Nude* as 'horrible', an 'insult to the

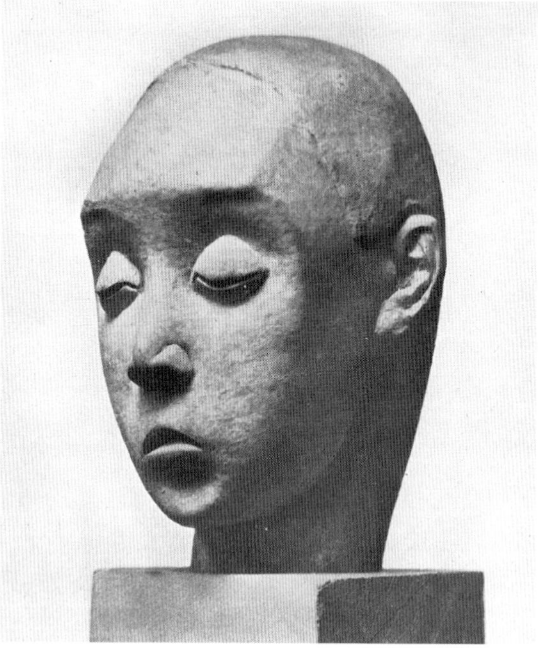

HENRY MOORE, *HEAD OF A GIRL,* 1923
REPRODUCED FROM AN ORIGINAL PHOTOGRAPH
THE HENRY MOORE FOUNDATION

human form'. One prominent member of an art committee from a city in the north, scoffingly enquired what that 'abortion' was doing in my gallery. I replied quietly, 'He that laughs last laughs longest.'

As the years went on the scoffers grew fewer and fewer. Gradually this *chef d'œuvre* wove its spell over many who had formerly disliked it. By the time public bodies began to acquire the work of Henry Moore, the need existed no longer to 'explain' it.

Frances Hodgkins

Another outstanding artist whose work thrilled me the better I knew it was Frances Hodgkins. I backed my admiration for her painting by consistently buying examples of it from the late 1920s onwards. I bought from her personally, I bought from Jackson's Gallery (Manchester), from the Claridge

Gallery, and from the St George's Gallery, and when Mr Arthur Howell, Director of the last named gallery, made a contract with her in 1930, I bought from him over the next half-year paintings for which I paid him over £400.

I flatter myself that my own enthusiasm communicated itself to many visitors to my gallery. I had a selection of her best watercolours and drawings beautifully mounted by Mr Stiles (whom I never knew go wrong on this difficult question) and it was my custom to show them on a portfolio stand which I kept for that purpose.

There is a *way* of showing watercolours: not as mere merchandise, but rather as rare expressions of the artist's own individuality.

I loved to make these experiments of 'putting them over', and it was not long before I had to my credit three public galleries as purchasers of Frances Hodgkins's work: the Salford Gallery, Lancashire, the Walker Gallery, Liverpool, and the Laing Gallery, Newcastle upon Tyne, as well as a number of distinguished private collectors, among them Sir Michael Sadler, who bought four from me, and Lord Ivor Spencer Churchill.

In spite of excellent notices from the critics – and I find among my press cuttings of this period (autumn 1930), much appreciation expressed in the *Spectator*, the *New Statesman*, *The Times* and the *Observer* – success came to this artist slowly. She was never a painter for the man in the street.

I have preserved rather more than a score of letters from her written between the time I made her acquaintance in Manchester when she was working as a designer for the Calico Printers' Association and the opening of my gallery in London. The letters make entertaining reading. Her pen is as facile as her brush, and whether she is describing a nursery tea with my little daughter and her nanny, or the painting of a bouquet of flowers in my flat to which she had added 'a couple of white lilies to give it a kick', her buoyant and vivid personality comes through, bent at all cost on overcoming obstacles and achieving recognition.

My friend, Sophie Thomson, wrote of her about this time, 'I'm afraid things have gone hardly with her, her vision having become rather too individual to be much liked in England.... She was very kind to me in those old Paris student days and I liked her very much. She had quite a successful class at Colarossi's before the War. She worked only in watercolour at that

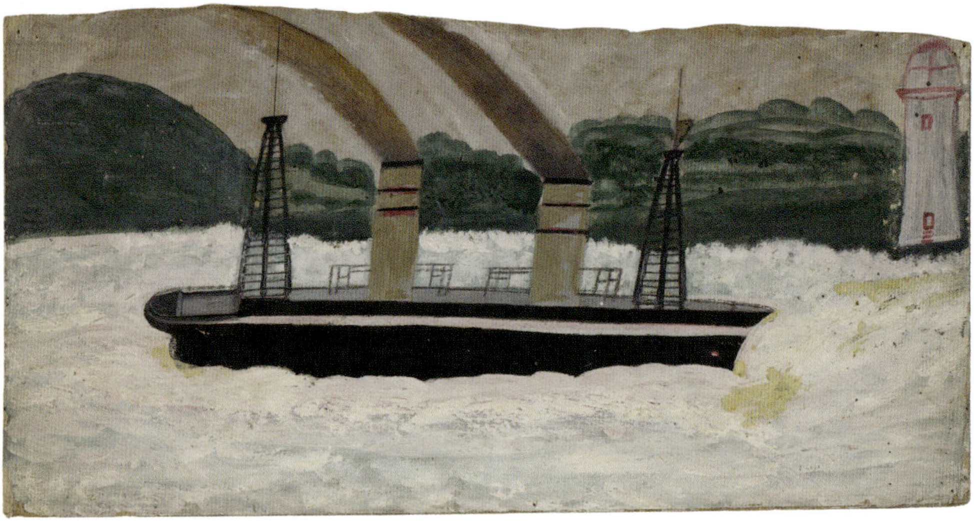

Alfred Wallis, *Steamer,* exhibited 1934
Towner Eastbourne, The Lucy Wertheim Bequest, 1971

time and was well thought of and well hung in Paris.'

Frances Hodgkins now enjoys a Civil List pension. Would not the accolade have been a well merited tribute to her genius?

Alfred Wallis

Alfred Wallis belongs to a very different type of painter. I became interested in his work during the years immediately preceding the opening of my gallery.

One summer I was staying with my friends Mabel Lenny-Smith and Sophie Thomson in their little house at St Mawes, and we had been talking of Wallis and his paintings, for which they both had a great enthusiasm.

I had no sooner expressed a desire to meet the Cornish fisherman than my friends had chartered a car to drive me over to St Ives the following day.

I found the old man in his little hovel (for it seemed to me no better), painting away with what appeared to be *boat paint* on odd bits of canvas, old photographs and scraps of cardboard. He had a special predilection for the ends and sides of Quaker Oats boxes!

He was surrounded by scores of his own paintings of all shapes and sizes.

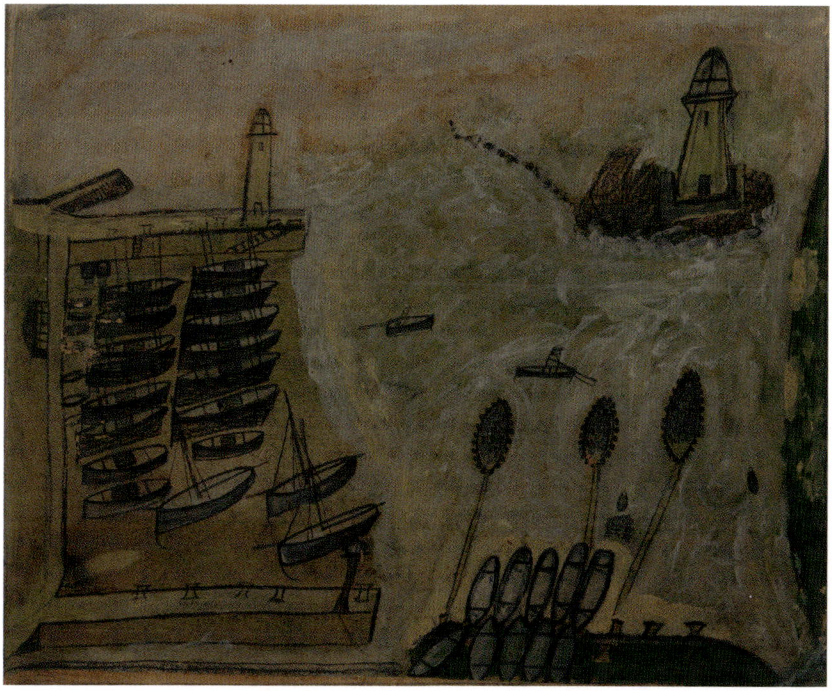

Alfred Wallis, *Boats in Harbour, St Ives*, c.1930
The Lucy Wertheim Estate

As the old man was almost completely deaf, it was not a very easy matter to 'talk business', but after much smiling and gesticulation he gathered that I was anxious to become the possessor of some of his paintings and was prepared to pay for them. He was so completely unmercenary that I believe he would have been satisfied with a tenth of the sum I gave him for the collection that he handed over to me. Some were hardly larger than a postage stamp, others of a size important enough to include in an exhibition.

I showed twenty of them in my gallery in the early spring of 1931. They did not cut much ice with either the public or the critics.

Now, after a number of years, Wallis is coming into his own and his work is frequently compared with that of Christopher Wood. Indeed, I have often heard it remarked that Wallis influenced the young painter.

As I possess a painting by Alfred Wallis done on the back of a photograph of one of Christopher Wood's pictures, I sometimes wonder if it was not rather the other way about!

War Clouds, 1938–9

There is little of importance to relate concerning these years. I kept going by the skin of my teeth, always hoping for happier times, times when I need no longer dread quarter-days with their recurring bills for rent and rates, insurance, printing and advertising expenses. Only my bank manager, that great-hearted Lancashire man, S.A. Smith, of Martins Bank, who gave me constant encouragement by his faith in my ultimate survival, and that suave, kindly Captain Adams, Secretary of Albany, who, saving my pride, never once pressed me unduly for my rent – only these two, apart from my secretary and Biddy knew how precarious was my position.

'Your gallery must surely be under some divine protection,' said a friend to me who knew of a succession of blows I had sustained by clients letting me down in 1938. Severest blow of all was the cancelling of an exhibition I had arranged of the work of the Mexican artist Diego Rivera. The political situation had become acute. Several exhibitions I had reserved dates for were called off. One artist, a wealthy Hungarian aristocrat, well-known to his embassy, decamped to America, owing me over £100. Another firm who had hired the gallery for an exhibition let me down for the same amount.

I reduced my expenditure to a minimum. Gone were the days of leisurely luncheons at the Berkeley or the Savoy. I came to know how excellent a meal of herring roes on toast (served piping hot) could taste at the quiet A.B.C., deserted after office hours, round the corner. I felt so disinclined for company, that often I spent my evenings in the two-and-threepenny seats of the cinema, sometimes falling asleep from sheer fatigue.

My husband knew nothing of these rigid economies. I still contrived to arrive home on a Friday evening, bland and smiling – though the smile was wearing a little thin towards the summer of 1939.

In June of that year I was approached by the secretary of a society of refugee artists, Fred Uhlman, representing Oskar Kokoshka, Max Ernst, Paul Hamann, Friedrich Feigl and others. Would I let the gallery to them for a few weeks on a commission basis? They would run their own exhibition. I agreed. The exhibition did well and to some extent established my finances. I was able to take a much-needed holiday.

On 1 September we hung an exhibition of drawings by a New Zealand artist. The private view was fixed for Tuesday 5 September. We had sent out two thousand invitations.

On Sunday 3 September, war was declared.

On Monday morning, 4 September, the police informed us of a regulation forbidding more than twelve people to congregate in one room. The artist dismantled the walls and gave up all thought of his exhibition.

On 5 September, the authorities declared they were taking over the gallery premises for an air-raid shelter. I removed all my belongings.

Notices were inscribed in the personal columns of *The Times* and the *Daily Telegraph*, requesting artists to collect their pictures.

The gallery was no more!

Paris, 1939.
Chinley, 1947.

WERTHEIM GALLERY 3-5 BURLINGTON GARDENS, BETWEEN REGENT ST. AND BOND ST., LONDON

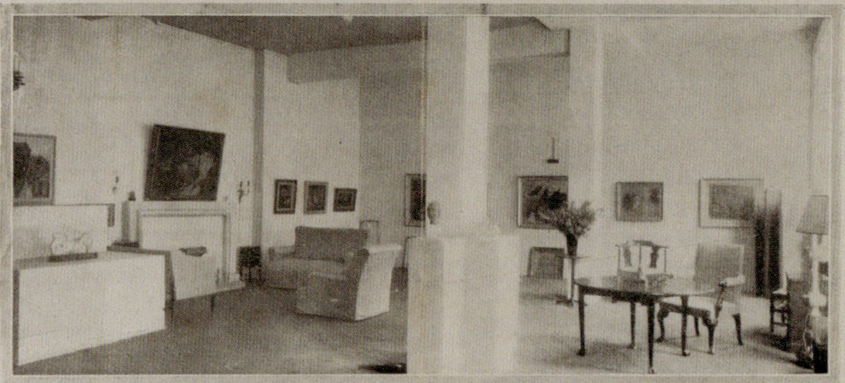

THE NEW WERTHEIM GALLERY, WHERE PICTURES ARE DISPLAYED AS IN A PRIVATE HOUSE

Always to be seen
Works by

CHRISTOPHER WOOD
MATTHEW SMITH
SICKERT
CEDRIC MORRIS
FRANCES HODGKINS
KOLLE
VIVIN
VAN HENGELAAR
ALEXANDRE ROBINSON
DAVID JONES
BERTRAM NICHOLLS
AND OTHERS

An
Art Gallery
in a
Drawing Room

WHAT better background for beautiful paintings could be found than the charming surroundings and quiet comfort of the Wertheim Gallery.

Here can be studied at leisure works by the foremost modern artists, also a good selection of old masters, drawings, lithographs, aquatints, etc.

ANNOUNCEMENT FOR THE WERTHEIM GALLERY, OCTOBER 1930. THE LUCY WERTHEIM ARCHIVE

Lucy Wertheim
Her Gallery in Context

FRANCES SPALDING

In October 1930, the Wertheim Gallery opened at 3-5 Burlington Gardens. Its owner had deliberately chosen a site that was in easy proximity to other West End galleries and with the Royal Academy of Arts in Piccadilly. She had also wanted it to be spacious, well-lit and comfortably furnished. Its white walls welcomed pictures, while comfortable armchairs, covered in what was almost certainly fashionable white Irish linen, offered the possibility of rest. Above all, Wertheim wanted to achieve an atmosphere that was democratic in spirit. 'The Wertheim Gallery,' the *Observer* opined on 12 October 1930, '... has nothing of the stodginess of the other London galleries; nothing of that awe-inspiring atmosphere which makes you talk in whispers and makes you rather shy, if there is not a crowd and you do not happen to be a buyer.... A visit to the Wertheim Gallery is more like going to see a friend and admiring his collection of pictures in the intimacy of a home.'

The woman who had conceived this gallery did so at a turning point in the history of British art. The individual creativity that had characterised art in the 1920s was replaced in the 1930s by an emphasis on group effort and experimentation. An opening up to new ideas and to influences from abroad created a fresh vitality. However, all this had taken time to emerge. The First World War had cut right across the cultural and artistic life of the nation, leaving in its wake an art world that was decentred and directionless. When Wyndham Lewis attempted to re-ignite the avant-garde by means of an exhibition titled *Group X*, which went on show in 1920 at the Mansard Gallery, London, it proved such a damp squib that Group X fizzled out. This same year, the Seven and Five Society held its first exhibition. Founded in 1919 with an initial grouping of seven painters and five sculptors, it had soon attracted more artists than its title suggests. However, it, too, made little initial impact. Its 1920 exhibition was accompanied by a mild, apologetic, uninspiring manifesto that did little to explain the group's purpose or identity. Not until the arrival of Ben and Winifred Nicholson in the mid-1920s did it begin to display a

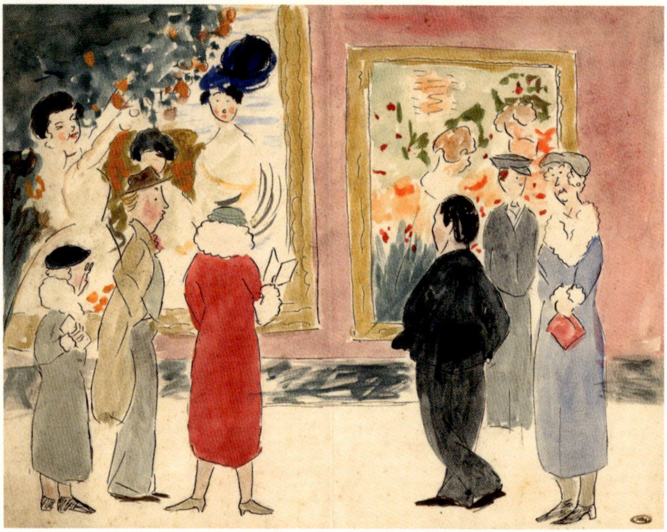

UNKNOWN ARTIST, *IN A PICTURE GALLERY*, C.1930
THE LUCY WERTHEIM ARCHIVE

fresh way of seeing the world, partly inspired by an interest in 'Primitivism', which challenged conventional methods of representation.

An interest in so-called 'primitive' art was by no means confined to Britain. It had begun before the First World War when certain artists in Paris and London looked to cultures outside the Western European tradition in order to invigorate their work. By the 1920s, the vogue for Primitivism meant that the self-taught painter Henri (Le Douanier) Rousseau had become highly rated, not just by Picasso and other artists, but almost as a fashionable figure in the Parisian art world. Christopher Wood assimilated his influence in the early 1920s while working in Paris and trying out a variety of styles. This was before he and Ben Nicholson discovered, in 1928, another so-called 'primitive', the former mariner and self-taught painter, Alfred Wallis, in St Ives, Cornwall. Wallis acted like a catalyst to both artists, his intuitive expressiveness affirming their desire to rid art of its staleness and decadence. After meeting with these two metropolitan sophisticates, Wallis found himself in communication with Nicholson's friend, H.S. (Jim) Ede, then a Tate curator, to whom he sent bundles of his paintings at intervals between 1929 and 1936. Ede showed these to artists, writers and collectors, thereby gaining for Wallis a discerning audience. In total, Ede himself acquired over one hundred works by Wallis, but he never made the journey to St Ives to meet him. The only dealer who did so was Lucy Wertheim, herself something of an outsider in the London art world and firmly committed to outsider art. She showed twenty of Wallis's pictures in her London gallery in 1931.

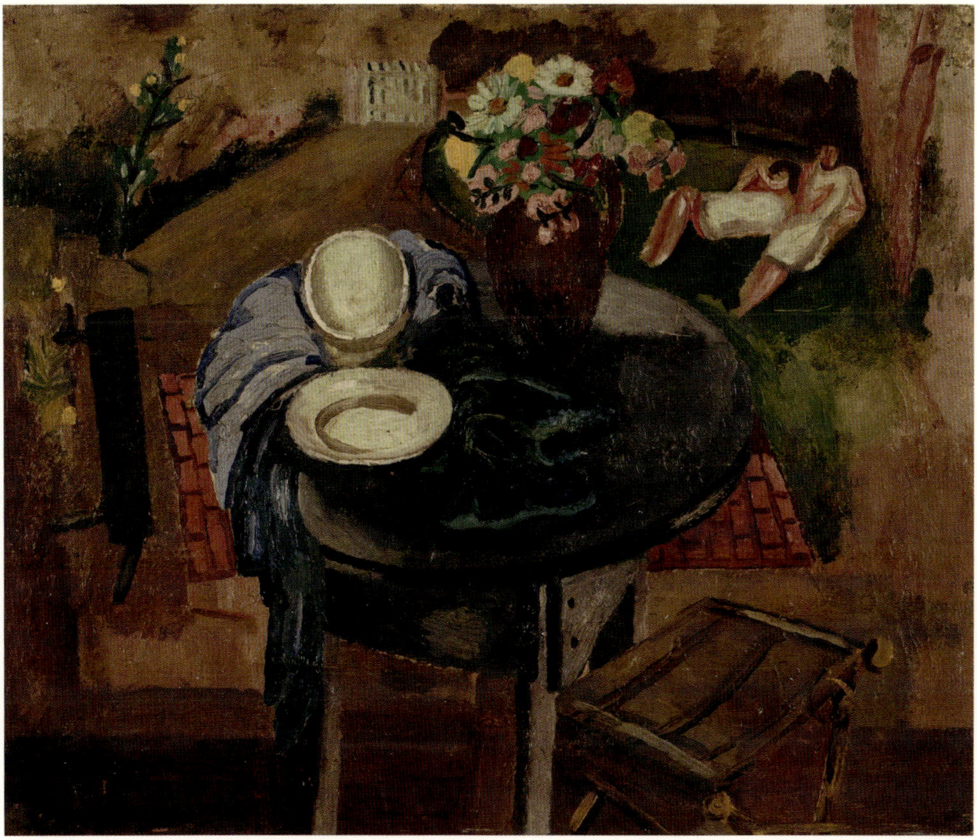

Frances Hodgkins, *Still Life, c.*1928
Towner Eastbourne, The Lucy Wertheim Bequest, 1971

Two of his pictures had been included in the annual Seven and Five Society exhibition in 1929. By this date, Ben and Winifred Nicholson had attracted into the Society a handful of artists – Christopher Wood, Cedric Morris, Frances Hodgkins and David Jones – thereby forming the first significant avant-garde group of the inter-war period. Their work was characterised by a new directness and freedom in their approach to their subjects; and if any particular component united them, it was a leaning towards a painterly lyricism. It encouraged Hodgkins to situate her still-lifes outdoors, in the landscape, thereby achieving more sonorous harmonies. Wertheim had first met her in Manchester, while Hodgkins was working as a textile design consultant for the Calico Printers' Association, and the two women had become friends. It was probably through Hodgkins that Wertheim met Cedric Morris. Both artists were invited to exhibit in her gallery's opening exhibition. Morris was aware that this might trouble his relations with

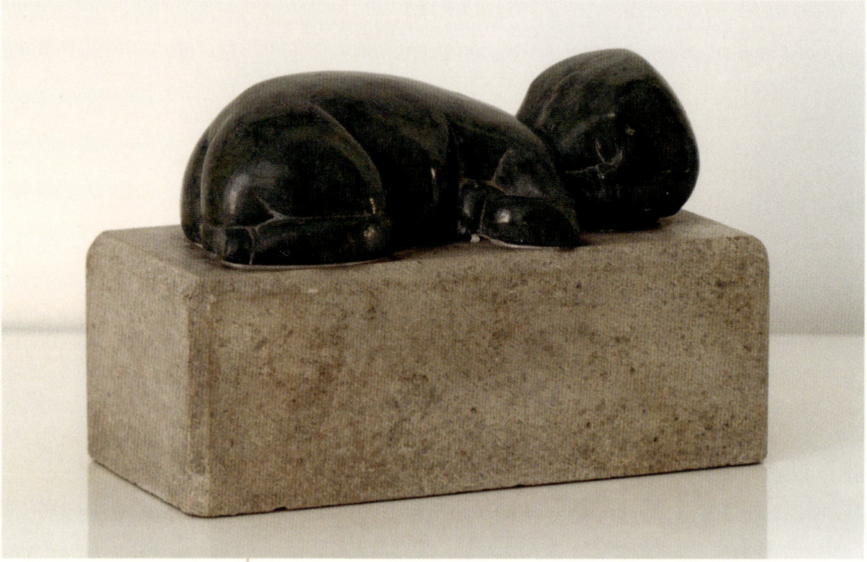

JOHN SKEAPING, *INFANT, c.*1929-30. THE LUCY WERTHEIM ESTATE

his dealer, but he enjoyed Wertheim's bold mix of artists. He wrote approvingly to Wertheim about Hodgkins and John Skeaping (in a letter in the Lucy Wertheim Archive): 'What is so good about them is that they really do work and are not namby-pamby – chicken hearted, affected, solemn fools like most so-called artists – sorry to get so violent, but they get on my nerves most of them.' In writing as freely as this, he must have been confident that in Lucy Wertheim he had found someone sympathetic to his anti-establishment views.

Unlike many other dealers, Wertheim refused to confine her choice of artists to those whose work was already recognised and accepted. She was prepared to take risks, especially in her attempt to identify new talent. Aware that talent did not necessarily come through training but could be innate, she early on gave an exhibition to Louis Vivin, known simply as Vivin, an elderly French ex-post office clerk who had spent most of his life travelling in a windowless carriage, sorting mail. Another untrained painter whom she promoted, with slightly more success, was the bus driver Henry Stockley, to whom she gave a solo exhibition in 1932. Later, in January 1939, he took part in one of her group exhibitions. It was titled *Pictures by Postmen, Gardeners, Sailors, Housewives etc., including the Ashington Group*. Stockley's ambition had been to paint royalty but in this exhibition he succeeded in showing his portrait of Neville Chamberlain. He also wrote to the Prime Minister, informing him that this portrait was hanging in the Wertheim Gallery and asking him to accept it.

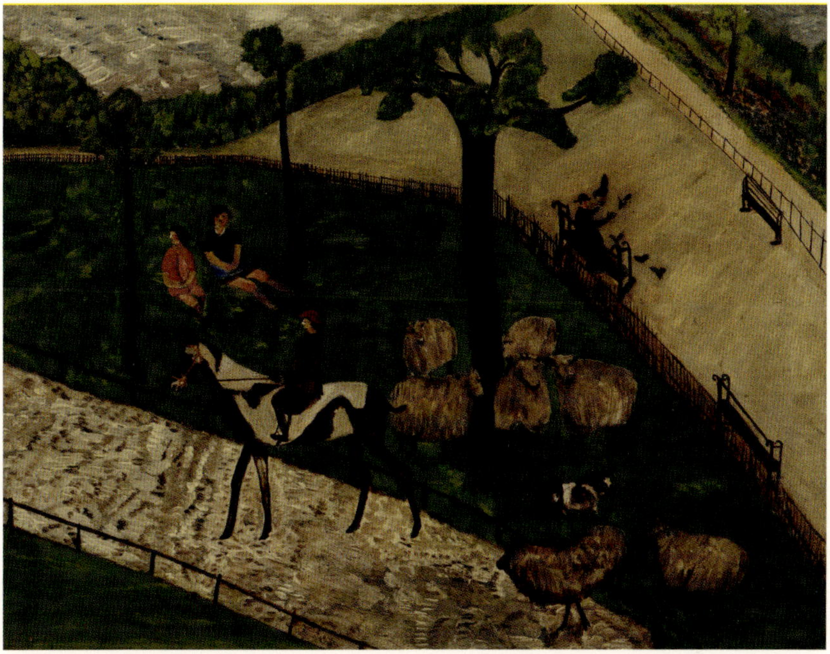

Henry Stockley, *Evelyn Laye in Hyde Park*, c.1933
Towner Eastbourne, The Lucy Wertheim Bequest, 1971

A gift for friendship, especially with artists, was undeniably one of Lucy Wertheim's strengths. Her friendship with Christopher Wood was firmly established on the day they first met. Soon afterwards she slipped into the position formerly occupied in his life by Winifred Nicholson, that of mentor, supporter and loyal friend. She also readily made friends with secretaries, typists, errand boys and apprentices; and she observed that the less well educated often made sounder aesthetic judgments than those who prided themselves on a knowledge of art. When she conceived the idea of opening a gallery, Wood became her most encouraging supporter. If there was a vein of self-interest in this support, he nevertheless saw clearly that her lively enthusiasm for art and her good judgment regarding pictures would ensure success.

Certainly, the gallery began well, with a flourish of notices in the press, the *Star* referring to it as 'the Drawing-Room Gallery'. A celebration party was held two days before it officially opened. George Bissill, the Nottingham miner-turned-painter, was delighted when Lady Millicent Hawes and Prime Minister Ramsay MacDonald each bought one of his paintings. However, in the wake of the Wall Street collapse it was not an auspicious moment to open a gallery. After the General Election of 1931, the Depression set in, at which point more galleries closed than opened.

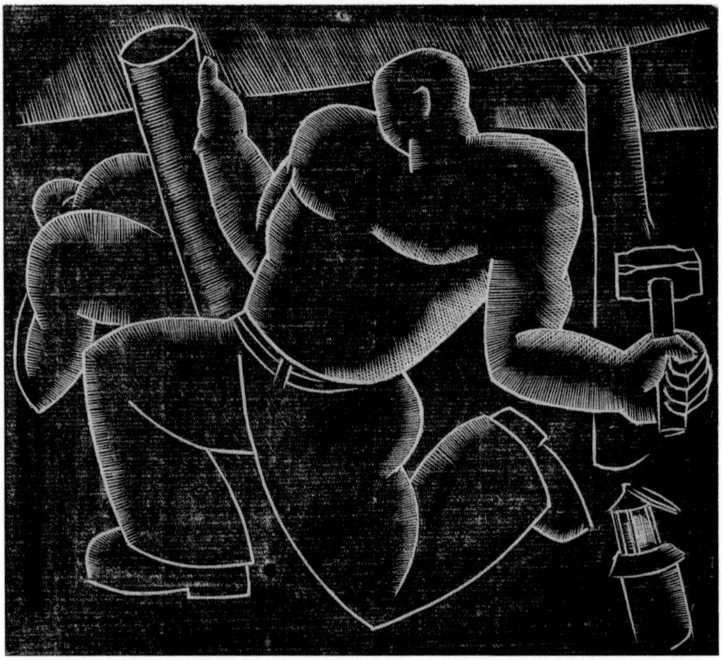

George Bissill, *Untitled (setting a timber prop),* post 1925
National Coal Mining Museum for England

However, if Lucy Wertheim's name is predominantly associated with the 1930s, her understanding of art had been formed in the previous decade. In the late 1920s, at a time when Henry Moore's innovations aroused dislike and incomprehension and J.B. Manson, having just taken over as director of the Tate Gallery, declared that no work by this artist would ever enter this institution under his leadership, Lucy Wertheim fell under Moore's spell. Within a year she was in possession of two statues, two smaller carvings and numerous drawings. In her memoir, *Adventure in Art,* she acknowledged that an exhibition in 1927, the *Daily Express Young Artists' Exhibition*, had opened her eyes to the amount of good work being produced by young artists. Simultaneously she noticed that very few London galleries were prepared to deal in modern English art. In this way she identified a gap that needed filling. From the start she knew it would be difficult to promote little-known or unknown artists, but her primary goal was to enhance the visibility of certain living artists rather than making money out of art.

Wertheim had gained instructive experience during a visit to the home of Edward and Fanny Wadsworth. The former Vorticist had in his house a 'den' filled with work by Wyndham Lewis. He also owned two works by Fernand Léger and was himself experimenting with abstraction. Wadsworth made Wertheim pay more attention to

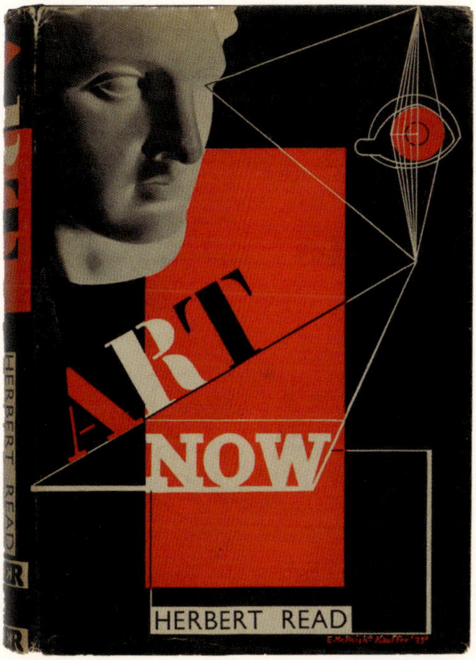

HERBERT READ, *ART NOW*, FIRST PUBLISHED 1933, THE COVER DESIGN BY EDWARD MCKNIGHT KAUFFER, THIS EDITION 1938. PRIVATE COLLECTION

Picasso and this would have left her better prepared for Herbert Read's seminal book, *Art Now*, published by Faber & Faber in 1933, which provided readers with a recent history of modern European art. The success of *Art Now* left Read much in demand for catalogue essays and for his support of new ventures. Yet Wertheim never became a modish follower of fashion and always pursued a line of her own. The absence of any mention in *Adventure in Art* of the Seven and Five Society's decision to move into pure abstraction in 1935, or of the 1936 *Abstract and Concrete* exhibition, the first international display of Abstract art mounted in this country, suggests that she had limited interest in it. And although she had shown in her gallery work by John Banting and John Bigge, two artists associated with Surrealism, she took only limited interest in this movement. Perhaps she shared Gertrude Stein's view that its complications belonged very much to the twentieth century, but its use of representation looked back to the nineteenth.

If Wertheim only intermittently kept her finger on the pulse of the avant-garde, her exhibition programme continued to surprise. On 27 July 1932, she opened an exhibition simply titled *27 Photographers*, which ran for six weeks and included work by Lázló Moholy-Nagy, Man Ray, Barbara Ker-Seymour and other 'creative photographers', as she termed some of the leading practitioners of the day.

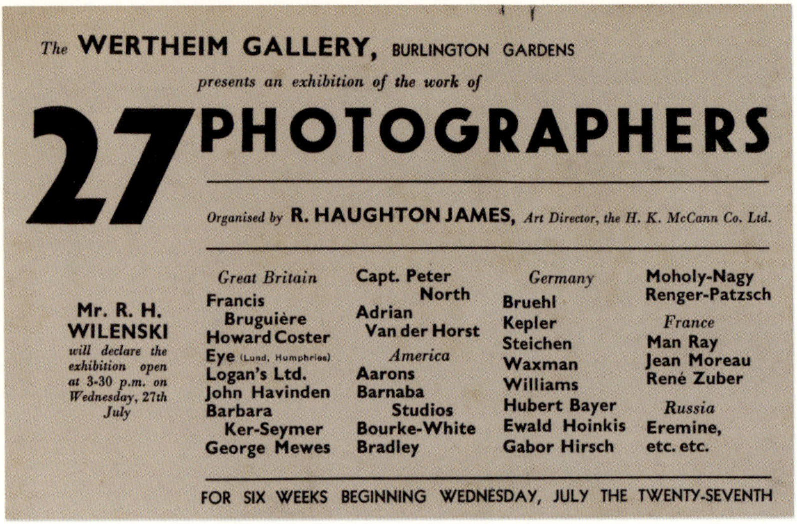

The **WERTHEIM GALLERY,** BURLINGTON GARDENS

presents an exhibition of the work of

27 PHOTOGRAPHERS

Organised by **R. HAUGHTON JAMES,** *Art Director, the H. K. McCann Co. Ltd.*

Mr. R. H. WILENSKI
will declare the exhibition open at 3-30 p.m. on Wednesday, 27th July

Great Britain
Francis Bruguière
Howard Coster
Eye (Lund, Humphries)
Logan's Ltd.
John Havinden
Barbara Ker-Seymer
George Mewes
Capt. Peter North
Adrian Van der Horst

America
Aarons
Barnaba Studios
Bourke-White
Bradley

Germany
Bruehl
Kepler
Steichen
Waxman
Williams
Hubert Bayer
Ewald Hoinkis
Gabor Hirsch
Moholy-Nagy
Renger-Patzsch

France
Man Ray
Jean Moreau
René Zuber

Russia
Eremine,
etc. etc.

FOR SIX WEEKS BEGINNING WEDNESDAY, JULY THE TWENTY-SEVENTH

EXHIBITION ANNOUNCEMENT CARD, *27 PHOTOGRAPHERS*, JULY 1932
THE LUCY WERTHEIM ARCHIVE

She explained to the *Star* newspaper: 'I am interested in every form and expression of art, and I am so impressed by the recognition that Germany, the United States, and France are giving to beautiful photographic slides that I decided to hold an international exhibition, and the astonishing material assembled on the walls is the result.' She also never let go of her interest in youth, mounting exhibitions titled *The Twenties Group*, which were intended to promote emerging artists. Hers was the only gallery at this time to promote work by students at the St John's Wood Art School, in 1938, in an exhibition from which she acquired, for her own collection, a landscape by the young John Minton. It was eventually bequeathed to Worthing Museum and Art Gallery.

Owing to her awareness of the need to educate others about art, Wertheim frequently sent out exhibitions from her gallery to schools and other institutions. This was at a time when conservative taste still dominated public imagination. Evidence of this could be found in the *Listener* in 1933. On 31 May it carried an illustration of a work by Picasso, on view at the Mayor Gallery in a mixed show, with the announcement that several artists (unnamed) were keen to have it bought by the Contemporary Art Society and gifted to a public gallery. The magazine's letters pages immediately filled up with angry protest. Picasso and his admirers were said to destroy beauty, truth and good craftsmanship. John Piper and Ben Nicholson rushed to his defence, and a battle of words over Picasso continued for three months before an editor drew it to a close.

A similar resistance governed the English attitude to Cézanne. This artist had come to be regarded in many countries as the father of Modern art, yet in 1921, at a time when no Cézanne could be found in a public collection in England, the Tate Gallery turned down the opportunity to accept on loan from Gwendoline Davies, the daughter of a Welsh coal and railway magnate, two paintings by Cézanne. The following year, the Tate rejected an opportunity to buy a portrait of Madame Cézanne, at a price of £8,000. It was offered again a year later at a reduced price of £7,000. Admittedly, the Tate's annual purchase grant at this date was very small, but the minutes for the Trustees Board meeting held on 16 November 1921 record that Sir Joseph Duveen was willing to provide the money for the purchase of a Cézanne, an offer that appears to have fallen on deaf ears. The situation regarding Cézanne would have been even more dire had not Samuel Courtauld taken steps to improve the Tate's holding in French art. At the time when it was preparing to open its newly built 'modern foreign galleries', it had scant treasures to showcase in these galleries. Courtauld stepped in and transferred £50,000 into a trust for the purchase of modern French art. This gift came with a list, naming the French artists whose work was to be acquired. It included Cézanne.

Wertheim's own patchy understanding of Modern art reflects the limitations of her day. Yet, from another perspective she was very much in agreement with progressive ideas. Her diverse programme of exhibitions suggests that she was aiming at wide appeal. Her outreach work also reflects her sympathy with the work of the Arts League of Service, especially with its aim 'to bring Art within the reach of all'. The 1920s had seen a proliferation of associations, societies and institutions dedicated to the arts, but the Arts League of Service was the most influential and did more than any other to bring the arts into closer relation with the public. Likewise, Lucy Wertheim, through her gallery, contributed towards the democratisation of art in the interwar period, thereby making an important contribution to English art. Her zest and enthusiasm, her excitement about art and her generous spirit were admired by many, not least by Christopher Wood, whose tragic death some weeks before her gallery opened in 1930 almost caused her to withdraw from the venture. She had discovered in Wood a romantic Modernist and an artist of lasting importance. The fact that throughout the 1930s work by him could always be seen in her gallery, even when it was not on immediate view, added to the gallery's reputation. It is one of the main reasons why the Wertheim Gallery, which had to close hurriedly once war began, is still remembered to this day.

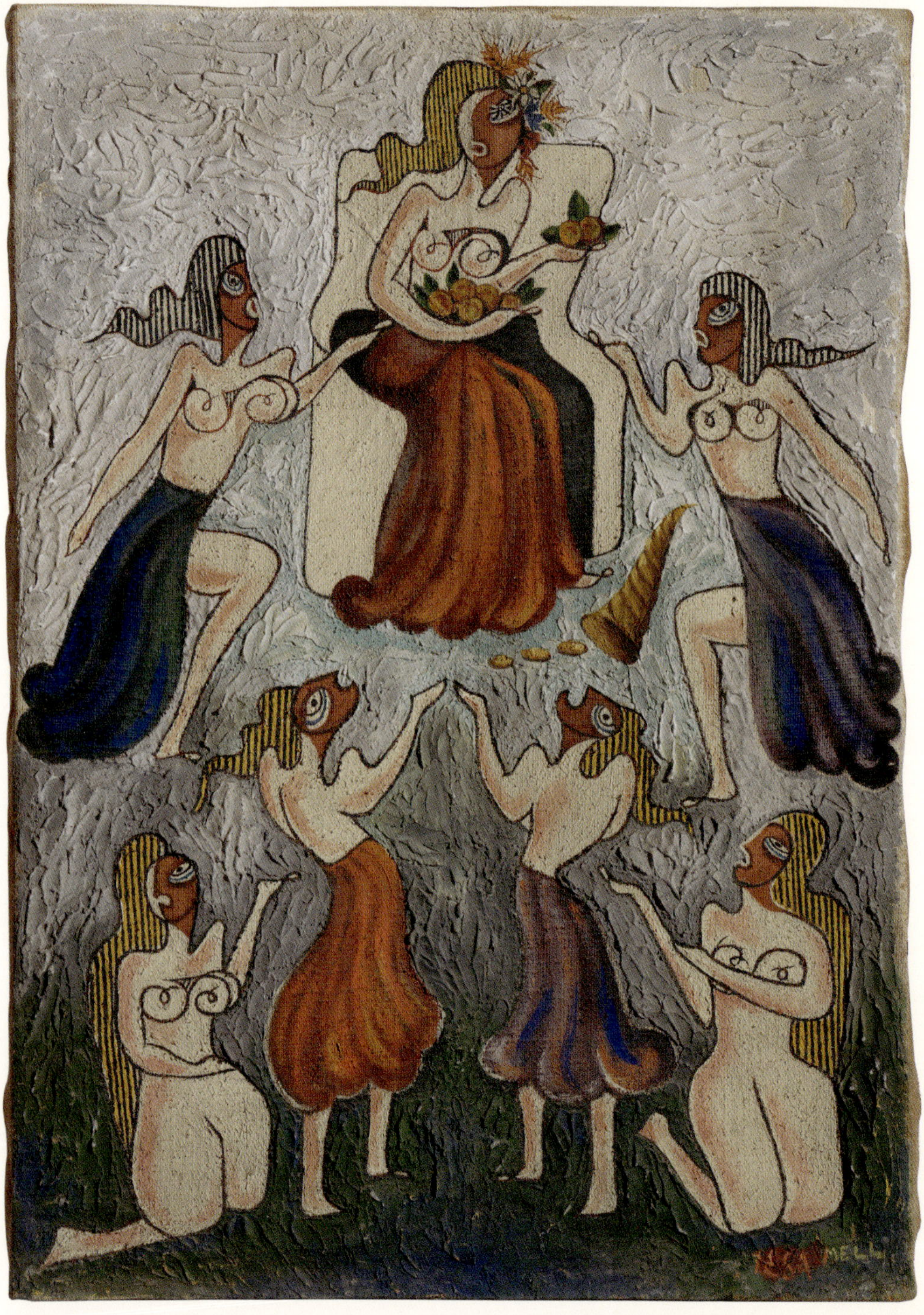

Ilsa Rodmell, *Allegorical Figures*, undated
The Lucy Wertheim Estate

Lucy Wertheim
A Pioneering Woman and her Contemporaries

ARIANE BANKES

Lucy Wertheim's gallery in Burlington Gardens was in its own way a phenomenon: the first gallery to be opened and run by a woman in London's West End. Not only did it break with convention in important ways, both in terms of ambiance and programme, but its opening in 1930 fired a salvo for a decade in which women would at last make a significant mark in the British art world. With her conventional and monied background, Wertheim was perhaps an unlikely champion of women's advancement, but she opened the door to a generation of powerful, independent spirits who relished the opportunities that now came their way and made the very most of them.

The dislocation and the de facto female emancipation that followed the First World War heralded the so-called Roaring Twenties, the era of the Bright Young Things, and the emergence of wealthy aristocratic women of a free-spirited, High Bohemian sensibility, such as Nancy Cunard and Lady Ottoline Morrell, who in their different spheres threw caution to the winds in pursuing their own creative and sexual freedom. They had the means and education to develop strong and independent personas, dressing flamboyantly – in Nancy's case with rows of her signature African bangles on each arm – and surrounding themselves with art from outside established collecting traditions. Lady Ottoline Morrell, whose name appears in the Wertheim Gallery visitors book in April 1931, had been instrumental, with Roger Fry, in founding the Contemporary Art Society in 1910 and remained one of its leading lights, and her frequent visits to Paris and close friendships with the Bloomsbury group only strengthened her enthusiasm for fresh ideas in the arts. She supported and promoted numerous artists – Jacob Epstein, Stanley Spencer, Henry Lamb and Mark Gertler among them – and arranged extravagant house parties at Garsington Manor to introduce them to further patrons and collectors in her wider social circle. Nancy Cunard, daughter of the flamboyant society hostess Emerald Cunard, struck out for Paris in 1920, where she developed her own distinctive style indebted to the contemporary rage for all things African. Paris was thrumming to the rhythms of the Jazz Age, personified by Josephine Baker and her barnstorming cabaret act, and Nancy immersed herself in the Surrealist and Modernist currents of the day, using her inherited wealth to found the Hours Press, where she published such radical writers as Samuel Beckett and Ezra Pound alongside Langston Hughes and Zora Neale Thurston.

Closer to home, the London art world, once the province almost exclusively of men, was opening up to the gentle but persistent influence of patrons such as Helen Sutherland and Margaret Gardiner, who befriended and supported the early Modernists Ben and Winifred Nicholson, Barbara Hepworth, and David Jones. The interior designer Syrie Maugham was boldly shaking up the decorative schemes of the wealthy from London to Palm Beach, and in 1922 Edith Sitwell's idiosyncratic spoken poem 'Façade', performed via megaphone through a hole in a curtain designed by John Piper, had bemused the public and been hailed by Siegfried Sassoon as 'Too Fantastic for Fat-Heads'.

Lucy Wertheim had none of the flamboyance of these disruptors, yet her influence was to be as wide-reaching, if more subtle. She came from an essentially conservative mercantile background, and she had a growing family and a husband with a respected role as Dutch consul in Manchester; but once she started to discover the art of her contemporaries in the mid-1920s, her taste and her life developed fast along independent lines. Her first reaction to the art of her brother-in-law's cousin Edward Wadsworth may have been negative and uncomprehending, but she soon revised her opinions about Vorticism and Surrealism and was to show the work of John Banting and John Bigge in 1931, five years before Roland Penrose and David Gascoyne staged the International Surrealist Exhibition in London. She quickly appreciated the genius of Alfred Wallis and was the only gallery owner to visit the former seaman and rag-and-bone man in his Cornish home in 1930, insisting on giving him a fair price for the works she bought: 'He was so completely unmercenary that I believe he would have been satisfied with a tenth of the sum I gave him,' she later recalled. She was enchanted by the work of the untutored and the 'naïve', the bus driver Henry Stockley, the French post office clerk Louis Vivin, and pavement artist David Burton among them, and she promoted them to the best of her ability throughout her time as a gallerist, pre-empting Helen Sutherland's patronage of the Pitman Painters, as the Ashington Miners came to be known. Both women also supported David Jones and Christopher Wood, and yet it is not recorded that they ever met.

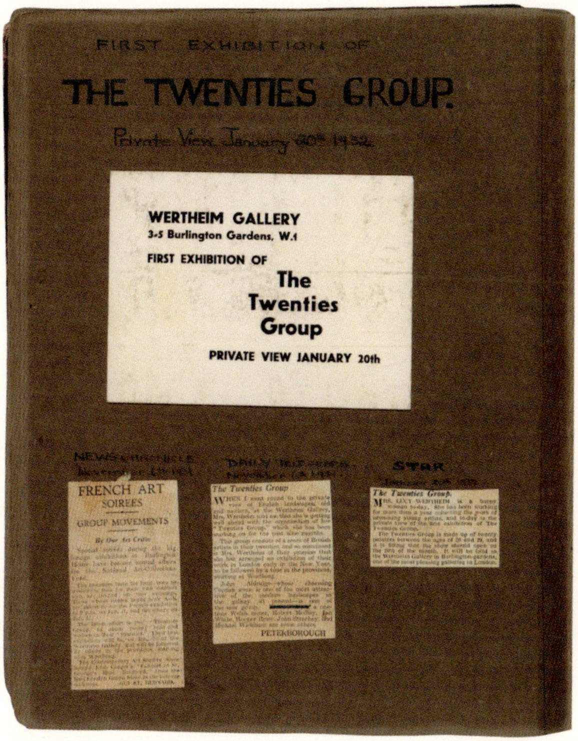
FIRST EXHIBITION OF
THE TWENTIES GROUP.
Private View January 20th 1932.

WERTHEIM GALLERY
3-5 Burlington Gardens, W.1
FIRST EXHIBITION OF
The Twenties Group
PRIVATE VIEW JANUARY 20th

FRENCH ART
SOIREES
GROUP MOVEMENTS

The Twenties Group

PETERBOROUGH

STAR

The Twenties Group.

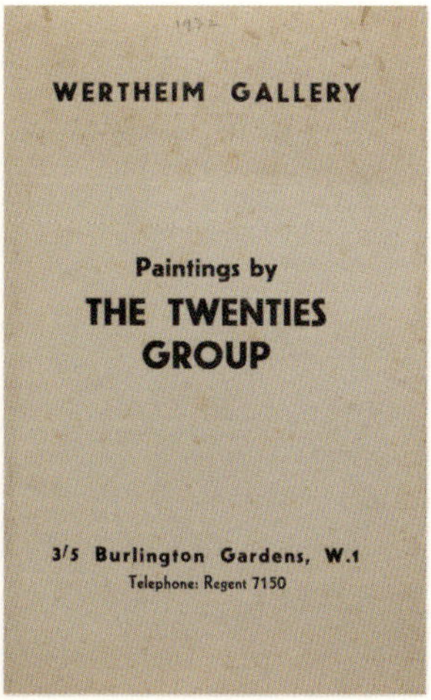
WERTHEIM GALLERY

Paintings by
THE TWENTIES GROUP

3/5 Burlington Gardens, W.1
Telephone: Regent 7150

LEFT: PAGE FROM *PRESS CUTTINGS*, VOLUME ONE (OF EIGHT), JANUARY 1932
RIGHT: EXHIBITION LISTING, *THE TWENTIES GROUP*, JANUARY 1932
THE LUCY WERTHEIM ARCHIVE

Wertheim's support too for young artists – which coalesced around her 'Twenties Group', formed in 1930 for those aged under thirty in whom Wertheim saw a promising future – was boldly ambitious at the time. The Twenties Group would include a significant number of women artists, perhaps most notably the young and still little-known Barbara Hepworth, whose work Wertheim first showed in 1930, and who first exhibited with the Twenties Group in January 1932. Wertheim's support gave opportunities to young women who did not necessarily achieve Hepworth's level of recognition but greatly valued the patronage. Kathleen Walne, for example was still in her teens when Wertheim first showed her work, and a relationship of trust was established that became a life-long bond.

It is interesting to ask what gave Wertheim the strength of her artistic convictions. The *"Daily Express" Young Artists' Exhibition* of 1927 was seminal in the evolution of her taste; it included Christopher Wood and Humphrey Slater, whose work appealed directly to her, but for whom there was as yet no accepted career path or market. Their prices were negligible, and they still had their whole careers ahead of them.

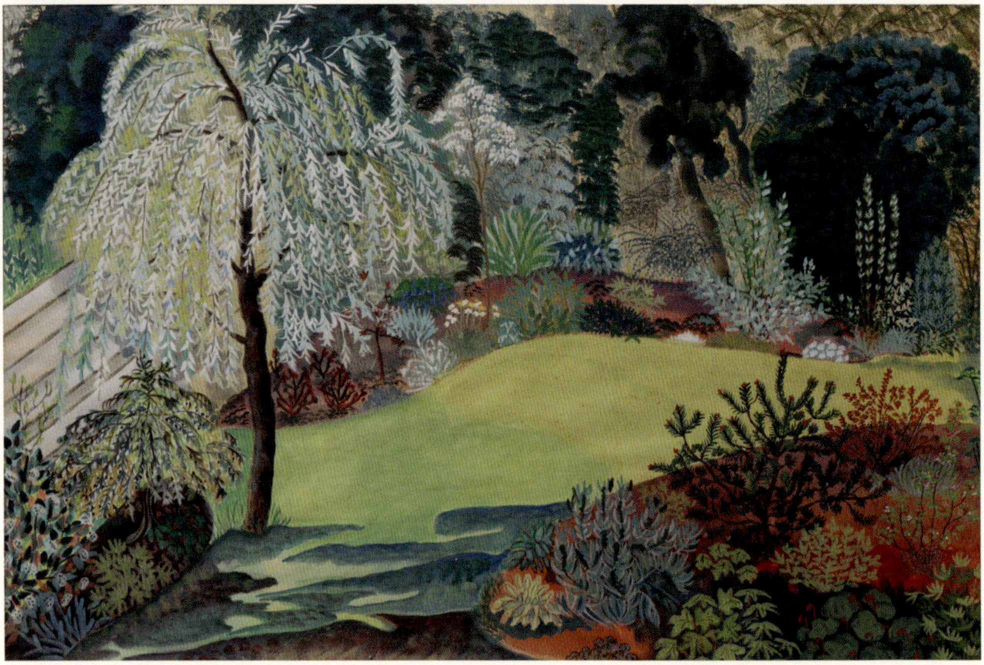

Kathleen Walne, *Garden*, undated. The Lucy Wertheim Estate

With the financial support of her husband Paul, who was otherwise uninvolved but happy to let his wife pursue her ambition, what was to stop her founding a gallery where she would put her then unorthodox taste to the test?

Wertheim was drawn to artists with a bold, naïve style, caring not a hoot whether they had already been acclaimed by others. She was a natural democrat, as happy to show the work of children or discoveries such as the untutored bus driver Henry Stockley as she was to promote the work of Matthew Smith or Lord Dunsany; what she considered artistic merit was her sole criterion. Her instinct to represent the unrepresented led her to scour the art schools for talent, and she found it in abundance. She gave the Grosvenor School of Modern Art its own show in 1936 and works by some of its most talented pupils, among them Suzanne Cooper and Rachel Reckitt, entered her own eclectic and ever-growing collection.

Looking through the records of the Wertheim Gallery from its inception, one is startled by the sheer range and energy of its programme. That one woman achieved this, initially single-handed, is astonishing. As is the fact that despite her indefatigable promotion of so much talent, she left less trace than many of her contemporaries. She blazed the trail for women in a world where all the other prominent galleries – Leicester, New Burlington, Tooth's, Mayor, Lefevre,

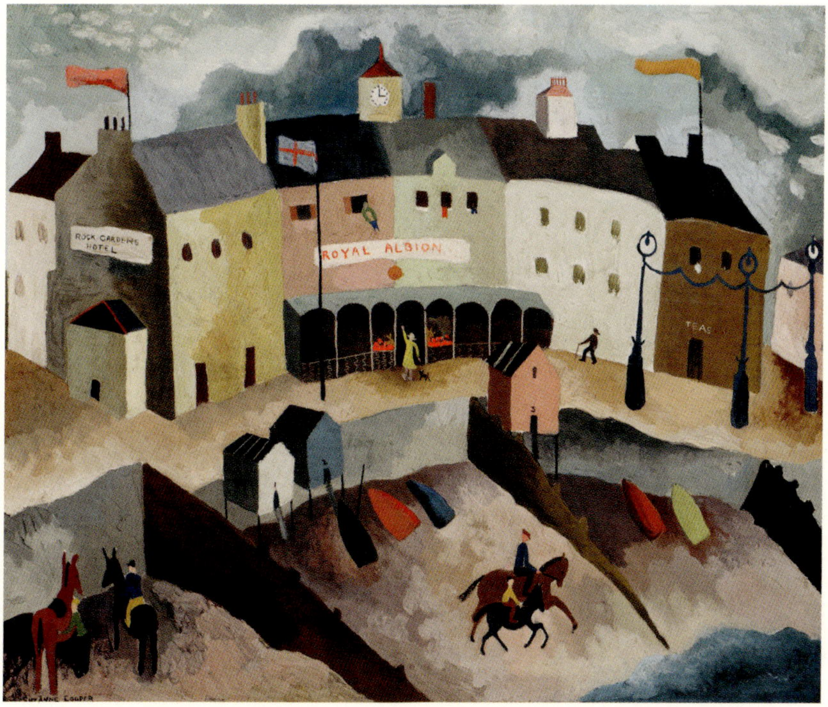

SUZANNE COOPER, *ROYAL ALBION*, 1936. AUCKLAND ART GALLERY
TOI O TĀMAKI, GIFT OF LUCY WERTHEIM, 1948

St George's, Leger, Zwemmer – were run by men, employing women only as secretaries or assistants. Helen Lessore joined Beaux Arts at its inception by her husband the sculptor Frederick Lessore in 1931, and was to graduate eventually from secretary to manager, becoming director after Frederick's death in 1951; but those women who did manage to establish a perch in the London gallery scene during the 1930s were more often than not émigrés from Europe – Erica Brausen, Lea Bondi-Jaray, and Ala Story among them.

Ala Story, whom Wertheim employed as secretary and sales assistant in 1932, was from Vienna, and had come to Britain in 1928 in her early twenties. She cut her teeth at Beaux Arts, later moving to the Redfern as secretary to Nan Kivell, before impressing Wertheim with her elegance, enthusiasm and continental connections. As Wertheim relates, 'Ala was at her best with chic and *soigné* notabilities of society and I was very content to leave this type in her hands.... She was an enthusiastic saleswoman, and it was a delight to witness her elation when she pulled off a sale.' Her assistant's predilection for a fashionable clientèle left Wertheim free to devote her time 'to the unknown and indigent, with whom [she] always had more in common.'

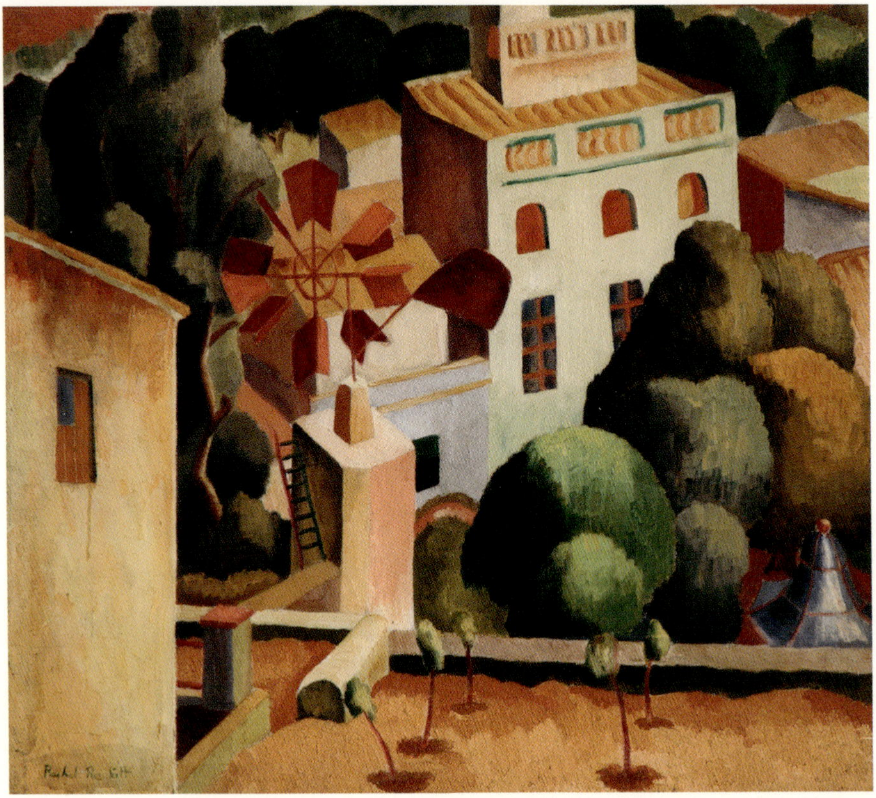

Rachel Reckitt, *House in Catalonia*, 1937
Salford Museum & Art Gallery, gift of Lucy Wertheim, 1939

Her talented and energetic protégée progressed from Wertheim's employment in 1933 to join a Mrs Cochrane in partnership at the Storran Gallery (an elision of their two names) in Albany Courtyard, next to the Royal Academy, where she showed a roster of fashionable artists such as the young Derek Hill, Gertrude Hermes, Duncan Grant, and Paul Nash. Story's enthusiasm for British Art accompanied her to New York in 1940, where she established the American-British Art Centre, and in her final post as Director of the Santa Barbara Museum of Art she was to significantly expand their European collection while discovering the rising stars of the American art scene.

The success of Wertheim and Story as discriminating dealers in contemporary painting opened the door to other women gallerists, but they were not emulated immediately. Lillian Browse had started work for Harold Leger at Leger Gallery in 1931, initially unpaid, and it was not until 1945 that she founded her gallery in Cork Street in partnership with Henry Roland and Gustav Delbanco. 'Peter'

(Noel Evelyn) Norton, married to the diplomat Clifford Norton, pitched into the London art scene in 1936, fired by her enthusiasm for the Bauhaus and particularly the International Surrealist Exhibition held at New Burlington Galleries that year. She opened the London Gallery in its wake, inspired by Roland Penrose and run by E.L.T. Mesens, to show fellow Surrealists and European Modernists such as Marcel Breuer. When her husband's posting took her to Poland in 1938, she sold the gallery to Penrose, and it continued to promote Modernism vigorously under the stewardship of Mesens until 1951.

It was as a consequence of the disruptions of fascism in Europe that other enterprising and ambitious women headed for London and its increasingly cosmopolitan art scene. Notable among these would be Lea Bondi Jaray and Erica Brausen, both of German Jewish origin. Brausen moved to London penniless at the outbreak of war, finding work in the early 1940s at Lea Bondi Jaray's St George's Gallery in Mayfair. Her inspired purchase of Francis Bacon's *Painting 1946* from his studio was to lead to a long and fruitful partnership with Bacon which initially underpinned her pioneering Hanover Gallery. This flourished as one of the most diverse and interesting galleries in Europe from 1947 until 1973. Lea Bondi Jaray, who had run a successful pre-war gallery in Vienna showing Egon Schiele among others, made St George's Gallery a contact point for German artists during and after the war, and was one of the first to show German Expressionist paintings.

Meanwhile, Peggy Guggenheim moved to London from Paris and opened Guggenheim Jeune (a nod to Paris's Bernheim Jeune) in Cork Street in January 1938. She had honed her taste in Paris under the influence of Marcel Duchamp and showed a sophisticated stable of prominent European Surrealists – Cocteau, Tanguy, Kandinsky, Calder, Arp, and her future husband Max Ernst among them. She acknowledged that she was entirely ignorant about art when she set out on this venture, stating in her memoir *Out of this Century* that she 'much preferred old masters'. Duchamp taught her the difference between abstract and Surrealist art and, more important, introduced her to the artists, more than one of whom became her lovers. Her account in *Out of this Century* showed how informal and arbitrary were her choices, and how the gallery got by more on luck than judgement, floated by Guggenheim's money and Paris connections, and managed by the efficient Wyn Henderson. Guggenheim coincidentally also mounted an exhibition of children's art, including three drawings by the young Lucian Freud, which proved an unexpected commercial success, but despite the proximity of their galleries there is no indication that Guggenheim and Wertheim ever met.

And Guggenheim Jeune was short-lived. It lost money despite its appearance of success, and in 1939 Guggenheim conceived a much more ambitious plan – to create a museum of Modern art, in which she eventually succeeded.

In comparison with all the above, Wertheim's enterprise might be seen as deliberately parochial; she lacked Guggenheim's continental contacts, or brazen flair for networking. Her focus was principally British but was nevertheless distinctive. During the 1930s her reach stretched across the English class system to include the largely untutored miners known as the Pitman Painters, first discovered by Tom Harrisson under his Mass Observation programme, and across the Channel to embrace Louis Vivin and Helmut Kolle, among a clutch of European figurative artists. She 'rediscovered' the Northumbrian painter Phelan Gibb, who had enjoyed considerable success in Paris before the First World War, alongside Picasso, Matisse, and Gris, and had a fund of anecdotes to prove it. It was through Gibb that she was introduced in 1931 to the formidable Gertrude Stein, one of Gibb's early champions, but their one encounter was dispiriting: Wertheim felt overpowered by Stein, commenting, 'I am often at a disadvantage with very brainy people.'

Wertheim's programme was eclectic, but she shied away from abstraction; and, with the exception of her exhibition of Banting and Bigge, she left forays into Surrealism and Modernism largely to her contemporaries. Her memoir, a spirited account of her own activities, makes no reference to certain prevailing currents of the day – to Unit One, for example, founded by Paul Nash in 1933 to promote Modern art, architecture, and design, or to the magazine *Axis,* founded in 1935 by Myfanwy Piper and Nicolete Gray to spread interest in continental Modernism. The latter's ground-breaking exhibition of 1936, *Abstract and Concrete*, which toured the country from Oxford, and the International Surrealist Exhibition were not aligned with her intuitive interests. She continued single-mindedly throughout the decade to focus largely on her stable of home-grown artists, young and old, celebrated and sidelined, with a determination and passion that knew no limits.

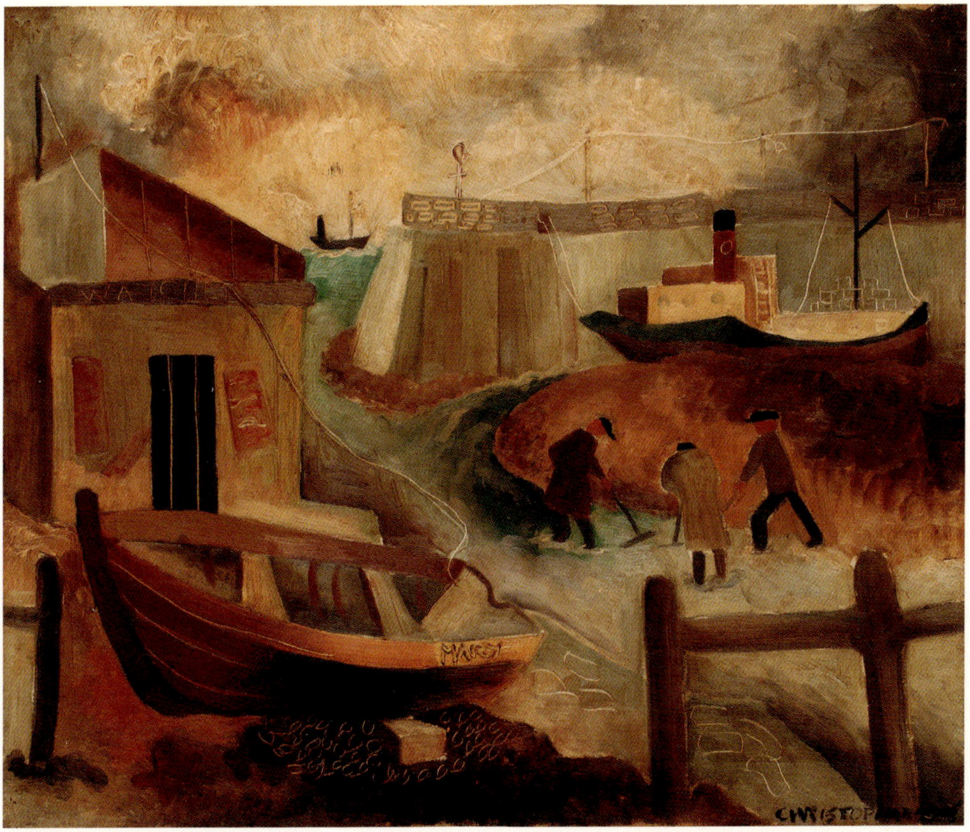

José Christopherson, *Watchet Harbour*, exhibited 1936
Private collection

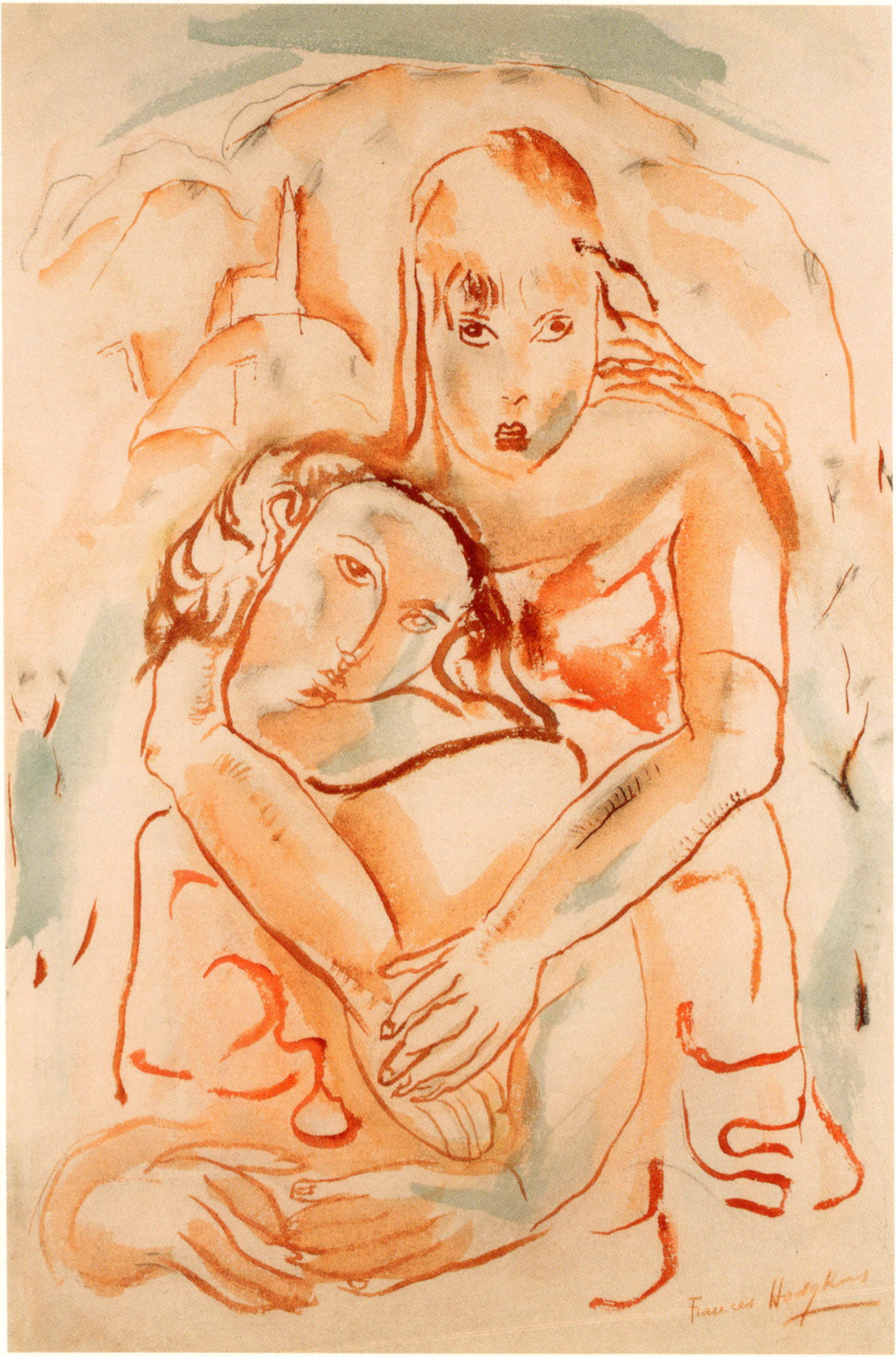

Frances Hodgkins, *Figures*, *c.*1927
Salford Museum & Art Gallery, gift of Lucy Wertheim, 1937

Lucy Wertheim
Her 'Forty-one Year Experiment' (1930–71)

KAREN TAYLOR

Lucy Wertheim's legacy quietly resonates from the art stores of public galleries and museums. Her gifts to regional, national and international collections reveal not only her own aesthetic and vision but also open a portal into the evolving sensibilities of Modern artists in 1930s Britain and Europe. Only with the comprehensive consideration of these gifts can the scale of her contribution to mid-twentieth-century art be recognised.

These gifts represent numerous overlooked and forgotten interwar artists who had emerged from art school in the 1930s, full of promise and aspirations, only to have their trajectory altered by the Second World War. Their early works, deposited in museums across the country and stored in plan chests or hung on racks, wait patiently to be discovered and appreciated by curators or scholars and, one hopes, inevitably by the public. These adventurous Modern paintings – that Wertheim tells us were deemed too difficult to understand and would often leave the audience baffled – have been collectively revealed in the 2022 exhibition, *A Life in Art* and *Reuniting the Twenties Group*, at Towner Eastbourne. Two questions occur to me as the curator of these exhibitions: Has the moment arrived, some ninety years later, for these overlooked artists to be acknowledged and appreciated? And will Wertheim's unwavering belief in her artists be vindicated fifty years after her death?

The objective consideration of Wertheim's legacy demands an understanding of the context within which she worked. Not only was it challenging as a woman with no formal art education to forge a path into the male-dominated art scene, but also as a woman in the social hierarchy of the 1930s. Her advantage was, of course, her social standing and her husband's financial backing. However, Paul Wertheim's support was not unconditional. He set out the boundaries for their financial arrangement, believing her enterprise would be a short-lived folly, often mocking her attempts to make the gallery a success. In her memoir, *Adventure in Art*, Wertheim acknowledges the commitment of their nanny who looked after

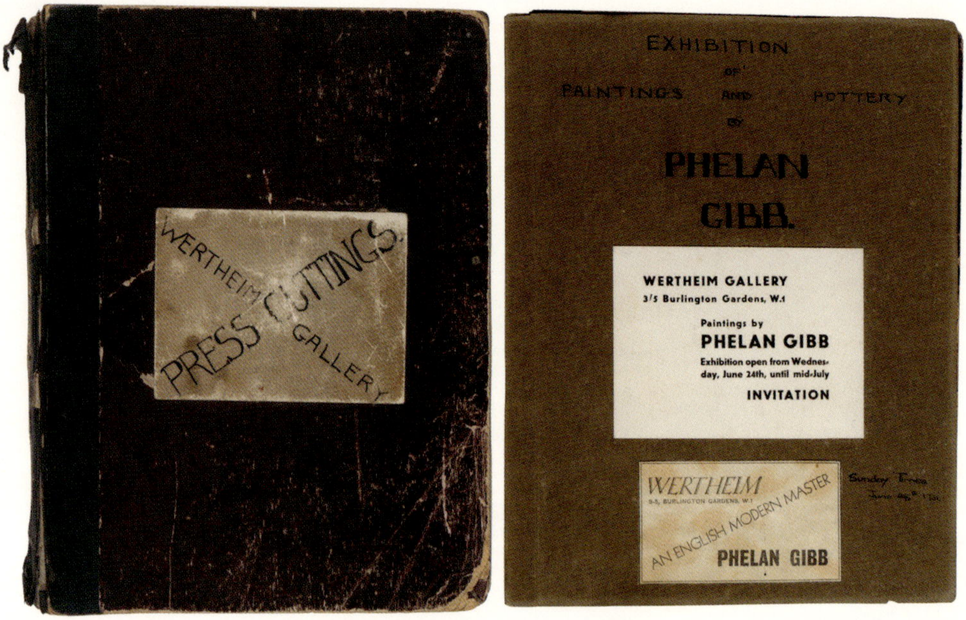

LEFT: *PRESS CUTTINGS*, VOLUME ONE (OF EIGHT), OCTOBER 1930–FEBRUARY 1932
RIGHT: PAGE FROM *PRESS CUTTINGS*, VOLUME ONE, JUNE 1931
THE LUCY WERTHEIM ARCHIVE

their children and ran the household. Acutely aware of her own privileged position, Wertheim felt compelled to help those who did not enjoy her advantages.

The Lucy Wertheim Archive – comprising her exhibition albums, invitations, press cuttings, photographs and hundreds of letters – reveals the individual plights of so many of the artists she championed, their hardships, their vulnerabilities, and how they turned to Wertheim for emotional and financial support. Generous with both her time and aid, she was driven by the artists' inherent dedication to create, and she was determined to enable them to do so, whether they were in their youth, straight from art school and full of expectation, or in their later years, overlooked and tired of rejection.

Wertheim passionately believed that young British artists should have the same opportunities as their European counterparts. She sought out young and unknown talent to represent and initiated the Twenties Group – an exhibiting collective for artists in their twenties. She relied on her emotional response to the artist's work and her own instinctive taste was reflected in the bold, vibrant, 'naïve' style that characterised the work of so many of the artists she represented. Concerned and frustrated by the art establishment's reluctance to show unknown artists, she was determined to address the problem. This defiant resolve and her appetite to exhibit

Modern art by emerging artists led to the opening of the Wertheim Gallery in London's Burlington Gardens in October 1930.

In an October 1937 press article, 'My Seven Year Experiment' (paper unknown; from the Salford Archive), she listed her key objectives: that the gallery was not to be primarily a commercial one, that her intention was to show only work she believed in and to build the reputations of living artists to enable them to sell their work during their lifetime. Her relentless dedication to those she referred to as 'my' artists, many of whom were represented in her personal collection, eventually spanned five decades. However, merely opening the doors of the Wertheim Gallery was not enough. It soon became apparent that the public found the Modern art on display difficult to understand and appreciate. It was too far removed from their experience and expectation. Wertheim needed to find a way to engage the public with Modern art, so to this end devised a programme reaching beyond the white walls of her Mayfair gallery.

She organised free touring exhibitions around the country, alongside a progressive schools' programme and loan scheme to expose the young mind to Modern art. Wertheim believed that if she gave the pupils the tools (the art) and opportunity to relate to these works without preconceptions, they would see its value, thus becoming future supporters. There were regular exhibitions aimed at children, and children were invited to make art to be shown at the Wertheim Gallery. Nan Youngman, a member of the Twenties Group, organised the first children's exhibition in 1931, a path that led to her being awarded an OBE in 1987 for her contribution to art education. The final stage of the dissemination was to place as many of Wertheim's artists as possible in public collections to infiltrate and influence the establishment.

Impassioned and forthright, Wertheim was candid when sharing her opinions, both in private and in public. In her journal, *Phoebus Calling*, she pleaded to the 'City Fathers', presumably the directors of public galleries and museums, 'Gentlemen, please wake up.... Give your own artists a chance. Your Art Galleries are packed with work which is dead and out of date.... Art is becoming a live and vigorous force that influences the lives of all of us, and it is the young artists who are leading the way...' Acknowledging their influence, she closed, 'Gentlemen, it is up to you.'

Despite the conservatism and institutional hierarchy that she faced, Wertheim understood the need for her artists to be appreciated and represented in public galleries; she vigorously pursued a dialogue with their curators with the intention of

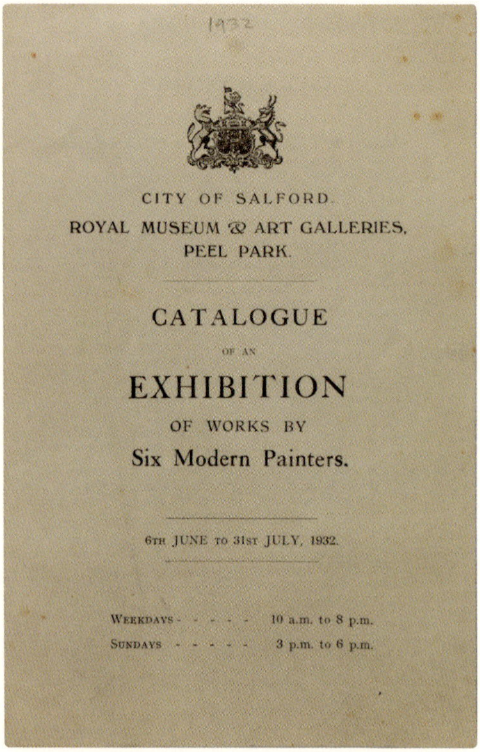
1932

CITY OF SALFORD.
ROYAL MUSEUM & ART GALLERIES,
PEEL PARK.

CATALOGUE
OF AN
EXHIBITION
OF WORKS BY
Six Modern Painters.

6TH JUNE TO 31ST JULY, 1932.

WEEKDAYS - - - - -	10 a.m. to 8 p.m.
SUNDAYS - - - - -	3 p.m. to 6 p.m.

SALFORD EXHIBITION CATALOGUE, *SIX MODERN PAINTERS*, JUNE 1932
THE LUCY WERTHEIM ARCHIVE

securing touring venues for her Twenties Group artists and others in her collection. Some of these negotiations were more successful than others, with one of the most important being the partnership she cultivated with the curator of the Peel Park Gallery in Salford. Their association began in 1932 when Wertheim's *Six Modern Painters* toured there and, following a watercolour exhibition in 1939, she gifted 106 works from the show to the gallery, now known as Salford Museum and Art Gallery.

Eager to secure a further venue for *Six Modern Painters*, Wertheim proposed the exhibition to Wakefield Art Gallery. The curator Charles Mosley politely declined, as the paintings were 'too advanced for either our committee or the general public to understand'. His reply was the catalyst for a very public debate in the *Daily Express*, in which Wertheim declared a 'Modern Art "tragedy"' and sent a 'Challenge to the Provinces' to 'Wake Up'. The article claimed that promising young artists were being driven from their native cities, hopeless, despairing and beset by intense poverty. Incensed by her actions, Mosely publicly replied, 'Mrs Wertheim has made unwarranted and unjustified charges against the gallery.' And he closed, 'I have no knowledge of any artist having left his native city in

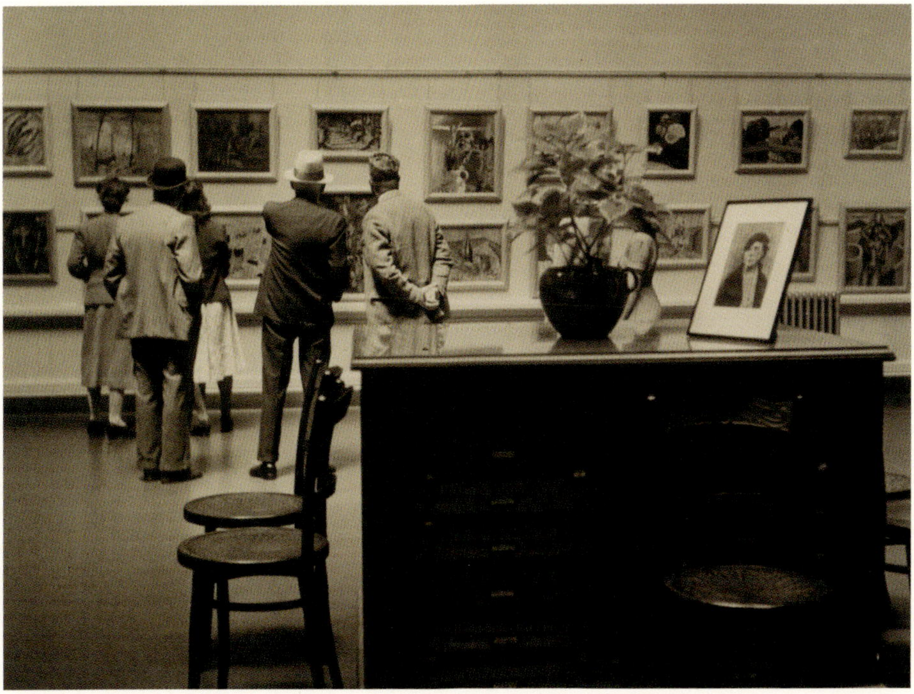

CITIZENS VIEW THEIR NEW HERITAGE, AUCKLAND ART GALLERY
PHOTOGRAPH FROM A COMMEMORATIVE ALBUM, 1948. THE LUCY WERTHEIM ARCHIVE

"sheer desperation"'. However, all was resolved by 1937 when the gallery agreed to exhibit one hundred watercolours and drawings from the Wertheim Collection, and a gift of eleven works was made via a public vote.

An opportunity to exhibit her collection internationally became possible when Wertheim met New Zealand writer, poet and critic Rex Fairburn. In the correspondence that followed, she offered to gift Modern paintings to his home city of Auckland. In 1948, Auckland Art Gallery accepted Wertheim's gift of 151 works by British artists. These paintings were to enrich the cultural lives of the 1920s influx of British immigrants in New Zealand.

In 1953, Tate director John Rothenstein wrote to Wertheim to decline the offer of a Christopher Wood painting, as they 'did not feel able to meet the conditions involved'. Wertheim's potential gift was made on the condition of Tate exhibiting her collection. In 1954, the Tate trustees declined to purchase a Wood painting from her collection, as they felt her prices 'even by prevailing standards, very high'. Such was her resolve to place an example of one of her Christopher Woods in the Tate collection that eventually, in 1962, she gifted *Boat in Harbour*, with no conditions attached.

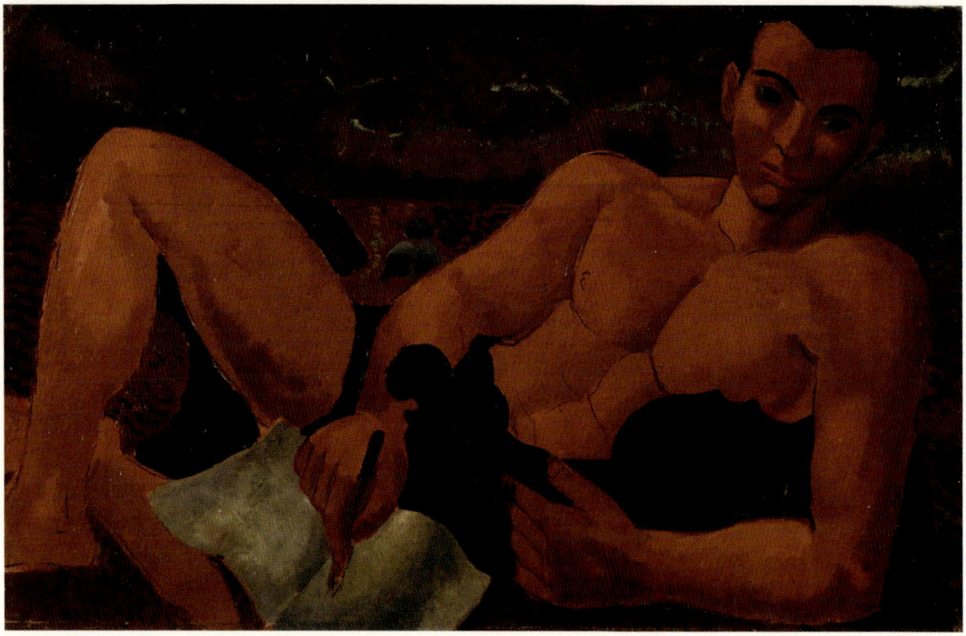

Christopher Wood, *Portrait of Constant Lambert*, 1927
Towner Eastbourne, gift of Lucy Wertheim, 1965

Wertheim's bequest of over fifty works to the Towner Art Gallery in 1971 followed exhibitions from her collection in 1965, 1968 and 1969. The first gift to the collection was a Christopher Wood portrait of the composer Constant Lambert. Once again, Wertheim suggested the public should vote for the painting they would like in 'their' collection, encouraging the audience to engage directly with the art and register their opinion. The Wertheim bequest featured key artists from her collection, among them Phelan Gibb, Frances Hodgkins, Helmut Kolle, Alfred Wallis and Christopher Wood. This was her final significant gift to a public collection.

Wertheim nurtured her relationships with her artists, and her extensive archive of letters confirms this. Adopting the role of patron, she offered emotional, financial and practical support. The boundaries of patronage and friendship were sometimes blurred, as is illustrated in the correspondence with Hodgkins and Wood, as well as in the letters from Henry Stockley, who over time confided the ways in which he would like to dispose of his neurotic, troublesome wife.

In Frances Hodgkins, Wertheim had met a woman of similar character – strong-willed, independent and proud. Initially, Hodgkins courteously accepted Wertheim's support of funds, food and clothes. Over time, however, she grew uncomfortable

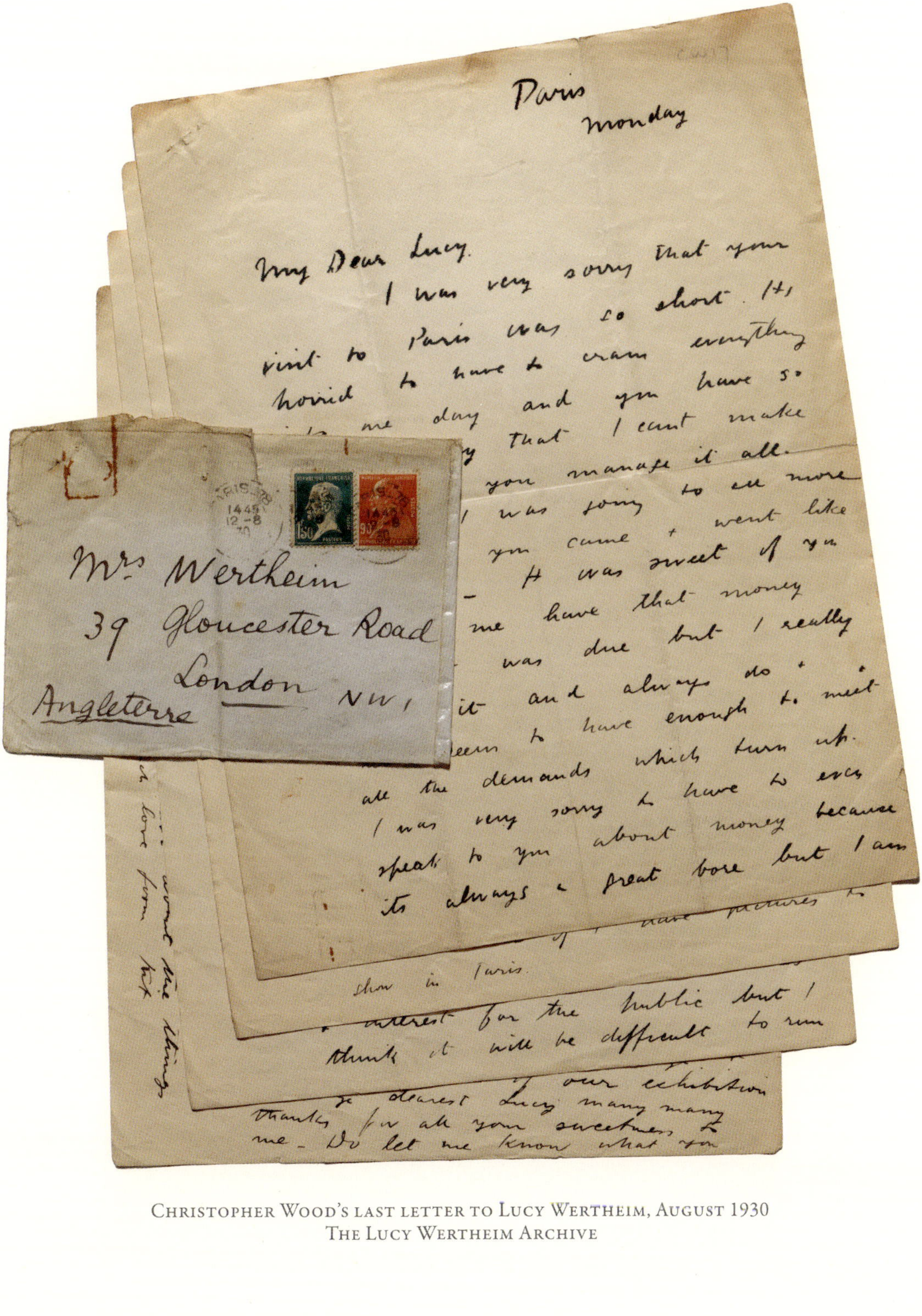

Christopher Wood's last letter to Lucy Wertheim, August 1930
The Lucy Wertheim Archive

with the charity, writing, 'I would be a pig to trade on your friendship and allow you to give me another penny.' Her remark was not heeded by Wertheim, who was hurt when Hodgkins eventually wrote, 'I feel I must not sponge or lean on you any longer, it is bad for us both. Perhaps you are changing from the Luce [sic] I knew in Manchester or perhaps I know you better.'

There is a notable difference in tone in the letters from Christopher Wood. He actively sought her aid, and in his charming manner appealed to Wertheim's sensibilities. Their close friendship began a year before Wood took his own life in 1930, but her commitment to his work and legacy lasted her lifetime. During this crucial year she acquired many of his paintings, including ten in exchange for settling his debts. The pair entered into an arrangement: she would send him funds to paint, so that he would be unencumbered by money worries, and the resulting paintings would be hers to sell and to launch the Wertheim Gallery. This arrangement did not end well, as after his suicide his mother laid claim to all the paintings he had made during this time. There followed a difficult ownership dispute. The paintings that Wertheim had invested in, and that Wood had intended for the opening, never materialised.

Henry Stockley's letters in the Wertheim Archive span thirty years. Stockley was a London bus driver whose 'naïve' paintings were adored by Wertheim, who believed them to be comparable in quality to those of Alfred Wallis. In his early letters, Stockley was enthused by her belief in his talent, producing paintings to themes she suggested. Wertheim gave 'Bus driver Stockley' a one-man show in 1932, and in 1934 exhibited his work alongside that of Christopher Wood. Over the years, Stockley's words became more fraught as he struggled to paint, exhausted from night shifts driving the bus and by the friction between him and his wife. 'I've no chance to paint,' he wrote, 'my hands are full of trouble, I've no paints and no brushes. If you have a Modern Henry Stockley show – I could not attend – I cannot paint here – it is finished.' Wertheim's support remained constant through Stockley's increasing frustrations.

Wertheim was drawn to the under-represented, whether this was based on youth, old age, sexuality or gender; the common denominator was the art they produced. She did not discriminate; her decision to represent or exhibit an artist was based on her emotional response to their work. She sought out promising young talent, visiting art schools, offering exhibitions to students not yet graduated, and inviting many to join her Twenties Group. The representation of women in the Twenties Group was significantly high for the 1930s when compared to the ratio of men to women represented in public collections at this time – and even today. Women

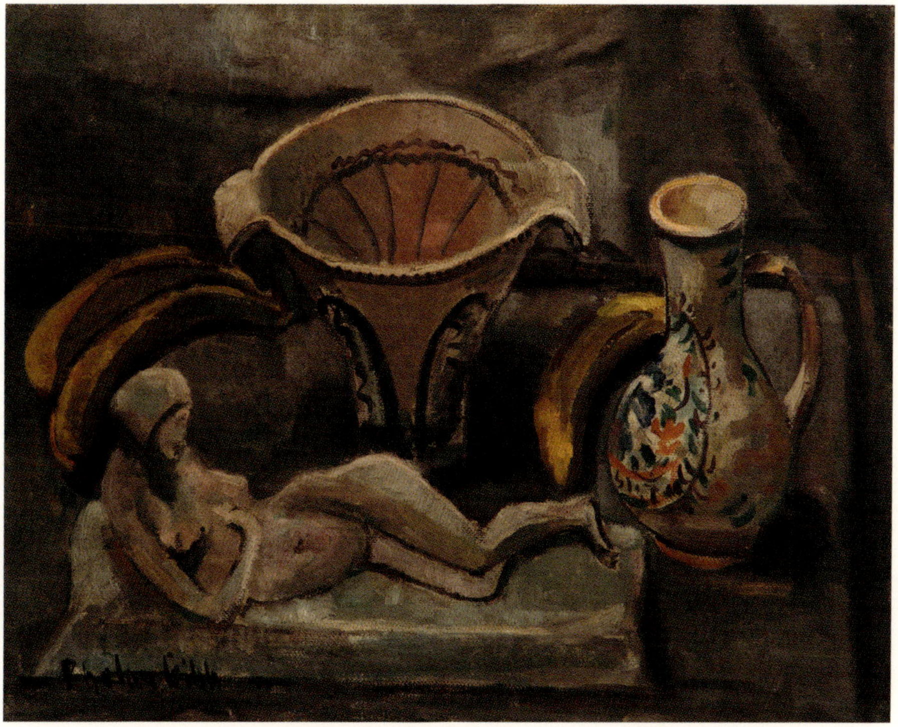

Phelan Gibb, *Still Life*, undated
Salford Museum & Art Gallery, gift of Lucy Wertheim, 1947

accounted for just under half the 112 documented members exhibiting between 1932 and 1937. Regrettably, the Second World War restricted the potential of many young women of the Twenties Group. By 1945, after six years of war, many of them, now married, put aside their aspirations to be artists to dedicate themselves to their families. Some found the only way to deal with this choice was to ignore their practice and not speak of their art. Without Wertheim's early patronage, these women would not be represented as artists.

A number of Wertheim's artists were homosexual; she does not openly acknowledge this in her memoir, so we do not know how open they were with her. However, it seems likely she was moved by their social vulnerability, among the repressed, the penniless, the sickly, the addicted, the trapped and the ignored. Many of her artists struggled and she felt a responsibility to help them because the art establishment would not. She was drawn in equal measure to this combination of artistic potential and powerlessness. Her artists needed her.

On 25 March 1964, the *Guardian* wrote, 'Mrs Wertheim has always seen herself as the servant of the artists whose work has attracted her. She manages to sound quite

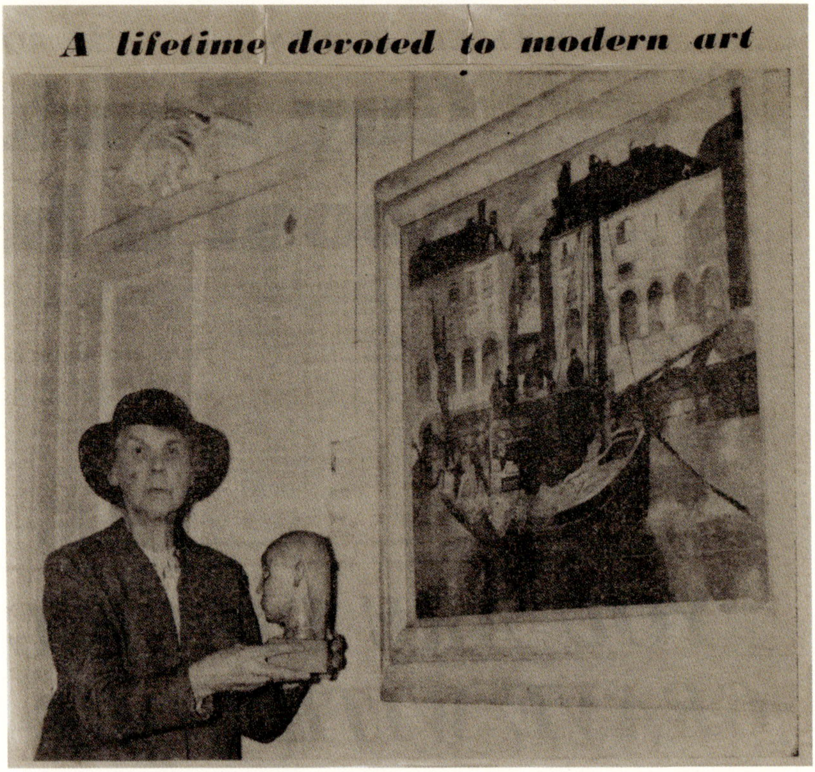

A lifetime devoted to modern art, *Evening Argus*, Brighton, 1 November 1960
The Lucy Wertheim Archive

humble when she says, "They still need someone like me."' This tendency to nurture led to her being dubbed 'Mama Lucy' in her later years.

Describing her encounter with the German artist Helmut Kolle in the summer of 1930, Wertheim wrote in *Adventure in Art*, 'My heart warmed to him as to a motherless child.' Kolle had suffered from a heart condition since 1922, and this was evident in his appearance. He lived in France with his partner and mentor, the art collector Wilhelm Uhde. She recounted, 'If l wrote here that I have loved and been loved by many artists the statement would be misconstrued. Nevertheless, there is a *sympathie* so intense between the creative artist and the sensitive "appreciator" that I think only the word love describes the emotion. I felt always in the presence of Kolle a deep tenderness mingled with humility and a passionate longing to serve him, or at any rate protect him from the hard, stupid, unseeing world. He seemed such a tragic, defenceless figure.' Wertheim gave Kolle his first English one-man show at her gallery in March 1931. The exhibition was not received well by the public or critics. In November that year Kolle died from his prolonged illness.

During her lifetime, more than ten public intuitions benefitted from Wertheim's generosity and enthusiasm to share her artists' Modern art. In all she gifted over 500 works to regional, national and international galleries and museums to cement her Modern artists in public collections. She played an important part in introducing Modern art to a wider audience, with over forty galleries, schools and libraries exhibiting works from her collection. Without Wertheim's tenacity, her loyalty to her artists and her foresight in gifting their works, there would remain little or no trace of many of these artists. The placing of a painting in a public collection anchors an artist within a context and allows their work to be located, researched and, most importantly, seen.

What Wertheim described as her 'Seven Year Experiment' in 1937 led to her devoting over forty years to this obsession. First and foremost, she was a patron and collector, dedicated to the support of struggling artists, and only selling her prized works by Christopher Wood or Henry Moore to finance her galleries and exhibition projects. Wertheim opened a total of eight galleries, from the opening of the Wertheim Gallery in 1930 to her last, Venture Eight in Brighton, in 1963. Sadly, her other galleries did not manage to replicate the groundswell of attention that the first drew over its nine years, perhaps because of the absence of the aspiring young artists from her Twenties Group.

Reflecting in the same Guardian article in March 1964, she observed, 'I have always been more of an impassioned collector rather than a dealer – completely unable to adopt the degree of detachment necessary for success.' Her motivation throughout remained the same, '... to do all [I] can to provide an opportunity for artists to gain recognition, while they are still fairly young and certainly before their death, when the vultures descent.'

Acknowledgements

The passion invested in the re-publication of *Adventure in Art* and in its related exhibition, led by Karen Taylor for Towner Eastbourne and Philippe Garner for the Lucy Wertheim Estate, has proved infectious and we extend our heartfelt thanks to all who have contributed to the fulfilment of these dual projects.

We thank: Lucy Duckworth at Unicorn for her initial approach to Towner Eastbourne with the suggestion of re-publishing *Adventure in Art* in parallel with the gallery curating an exhibition; Lucilla Garner for her faith and quiet guidance; her father, the late James Hume, who so diligently brought order to the Lucy Wertheim Archive as the first advocate for, and guardian of, Lucy's legacy; Edward and Polly Hutchinson and other members of the extended Wertheim family who have supported the projects with such enthusiasm; the artists' representatives who have responded so generously with trust, resources and permissions, notably Hilary Ward, Kathleen Walne's daughter, for locating her mother's painting *Ballet Dancers*, which featured in the 1947 edition of this book; conservator Corinne Farmer, who patiently revived many of the paintings illustrated; Fraser Marr for his expertise in documenting the conserved works; and Tony Fisher for his skill and care in photographing works from the Lucy Wertheim Estate and the Lucy Wertheim Archive.

Our thanks go also to the many curators, specialists, gallerists and museum professionals who have assisted our research and offered access to their collections, notably: Peter Ogilvie, Salford Museum & Art Gallery; Mary Kisler, curator of *Frances Hodgkins: European Journeys*, 2019, Auckland Art Gallery Toi o Tāmaki; Dr Abi Shapiro, The Hepworth Wakefield; Dr Hannah Higham, Henry Moore Foundation; Richard Selby, of the Redfern Gallery for his support and access to Redfern's Christopher Wood records; Katy Norris and Christopher Penn for their assistance in locating Wood's paintings; Nick Orchard of Christie's; and Mary Rose Rivett-Carnac, Art UK, for all her help in contacting the many artists' estates.

We thank the Paul Mellon Centre, whose funding enabled in-depth research; the team at Towner Eastbourne and specifically Sara Cooper for her support and guidance; Felicity Price-Smith for her elegant design; Frances Spalding and Ariane Bankes for contextualising Lucy among her female peers and the art scene of the 1930s; and those collectors who have generously shared their works, helping shape the publication and the exhibition, as Lucy Wertheim's endeavours helped shape their own collecting sensibilities.

Towner Eastbourne and the Lucy Wertheim Estate

Picture Credits

2, 4, 6, 8, 33, 56, 99, 107, 125, 144, 154, 156, 161, 162, 167, 176, 178, 179, 181, 184 Photo The Lucy Wertheim Archive; **10** ©The Estate of Roland Pitchforth/Auckland Art Gallery Toi o Tāmaki; **13** Fletcher Trust Collection, Aotearoa New Zealand/Photo Jennifer French, courtesy of Auckland Art Gallery Toi o Tāmaki; **14, 22, 29, 46, 49, 62, 64, 66, 150, 157, 180** Towner Eastbourne; **15** Ravenscar Trust/Image courtesy Canterbury Museum, New Zealand; **17, 37** Photo ©Tate; **21** Jerwood Collection; **25, 31** Private Collection; **28, 44** Image Lund Humphries; **39** Reproduced courtesy of Leicester Arts and Museums Service; **41, 51, 69, 92, 97, 119, 121, 151** Photo The Lucy Wertheim Estate; **45** Image reproduced with the kind permission of HRH The Prince of Wales; **55** ©SCC Cultural Services; **70** The Lucy Wertheim Estate/Image courtesy of Christie's; **74** ©The Estate of John Bigge/Photo ©Tate; **75** ©The Estate of John Banting/All rights reserved 2022/ Bridgeman Images/Photo Fraser Marr/Salford Museum & Art Gallery; 77, **159** ©The Estate of Henry Stockley/Towner Eastbourne; **88** ©The Estate of Michael Wickham/ Salford Museum & Art Gallery; **91** ©The Estate of Katharine Church/Courtesy The Katharine Church Family Archive; **93** ©Elizabeth Rivers/Courtesy of Karen Reihill & David Britton; **94** ©The Estate of Suzanne Cooper/Private Collection; **95** ©The Estate of William Townsend/Salford Museum & Art Gallery; **101** ©The Estate of John Melville/ Photo The Lucy Wertheim Estate; **102** ©The Estate of Robert Greenham/Photo The Lucy Wertheim Estate; **103, 124** ©The Estate of Kathleen Walne/Towner Eastbourne; **105** ©The Estate of Henning Nyberg/Salford Museum & Art Gallery; **116** (top) Image courtesy of whytes.com; **116** (bottom) ©The Estate of David Gommon/Towner Eastbourne; **118** Photo Fraser Marr/Private Collection; **123** ©The Estate of David Gommon/Photo The Lucy Wertheim Estate; **141** ©The Estate of Billie Waters/Photo The Lucy Wertheim Estate; **147, 148, 190** (centre right) Reproduced by permission of The Henry Moore Foundation; **158** ©The Estate of John Skeaping/Photo The Lucy Wertheim Estate; **160** ©The Estate of George Bissill/National Coal Mining Museum for England; **164** ©The Estate of Ilsa Rodmell/Photo The Lucy Wertheim Estate; **168** ©The Estate of Kathleen Walne/Photo The Lucy Wertheim Estate; **169** ©The Estate of Suzanne Cooper/Auckland Art Gallery Toi o Tāmaki; **170** ©The Estate of Rachel Reckitt/Salford Museum & Art Gallery; **173** ©The Christopherson Estate/Photo Fraser Marr/Private Collection; **174** Photo Fraser Marr/Salford Museum & Art Gallery; **183** Salford Museum & Art Gallery; **189** (top middle) ©The Christopherson Estate; **190** (centre left) ©The Estate of Mostyn Lewis; **190** (centre middle) ©The Estate of John Melville; **190** (bottom left) ©The Estate of Justin Pieris; **190** (bottom middle) ©Basil Rákóczi; **190** (bottom right) ©Elizabeth Rivers/Courtesy of Karen Reihill & David Britton; **191** (top middle) ©The Estate of Humphrey Slater; **191** (top right) ©The Estate of Henry Stockley; **191** (centre left) ©The Estate of Rowland Suddaby.

Additional plates
from the 1947 edition

The following plates document, in alphabetical sequence by artist, all those works illustrated in the original edition of *Adventure in Art* that we have not been able to illustrate within the body of the present re-edition. The titles are those given in the original publication.

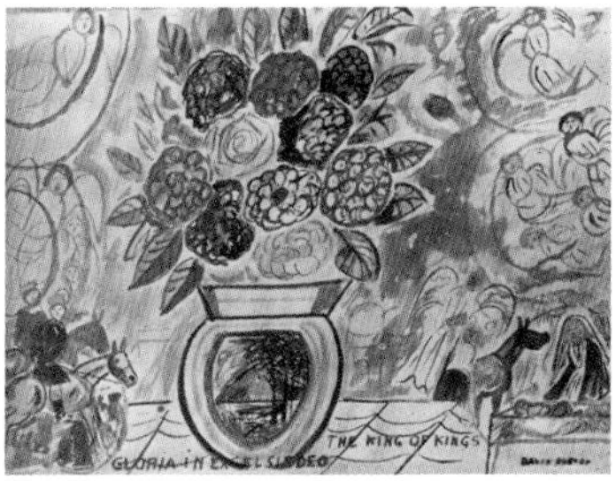

David Burton,
Gloria in Excelsis Deo

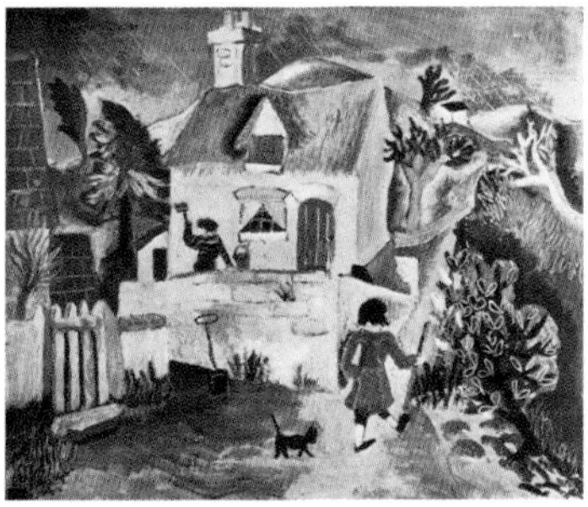

José Christopherson,
Fairy Tale

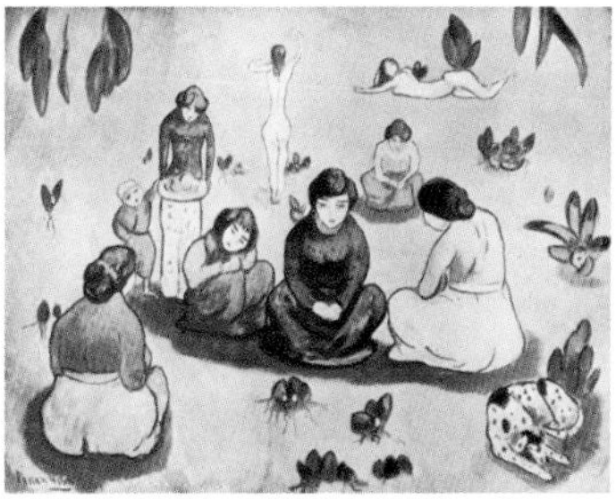

Phelan Gibb,
Picnic

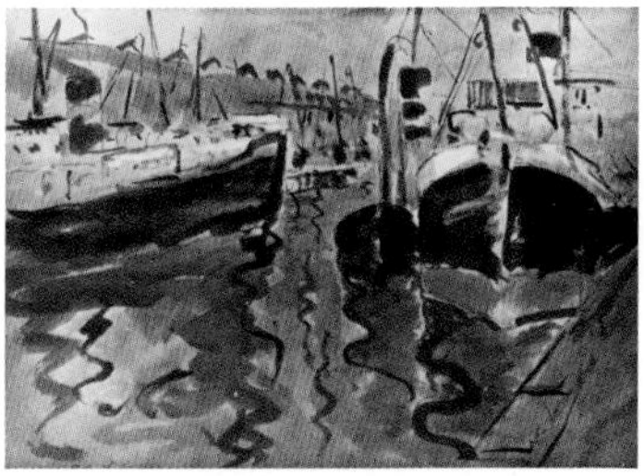

Phelan Gibb,
Ship Canal

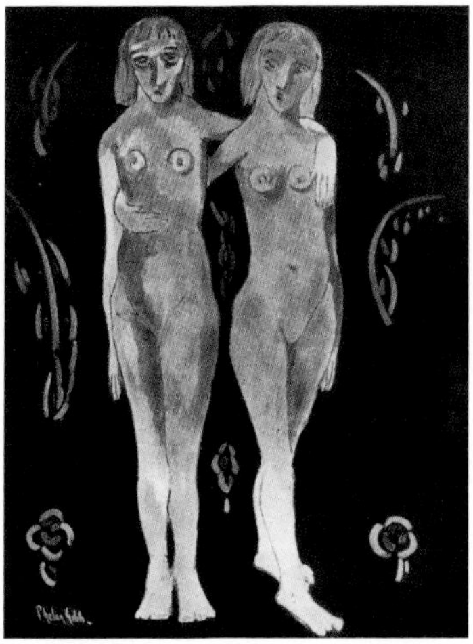

Phelan Gibb,
Two Nudes

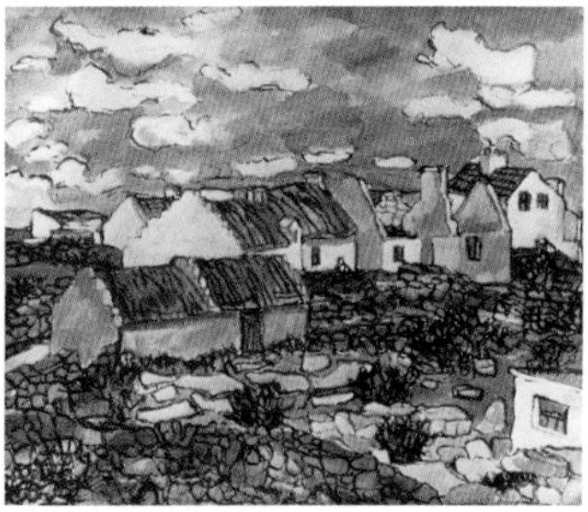

Kenneth Hall,
Aran Islands

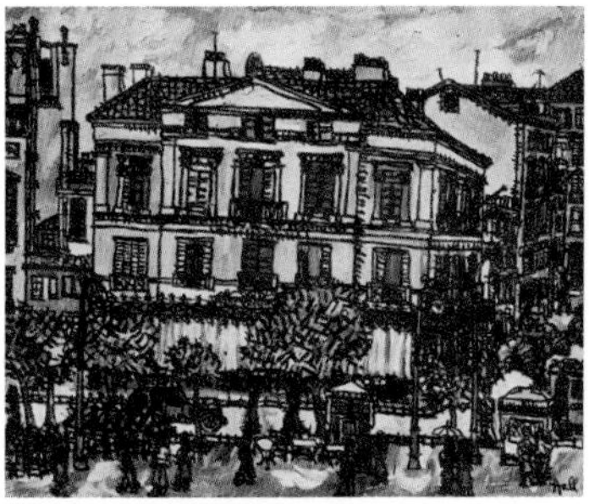

Kenneth Hall,
Athens

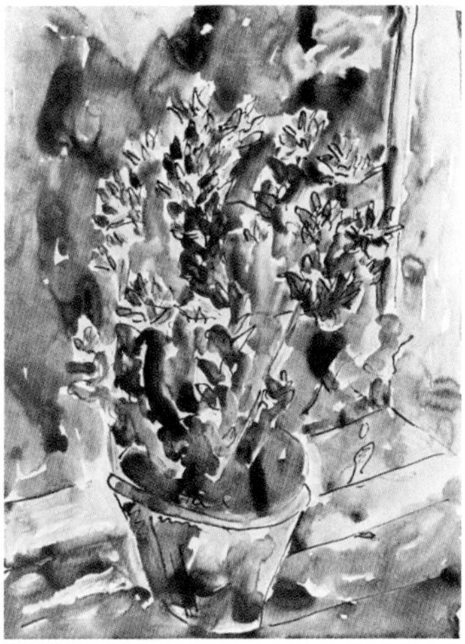

Kenneth Hall,
Flower Piece

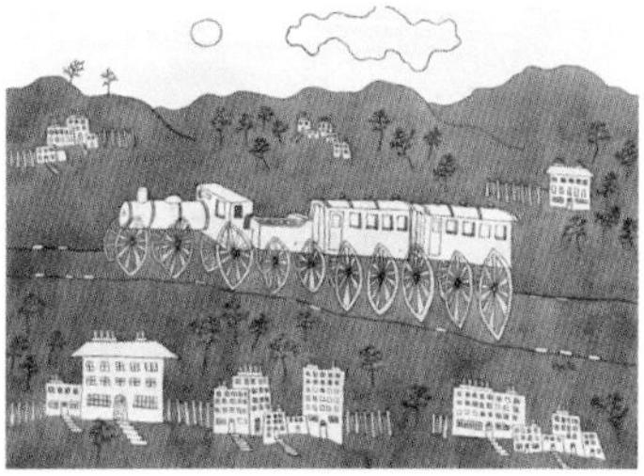

Kenneth Hall,
The Train

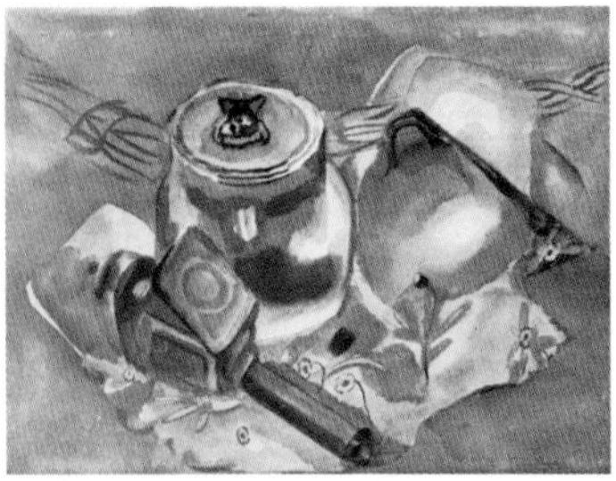

Frances Hodgkins,
The Brown Vase

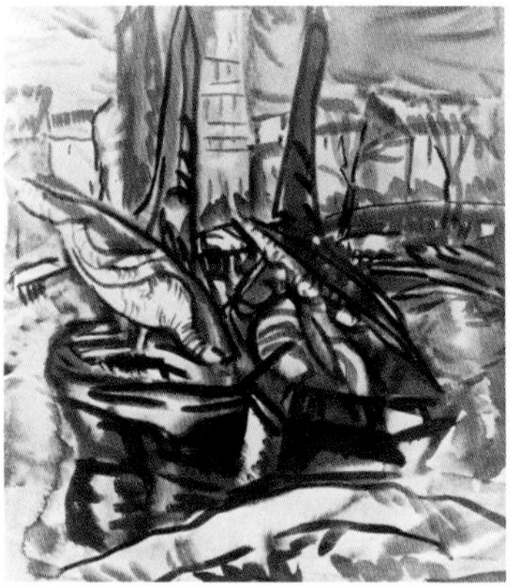

Frances Hodgkins,
Fishing Smacks

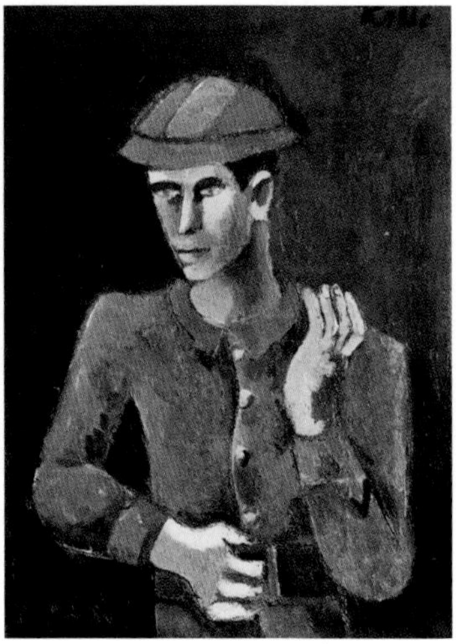

Helmut Kolle,
Soldat

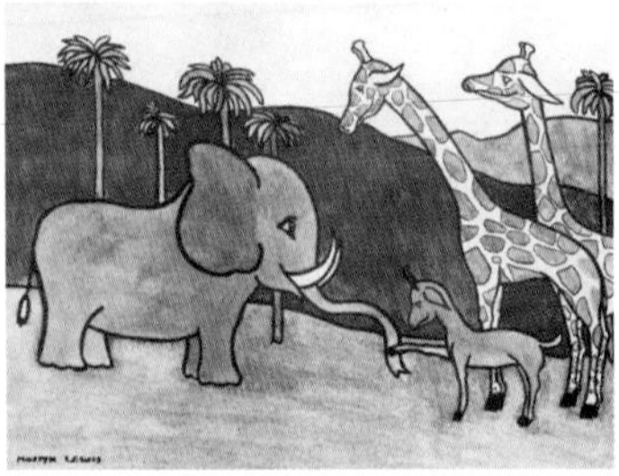

Mostyn Lewis,
Nursery Picture

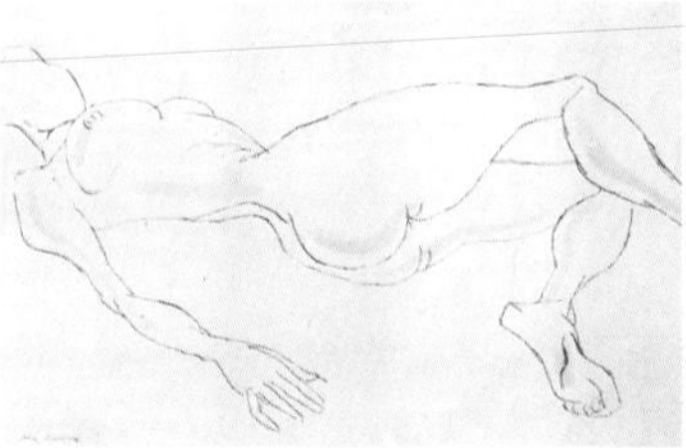

John Melville,
Drawing

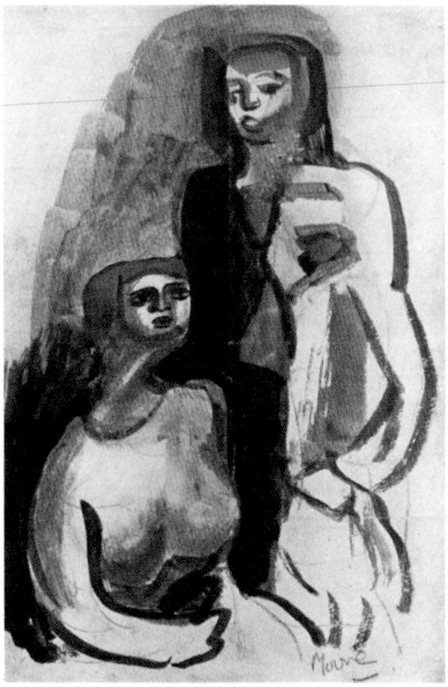

Henry Moore,
Two Women

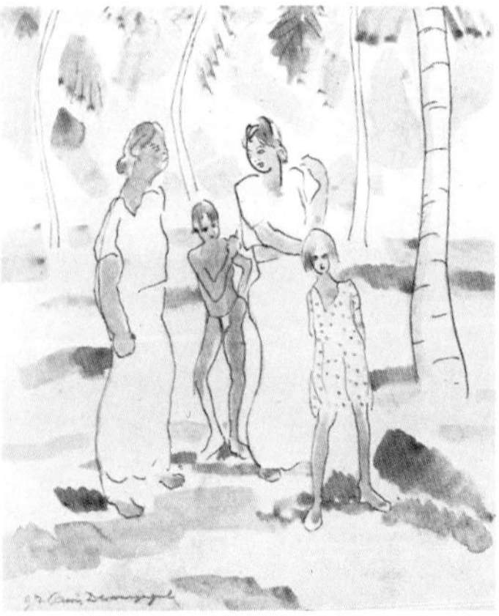

Justin Pieris,
Watercolour

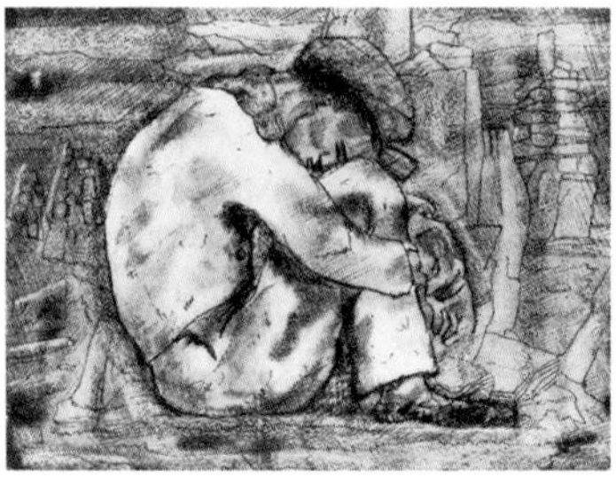

Basil Rákóczi,
Aran Islander

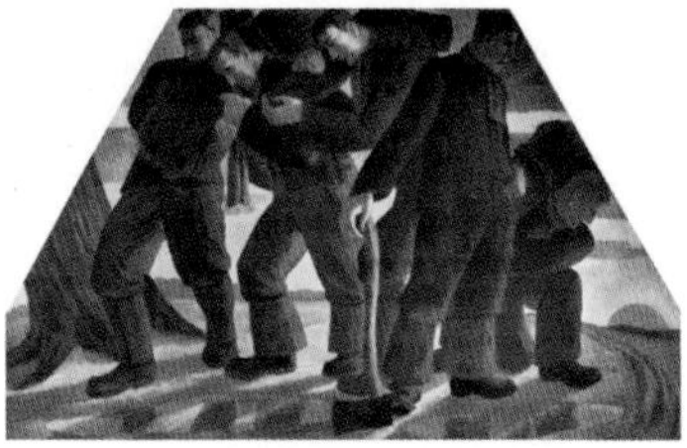

Elizabeth Rivers,
Mural Design

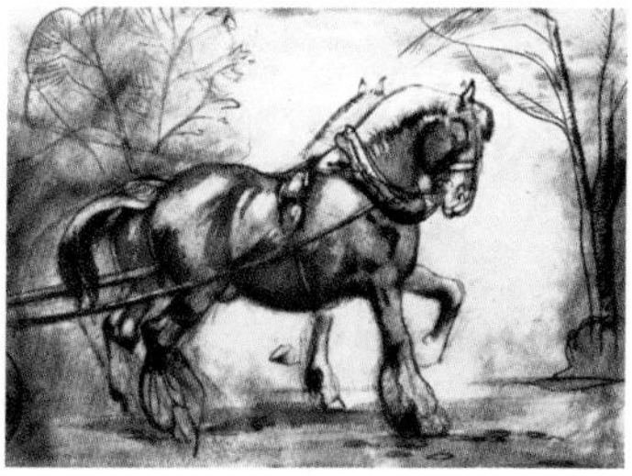

LANCELOT D. RUST,
L.M.S. HORSES

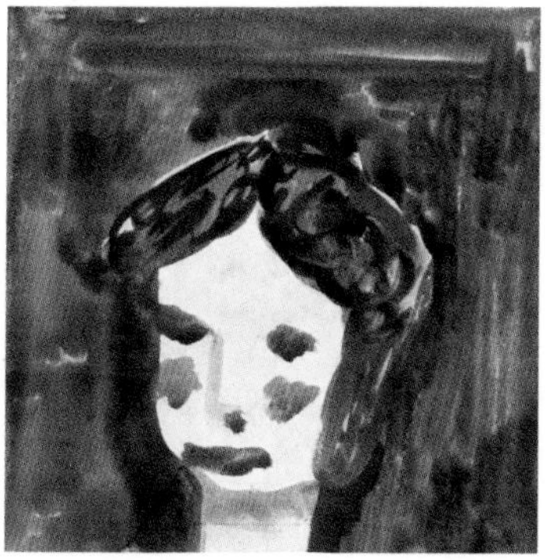

HUMPHREY SLATER,
HEAD OF GIRL

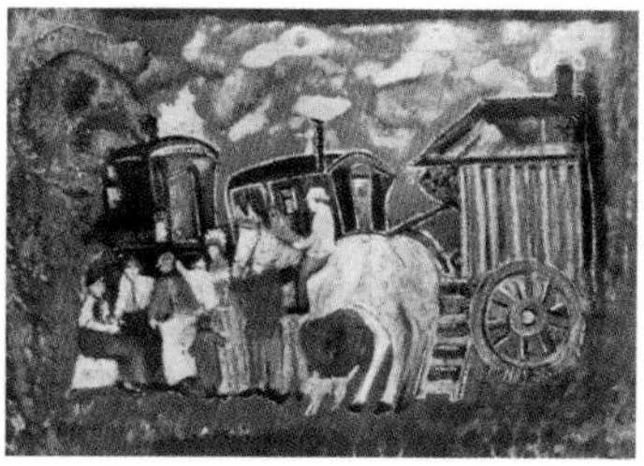

HENRY STOCKLEY,
THE CIRCUS

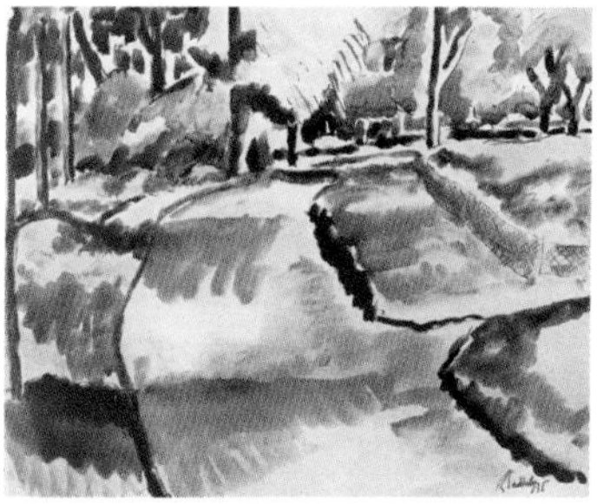

ROWLAND SUDDABY,
WINTRY SCENE

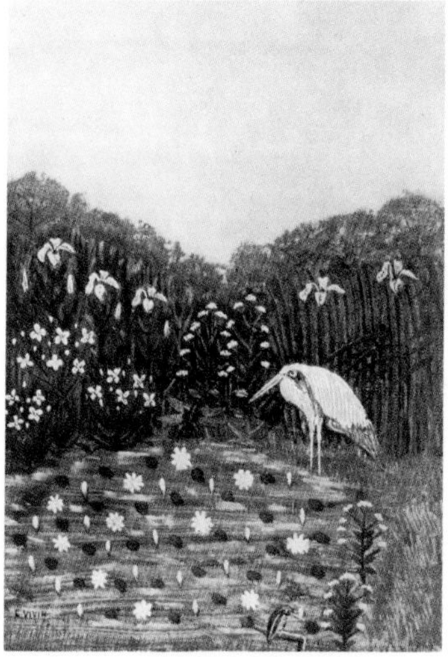

LOUIS VIVIN,
LILY POND

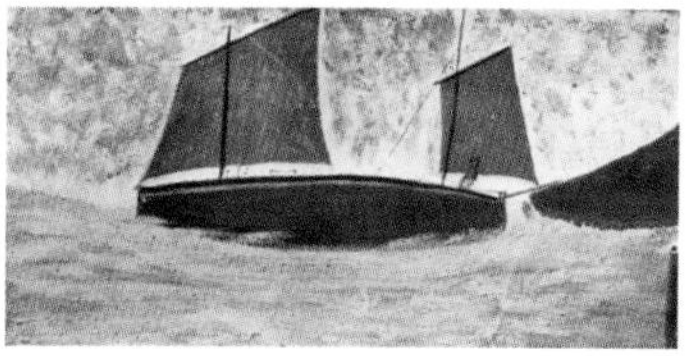

ALFRED WALLIS,
FISHING BOAT

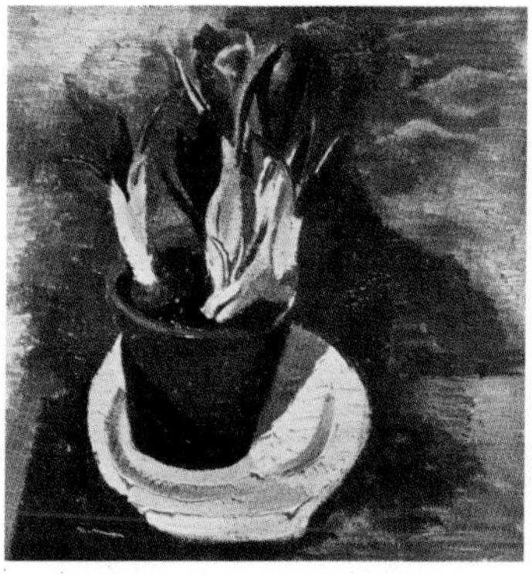

CHRISTOPHER WOOD,
THE CROCUS

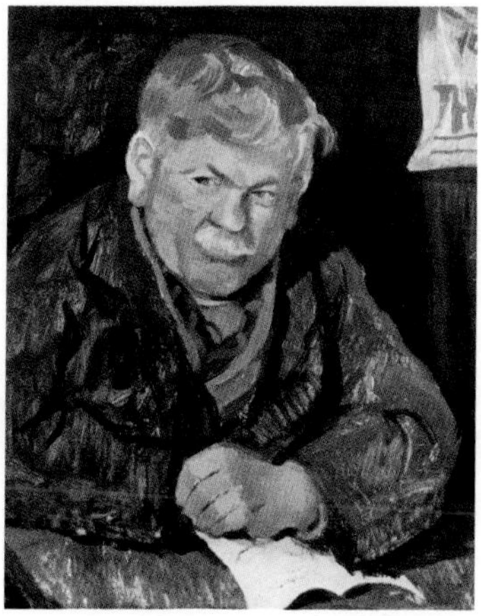

CHRISTOPHER WOOD,
THE INNKEEPER

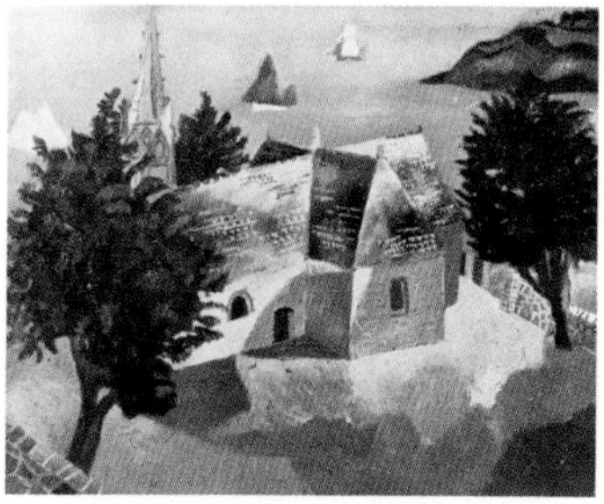

CHRISTOPHER WOOD,
LITTLE CHURCH BY THE SEA

Publisher's Note

Lucy Wertheim's original text has been faithfully transcribed, respecting her today-outmoded use of certain words and her styling of certain institutional or exhibition names (such as the *"Daily Express" Young Artists' Exhibition* of June 1927 at the Royal Society of British Artists, which she refers to as *English Artists under Forty*). We have restricted our interventions to the modernising of archaic punctuation, the correction of the very few spelling or factual errors that we found, and the addition of a number of given names which Wertheim had omitted but which we believe will be of help to the reader.

Published in 2022 by Unicorn, an imprint of Unicorn Publishing Group Ltd
Charleston Studio, Meadow Business Centre Lewes BN8 5RW
www.unicornpublishing.org

ISBN 978-1-912690-17-6
10 9 8 7 6 5 4 3 2 1

Designed by Felicity Price-Smith
Printed by Fine Tone Ltd